AF262548

Matisse's
Femme au chapeau

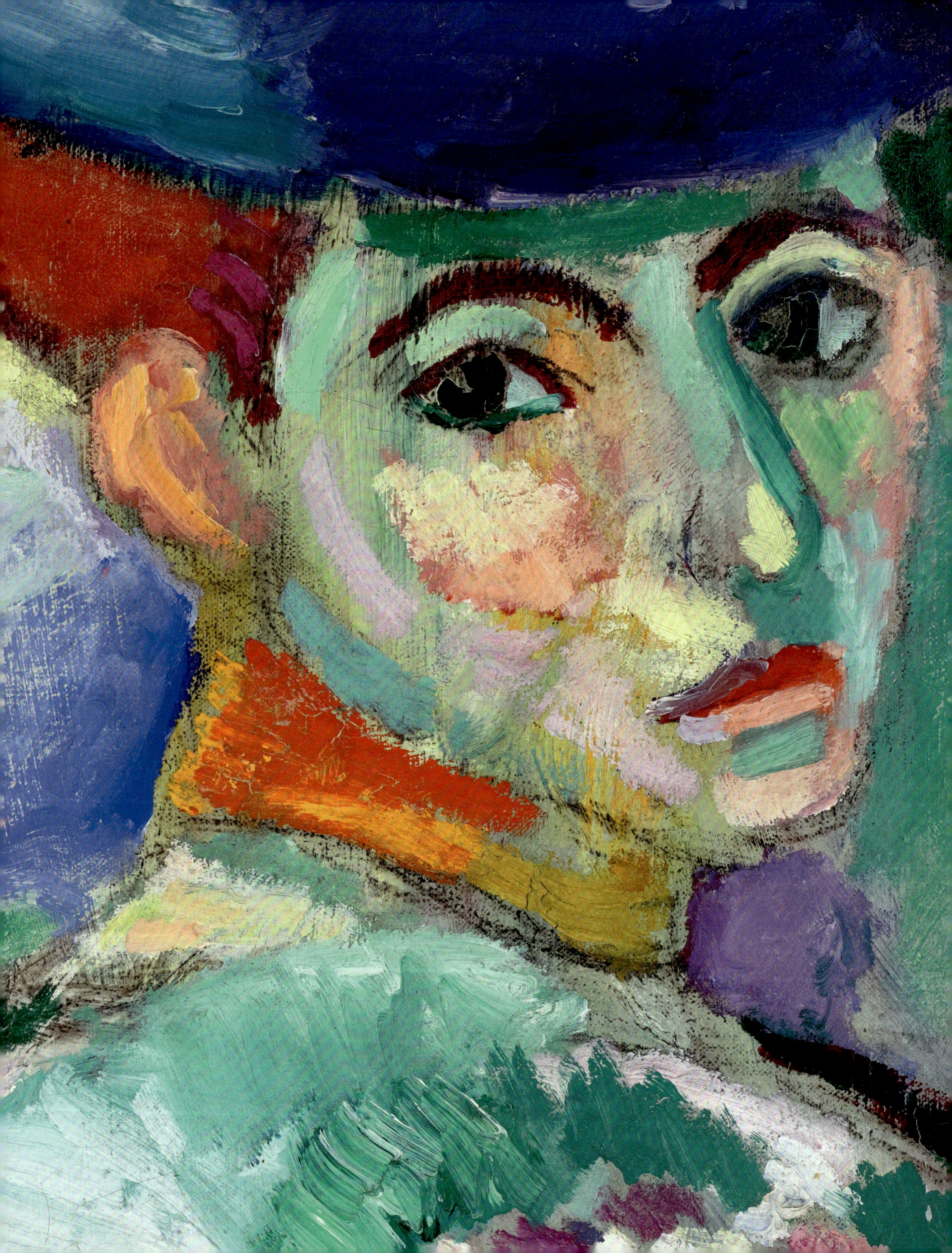

Matisse's *Femme au chapeau*

1905 TO TODAY

Edited by Janet Bishop
and Maria Castro

San Francisco
Museum of Modern Art
in association with
DelMonico Books • D.A.P.

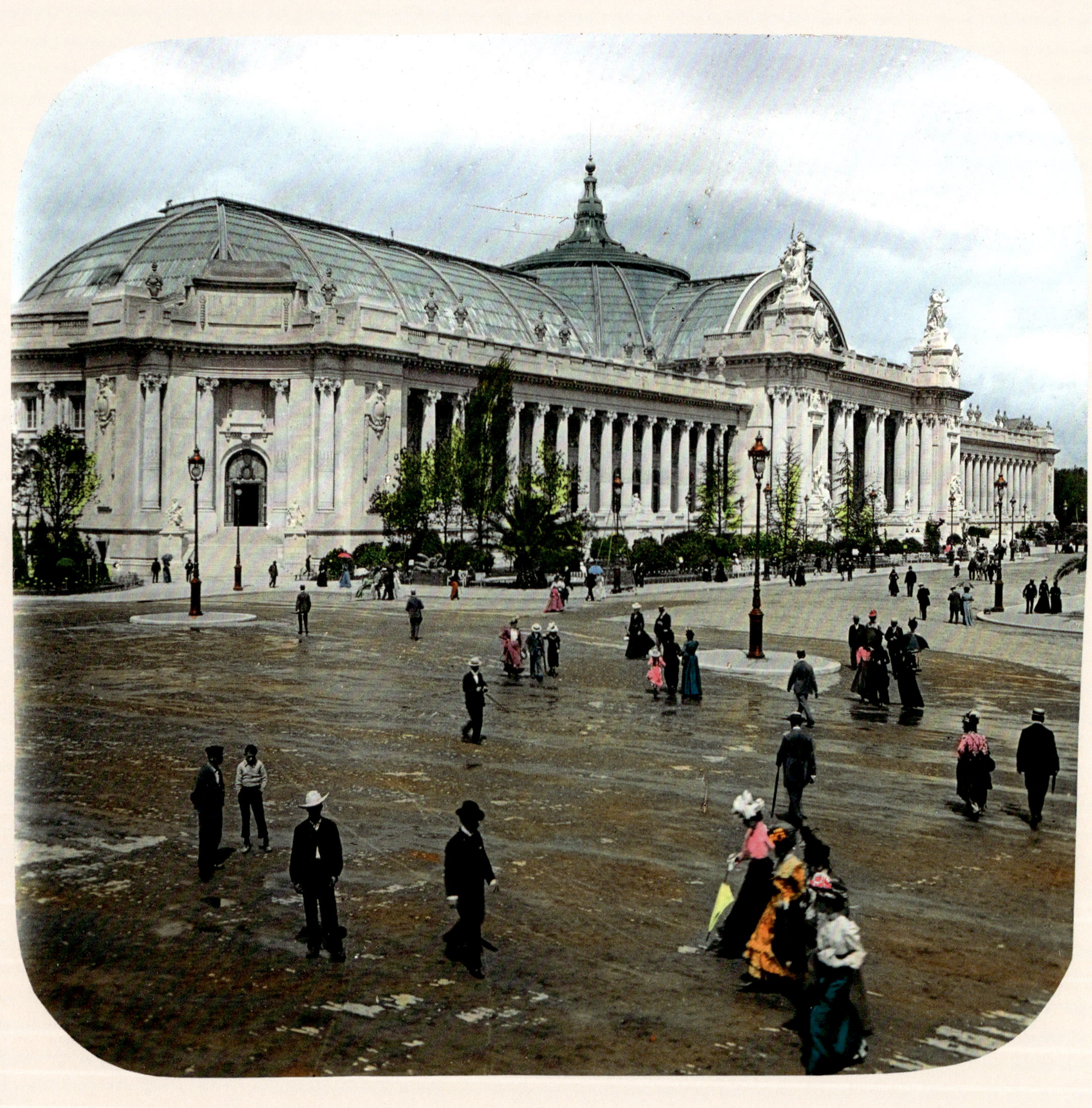

Paris Exposition: Grand Palais, Paris, France, 1900, 1900. Lantern slide, 3¼ × 4 in. (8.3 × 10.2 cm). William Henry Goodyear Collection, Brooklyn Museum Libraries and Archives

CONTENTS

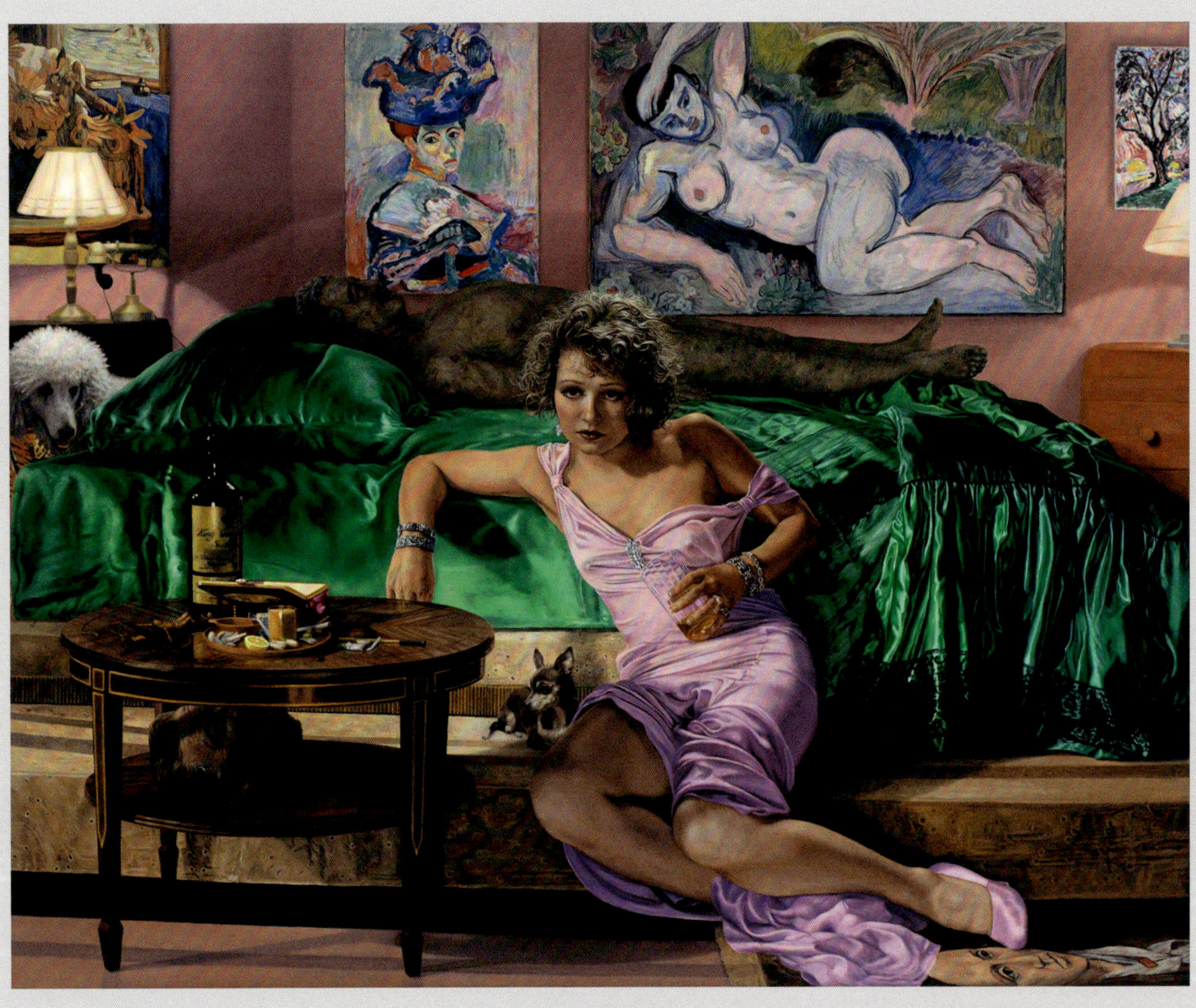

Hilary Harkness, *Answered Prayers*, 2024. Oil on linen mounted on panel, 16 × 20 × 1⅛ in. (40.6 × 50.8 × 2.8 cm). Collection of KAWS

FOREWORD

Since its sensational public unveiling in Paris at the Salon d'Automne in 1905, Henri Matisse's *Femme au chapeau* (Woman with a Hat) has persistently exerted its influence. This iconic work has been part of the history of the San Francisco Museum of Modern Art nearly since the beginning; it was first exhibited here in 1936, one year after the institution's founding. Decades later, it joined our collection as part of a transformational 1991 bequest from Elise S. Haas, quickly becoming a visitor favorite in our galleries. The present exhibition and catalogue build on a long legacy of engagement with *Femme au chapeau* at SFMOMA, deftly bringing Matisse's work into dialogue with that of his contemporaries, later generations, and artists working today to explore the painting's enduring impact.

In the great philanthropic tradition of Elise S. Haas, an extraordinary group of donors came forward to support this project. I extend my gratitude to the Mimi and Peter Haas Fund; Bank of America and Dana and Bob Emery; the Neal Benezra Exhibition Fund, Carolyn and Preston Butcher SFMOMA Exhibition Fund, and Davidow Family Fund for Exhibitions of Modern Art; Mary Jane Elmore, Christine and Pierre Lamond, The Elaine McKeon Endowed Exhibition Fund, Deborah and Kenneth Novack, and an anonymous donor; Alka and Ravin Agrawal, Dolly and George Chammas, Laurie and Jim Ghielmetti, Robert Lehman Foundation, Stuart G. Moldaw Public Program and Exhibition Fund, Nancy and Alan Schatzberg, Thomas W. Weisel and Janet Barnes, Bobbie and Mike Wilsey, Pat and Bill Wilson Exhibitions Fund, and an anonymous donor. Finally, support for this catalogue is provided by Furthermore: a program of the J. M. Kaplan Fund.

On the occasion of the Haas bequest, Dr. John R. Lane, SFMOMA's director from 1987 to 1997, wrote of the painting: "The controversy that originally surrounded this audaciously colored portrait is a vivid reminder to us of our continued responsibility as a museum committed to contemporary art to be responsive to the most challenging work of our own day." I am immensely proud that SFMOMA has heeded this advice. *Matisse's Femme au chapeau,* which re-creates the pivotal 1905 scandal at the Salon d'Automne, also crucially looks forward to today—both to track the influence of Matisse and to remind us afresh of the ways contemporary art can provoke us and expand our thinking. I am grateful to Janet Bishop, Thomas Weisel Family Chief Curator; Maria Castro, Jacques & Natasha Gelman Associate Curator in Modern and Contemporary Art at The Metropolitan Museum of Art, New York (and former SFMOMA Andrew W. Mellon Foundation Associate Curator of Painting and Sculpture); and Alison Guh, Assistant Curator of Painting and Sculpture along with the SFMOMA staff members and other colleagues listed on pages 9 to 13, for bringing this project to life so vividly.

CHRISTOPHER BEDFORD
Helen and Charles Schwab Director, San Francisco Museum of Modern Art

HENRI-MATISSE

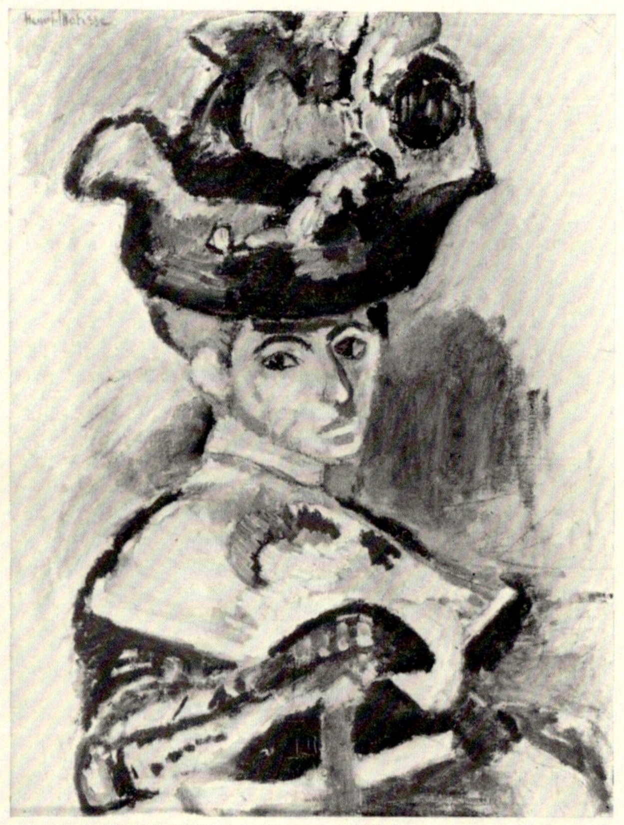

9 WOMAN IN A BLUE HAT. 1905   LENT BY MR. AND MRS. MICHAEL STEIN

PAINTINGS   DRAWINGS   SCULPTURE
JANUARY 11 - FEBRUARY 24, 1936

SAN FRANCISCO MUSEUM OF ART
WAR MEMORIAL   CIVIC CENTER

One year after the 1935 founding of the San Francisco Museum of Art (now SFMOMA), its director, Dr. Grace L. McCann Morley, inaugurated a major Henri Matisse exhibition. Illustrated on the cover of its accompanying brochure was *Femme au chapeau* (Woman with a Hat) of 1905, announcing the show's promise of presenting to San Francisco audiences paintings, drawings, and sculptures from the period when "the work of the artist and his young colleagues was stirring the world of painting to its depths."[1] Morley's project marked the first time the painting was exhibited publicly in the United States, after it made its way from Vaucresson, outside Paris, to Palo Alto, California, the previous year in the collection of Sarah and Michael Stein. After entering the museum's holdings as a bequest of Elise S. Haas in 1991, it has been on view almost continuously, effectively marking the beginning of modern art narratives the museum has proposed over time.

When Matisse first presented *Femme au chapeau* in Gallery VII of the Salon d'Automne in Paris, shortly after applying the final dabs of paint in the early fall of 1905, the canvas was received with laughs and jeers from visitors, confusion and skepticism from critics, but also with admiration for its innovation. The American expatriate collector Leo Stein encompassed both sides of the argument, calling the painting "the nastiest smear of paint [he] had ever seen," and then going on to purchase the work, with his sister Gertrude Stein, on the last day of the exhibition.[2] The Steins promptly exhibited it in their tiny Paris apartment, where it became the foundation for a growing collection that attracted visitors from both sides of the Atlantic to their lively Saturday night salons. This book and the exhibition it accompanies return to October 1905 to tell the full story of this groundbreaking painting and shed new light on how this portrait of Amélie Matisse made and continues to make its mark on art history.

At the heart of our exhibition, a gallery restages *Femme au chapeau*'s debut at the Salon d'Automne. Maria Castro's essay in this volume expands on the careful research identifying the works that were shown alongside Matisse's and explores the original setting of its presentation. Plates illustrating works by the ten artists on view in Gallery VII follow, including many identified as those shown in the salon and, when identifications were not possible, some that represent those artists' output at the time. Ordered alphabetically by artist as in the salon's catalogue, this section of plates contextualizes *Femme au chapeau* alongside works by Matisse's peers. Throughout this volume, we illustrate artworks included in the exhibition as well as others that are central to telling the full story of *Femme au chapeau*. Claudine Grammont's essay examines the subject of Matisse's canvas—his wife, Amélie Matisse—illuminating her biography and creative endeavors, while also positioning her as a collaborator in the making of *Femme au chapeau*. Popy Venzal posits a dialogue between Matisse's painting and Gertrude Stein's writings in the period when the work hung in her apartment. Janet Bishop considers the impact of

Matisse's painting, from works made by his peers to those by subsequent generations of artists, in testament to its enduring appeal. An illustrated timeline by Alison Guh traces the work's provenance and exhibition history.

This exhibition would not have been possible without the expertise and support of colleagues across the United States and Europe. The process of identifying works shown in Gallery VII of the Salon d'Automne relied on the foundational research and stewardship of artists' estates and archives. We are deeply grateful for their steadfast partnership and unfailing enthusiasm for our proposal to revisit that presentation. We extend heartfelt thanks to Georges Matisse, Anne Théry, and Gwenaëlle Fossard at the Archives Henri Matisse, Issy-les-Moulineaux, France, whose deep knowledge and generous spirit enable ever new perspectives on Matisse's work and legacy.

We are likewise indebted to Assia Quesnel at the Archives Camoin; Isabelle Monod-Fontaine and Jacqueline Munck of the Comité Derain; Evelyne Dartiguelongue at the Archives Pierre Girieud; Jean-Pierre and Sylvie Manguin; and Sandrine Canac, Claude Jacir, and Janet Lee, and the Albert Marquet Research Archives at The Wildenstein Plattner Institute. Our research was at every turn a team effort. We thank Robert McDonald Parker for sharing his time, contacts, and expertise and for his diligent research.

We are deeply grateful to colleagues who offered guidance on our search for original materials. Caroline Dubail, former historian of the Grand Palais, provided new insights on the interior design of the 1905 Salon d'Automne galleries that inspired our designers' approach to the current exhibition. Although photographs of the original presentation in Gallery VII, if any exist, have yet to be discovered, McDonald Parker's exhaustive search was assisted by numerous generous colleagues: Bérengère de l'Épine and Delphine Desveaux, Bibliothèque Historique de la Ville de Paris; Flora Triebel, Bibliothèque Nationale de France; Christelle Chefneux, Institut National d'Histoire de l'Art; Bruno Martin, Médiathèque du Patrimoine et de la Photographie; Christophe Soulier, Musée Carnavalet; Ines Rotermund-Reynard and Thomas Galifot, Musée d'Orsay; and Isabelle Le Guern, Paris Musées. Likewise, we extend our gratitude to those who supported our search for images of the Marque sculpture presented in Gallery VII, especially Catherine Chevillot; Laure de Margerie; Eve Turbat, Galerie Malaquais; Amandine Delcourt and Bruno Gaudichon, La Piscine – Musée d'Art et d'Industrie André Diligent; Antoinette Le Normand-Romain; and Dominique Lobstein. We are also grateful to Annie Chollet and her team at the Société du Salon d'Automne. We thank the many archives and libraries that hosted visits, in addition to those named above: the Archives de la Ville de Paris; the Archives Nationales; the Frick Art Research Library; the Institut National d'Histoire de l'Art; Laura Camerlengo at the Joan Diehl McCauley Textile Study Center at the de Young; Marie-Josephe Lesieur at the Musée d'Orsay; The Museum of Modern Art Archives, New York; and the UC Berkeley Library.

We also extend thanks to the specialists who contributed their expertise about the artists and subjects featured in this book and the exhibition, including Emily Banas, RISD Museum; Gunhild Bauer, Albertina; Véronique Bedouelle; Simon Crameri, Fondation Beyeler; Nadine Engel, Museum Folkwang;

Helen Faulkner, Delius Trust; Marina Ferretti-Bocquillon; Jérôme Fourmanoir, Château-Musée de Nemours; Gaëlle Guérin and Pauline Lucet, Centre National des Arts Plastiques; Emily Jones, Woodstock Artists Association and Museum; Martin Lee-Browne; Artur Ramon Navarro; Camille Philippon; Jaume Quintanilla, Colección de Arte Banco Sabadell; Lucien Roux, Raphaël Roux dit Buisson, and Camille Roux dit Buisson, Comité Jacqueline Marval, Paris; Francisca van Vloten; and Tom Wolf, Bard College.

For their support of our research on the exhibition and circulation history of *Femme au chapeau*, we extend thanks to Maggie Dethloff and Josh Schneider, Stanford University; Allyson Healey, Santa Barbara Museum of Art; Zoe Heinsohn, Dallas Museum of Art; Nikki Macháček, Museum of Fine Arts, Houston; Maureen Melton, Museum of Fine Arts, Boston; and JT de la Torre, the Art Institute of Chicago.

Several friends and colleagues have brought to our attention works of art that were directly inspired by *Femme au chapeau*. We are grateful to Lizanne Suter for sharing an auction listing for Elizabeth Peyton's *The Stein's Collect and Flowers* (2011), to Carol Greene for alerting us to Rachel Harrison's *Hoarders* (2012), and to Jared Ledesma for telling us about Yasuo Kuniyoshi's *Untitled* (1934), a still life incorporating an image of *Femme au chapeau*. These works sparked our decision to dedicate a portion of our project to the impact Matisse's picture has had since its making, as did collaborating with Katy Rothkopf of the Baltimore Museum of Art on the 2016–17 exhibition *Matisse/Diebenkorn*. We are honored to share the relevance of Matisse's work today through contemporary voices including Harrison and Peyton, as well as Hermine Ford, Hilary Harkness, David Hockney, and Mickalene Thomas.

Our project is indebted to numerous Matisse curators and scholars. We recognize in particular Dorthe Aagesen, Dita Amory, John Cauman, T. J. Clark, Stephanie D'Alessandro, Cécile Debray, Ann Dumas, John Elderfield, Arthur Fink, Claudine Grammont, Josef Helfenstein, John Klein, Rebecca Rabinow, Gail Stavitsky, Ann Temkin, and Gary Tinterow.

We are deeply grateful to the institutions who parted with their artworks to graciously lend to our exhibition. We thank Susan M. Cary and Anne Helmreich, Archives of American Art, Smithsonian Institution; Jay Dandy, Caitlin Haskell, Paulina Pobocha, and James Rondeau, the Art Institute of Chicago; Christina Frank, Kevin Jones, and Dennita Sewell, ASU FIDM Museum; Asma Naeem, Katy Rothkopf, and Jamiee Shim, Baltimore Museum of Art; Rebecca Hatcher and Lucy Mulroney, Beinecke Rare Book and Manuscript Library, Yale University; Kate Eilertsen and Katie Kime, di Rosa Center for Contemporary Art; David Hockney, Megan Mueller, and Elise Wille, The David Hockney Foundation; Lee Anne Chesterfield, Liz Rodgers, Dulce M. Román, and Jessica Uelsmann, Harn Museum of Art, University of Florida, Gainesville; Brenda Danilowitz, Samuel McCune, Jeannette Redensek, and Nicholas Fox Weber, Josef and Anni Albers Foundation; Charlotte Barat-Mabille, Claire Böhm, Solène Delanoue, Fabrice Hergott, and Jacqueline Munck, Musée d'Art Moderne de Paris; Armelle Bonneau-Alix and Sylvie Ramond, Musée des Beaux-Arts de Lyon; Catherine Bailly-Basin,

Sophie Bernard, Sébastien Gokalp, Joëlle Vaissiere, and Isabelle Varloteaux, Musée de Grenoble; Claire Gooden, Aymeric Jeudy, and Florence Perez, Musée Matisse, Nice; Noëlle Albert, Raphaële Bianchi, Claudine Grammont, Marion Julien, Frédéric Paul, and Xavier Rey, Musée National d'Art Moderne and Centre Pompidou; Christophe Cherix, Lily Goldberg, and Ann Temkin, The Museum of Modern Art, New York; Jacques Bedossa, Coralie Delcambre, and Chloé Leray, Mairie-Musée de Grez-sur-Loing, France; Caren Jones and Roman Zieglgänsberger, Museum Wiesbaden; Andrew Bolton, David Breslin, Mary Chan, Emily Foss, Max Hollein, Marci King, Julie T. Lê, Ken Soehner, Kelsey Talbot, and Tracy Yoshimura, The Metropolitan Museum of Art; Harry Cooper, Margaret Doyle, Kaywin Feldman, and Rebecca Myles, National Gallery of Art, Washington, DC; Carin Adams, Lori Fogarty, and Meredith Patute, Oakland Museum of California; Alessandra Carnielli, The Pierre and Tana Matisse Foundation; SFMOMA Library; Gurudarshan Khalsa and Robert G. Trujillo, Special Collections, Stanford University Libraries; and Maria Balshaw and Olivia Maguire, Tate.

We are moreover grateful to the many private collectors who generously lent works to our exhibition: AAA Fondation; Artur Ramon Navarro and Giulia Violino, Artur Ramon Art, Barcelona; William J. Ashton and the Estate of Daniel M. Stein; Glenn and Amanda Fuhrman and the FLAG Art Foundation; Galerie MASUREL; Hans Gallas and Vishwa Marwah; Michel Giraud; KAWS; Vicki and Kent Logan; Dr. Harald Link; M. S. Rau Art and Antiques, New Orleans; Stuart Smith; and those who wish to remain anonymous. We further extend thanks to our colleagues in galleries and auction houses whose support proved essential to our effort: Samantha Koslow and Katherine Mandel, Christie's; Florence Chibret-Plaussu, Galerie de la Présidence; Carol Greene, Cory Nomura, and Lauren Vallese, Greene Naftali; Annegret Thoma, Karl & Faber; Margaux Bruneteau, Millon; Pauline Chanoit, Oger-Blanchet; Giulia and Alexis Pentcheff; Ella Blanchon and Wendy Olsoff, P·P·O·W; and Edith Eustis, David Galperin, Becky Heldfond, and Sharon Kim, Sotheby's.

Ours is a story profoundly connected to the history of SFMOMA; realizing it has been a highly gratifying collective effort. We are grateful, first and foremost, to Christopher Bedford, our director. Early in his tenure, Chris invited us to propose a Matisse-related exhibition and he has championed the project at every step. We are likewise appreciative of SFMOMA's executive leadership team: Rodimiro Coronado, Cheryl Ewers, Gamynne Guillotte, Dee Minnite, Sheila Shin, Adine Varah, and Peter Wilch. For their support and advice, we thank current and recent colleagues in SFMOMA's Curatorial division: Jacqueline Belloso, Jenny Gheith, Nancy Lim, Shana Lopes, Sarah Roberts, Marin Sarvé-Tarr, Ann Marguerite Tartsinis, and especially Alison Guh, who was an essential partner throughout.

We appreciate many SFMOMA staff members, past and present, for the passion, expertise, and commitment they brought to this endeavor as they supported our ability to share it with the broadest possible audience. We offer our warmest thanks to our colleagues in the Collections, Exhibitions, and Design division: Sriba Kwadjovie Quintana, Meg Ocampo, Don Ross, Jessica

Teters, and Rebecca Weisberg, Archives and Art Resources; Alex Dangles and Steve Dye, Collections Technical; Michelle Barger, Jennifer Hickey, Amanda Hunter Johnson, and Natalya Swanson, Conservation; Sarah Choi, Hana Ishijima, Jenn Livermore, Gail Sheerin, and Edward Whelan, Design Studio; David Funk and Angelo Hallinan, Exhibitions Project Management; Nahshon Clark and Jill Santos, Finance; Brian Caraway, Graciela Espinoza, Juli Gamble, Frederick Gums, Claire LaMont, Brandon Larson, and Kayla Pierce, Gallery Infrastructure and Fabrication; Ian Claussen, Ximaps Dong, Doug Kerr, Martin Malvar, Evan Mulitauopele, Jeanine Parish, Rico Solinas, Brooke Valentine, and Dale Verga, Installation; Abby Bridge, Erin Parker, and David Senior, Library; Courtney Costello, Garzo Garcia, Walter Logue, and Tim Tengonciang, Operations; and Andrew Haller and Maren Jones, Registration.

Additional staff who contributed expertise include Erica Gangsei, Santino Gonzales, Michael Kasian-Morin, and Tiffany Yau, Interpretation. Shannon Morzov partnered with our Interpretation team and Google Arts and Culture to produce the exhibition's animations. Thanks also go to Mei Li, Legal; Sylvia Castillo, Cristina Chan, Komal Desai, Dyemond Dye, Stephanie Gianni, Clara Hatcher Baruth, Colin Howard, Julie Lamb, Alexandra Nguy, and Andrea Wang, Marketing and Communications; Alison Bowman, Laura Cunniff, Katy Silva, and Suzy Varadi, Philanthropy; Kathleen Maguire, Public Engagement; Derrick Bowman, Walter Coupland, and the Security team; Anne-Marie Conde, Elena Gurule, Virginia Lee, Tobey Martin, and Shane Salvata, Museum Store; and Nicole Meshack and the Visitor Experience team.

This beautiful volume, designed by Barbara Glauber, was deftly overseen by SFMOMA's stellar publications team: Kari Dahlgren, Amanda Glesmann, and Katie Lindsey. We are grateful to translators Fabienne Adler and Annie Levine. Jennifer Snodgrass carefully edited the manuscript, while Emily Bowles and Juliet Clark provided invaluable editorial support at the end of the project. Mary DelMonico at DelMonico Books • D.A.P. championed this book as its copublisher. The expert team at Verona Libri oversaw its production. We likewise wish to thank Ondrea Vicklund for her inspired reimagining of the Grand Palais's turn-of-the-century wall covering, an essential component of the book's cover design and of the exhibition, and Holly Baxter for generously connecting us.

It has been our great pleasure to delve deeply into the history and impact of what is not only SFMOMA's most famous painting but one of San Francisco's greatest treasures. We reserve our principal thanks for Elise S. Haas and her heirs, whose generosity and foresight ensured that *Femme au chapeau* would have a perpetual public life, enriching the experience of all who encounter it.

JANET BISHOP
Thomas Weisel Family Chief Curator,
San Francisco Museum of Modern Art

MARIA CASTRO
Jacques & Natasha Gelman Associate
Curator in Modern and Contemporary Art,
The Metropolitan Museum of Art

1   Grace L. McCann Morley, *Henri Matisse: Paintings, Drawings, Sculpture*, exh. cat. (San Francisco: San Francisco Museum of Art, 1936).

2   Leo Stein, *Appreciation: Painting, Poetry, and Prose* (New York: Crown Publishers, 1947), 158.

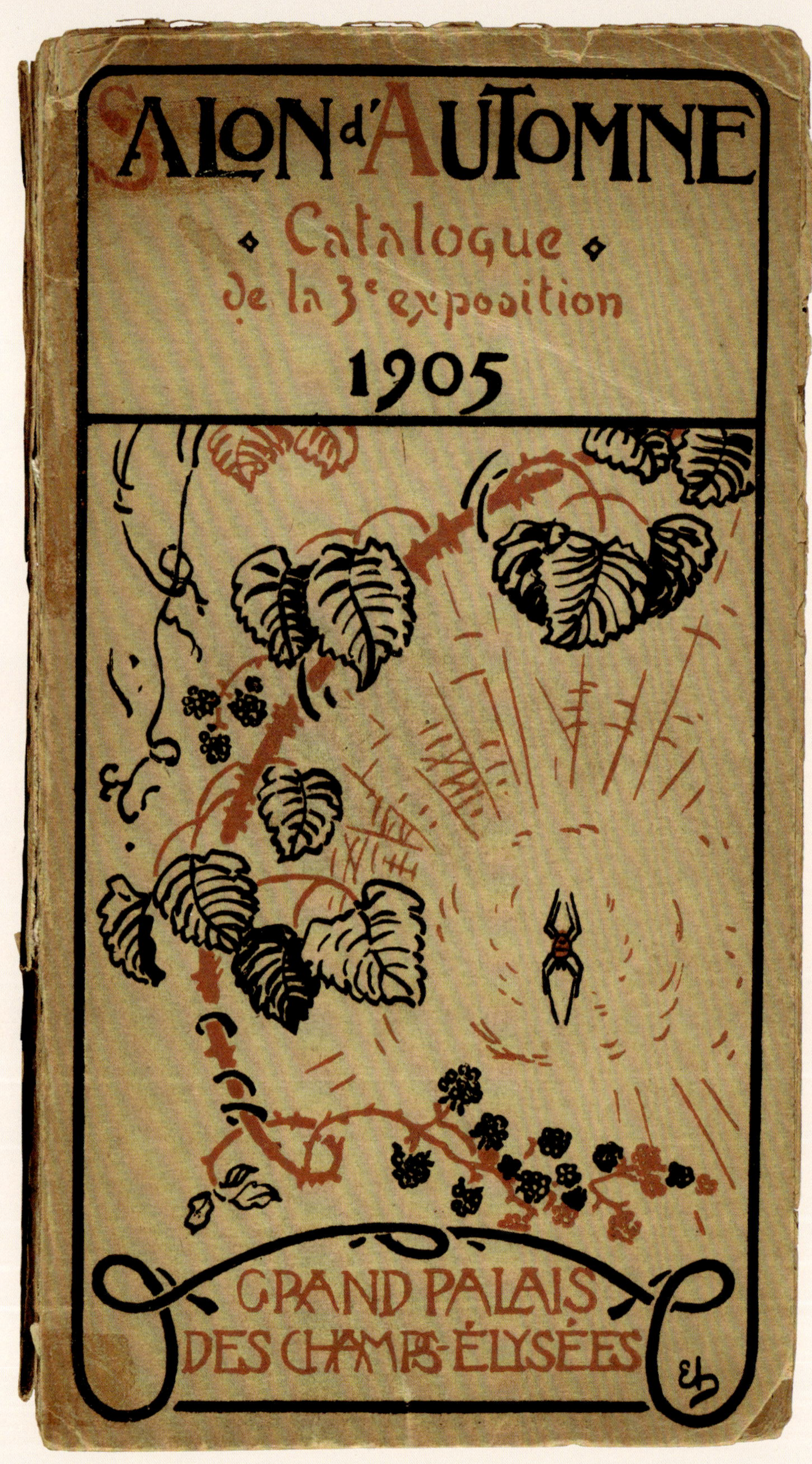

Cover of the exhibition catalogue for the third Salon d'Automne at the Grand
Palais des Champs-Élysées, Paris, 1905. Miscellaneous art exhibition catalog collection,
1915–1925, Archives of American Art, Smithsonian Institution, Washington, DC

A Modern Scandal: The 1905 Salon d'Automne

MARIA CASTRO

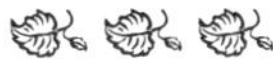

Before the label "Fauves" (Wild Beasts) stuck, other expressions circulated among critics and the public to describe the presentation in Gallery VII of the 1905 Salon d'Automne at the Grand Palais in Paris—from reviews that dubbed it the "room of incoherents" to an unsanctioned sign allegedly posted outside the entrance designating it as the "gallery of dangerous madmen."[1] The gallery featured fifty-five works by ten artists, but one elicited the most passionate reactions, and over time has come to represent this infamous occasion. This was Henri Matisse's *Femme au chapeau* (Woman with a Hat)—or, as one critic described it, "a certain figure of a woman in green, green-cheeked, the greenest attack upon taste and common sense I've ever witnessed."[2] The history of modern art is punctuated with moments of rupture with the past, mythologized first by critics and later by art historians. The 1905 salon was almost immediately understood as one such moment, an art-world scandal that identified and named the first avant-garde expression of twentieth-century Paris. The story of the public debut of Matisse's painting has been rehearsed in countless studies, yet many of the details and much of the context of its original presentation are now unknown.

To date, no photographs of the interior of the Salon d'Automne galleries have been located, and because the catalogue of the exhibition lists artworks in alphabetical order, it is not possible to identify all of the works that appeared alongside *Femme au chapeau*.[3] Reviews of the salon are the best sources available. One article in particular had an outsize impact on its reception: an extensive review by Louis Vauxcelles, published in the daily periodical *Gil Blas* the evening before the exhibition opened to the public. Vauxcelles, a prolific critic of contemporary art, was also a member of the Salon d'Automne.

Vauxcelles characterized Albert Marque's cherubic sculptures in the center of Gallery VII as "Donatello chez les fauves" ("Donatello at home with the wild beasts"), and in so doing named the Fauves (for works by Marque on similar subjects, see pp. 42 and 43).[4] His recap of Gallery VII describes works by Charles Camoin, André Derain, Pierre Girieud, Henri Manguin, Albert Marque, Albert Marquet, Henri Matisse, Ramon Pichot, Jelka Rosen, and Maurice de Vlaminck.[5] Scholarly attention to the Salon d'Automne has not been equally distributed—while Matisse and Derain have been subjects of numerous studies and exhibitions, other artists have been all but forgotten.[6] Bringing light to the full range of art on view, as well as to the Grand Palais as an influential exhibition venue in the period, reveals that the scandal surrounding Matisse's painting was propelled by its context as part of a broader progressive, anti-establishment effort with social, political, and aesthetic implications.

The Salon d'Automne was one of four seasonal salons in Paris in 1905, each with its own structure. It was the youngest, in only its third iteration that year. After surviving the inhospitable basement of the Petit Palais—damp and dark, deemed fit only for "mice, rats, spiders, and woodlice"—in its debut exhibition, the salon had secured enough support to move into the Grand Palais in 1904.[7] The salon's organizers in these first two years—chief among them the architect Frantz Jourdain, who would be its president for more than three decades—weathered attacks by the leaders of the Société des Artistes Français and the Société Nationale des Beaux-Arts.[8] Such condemnation is not surprising, as Jourdain deliberately positioned the new salon against those institutions' more established and conservative-leaning exhibitions, "whose initial liberalism had gradually cooled," in his words.[9] The reactions of the rival salons were especially stoked by the Salon d'Automne's admission into the Grand Palais, the venue for both societies' spring exhibitions, and a building dedicated to the "glory of French art."

The Salon d'Automne embraced a progressive agenda throughout the organization of its exhibition. Unlike the Salon des Indépendants, another annual that likewise promoted new art, its exhibitions were curated by a rotating jury of its members, which included artists as well as architects, art critics, and "art lovers."[10] The galleries were organized by a different artist member each year, who imposed a cogent arrangement on the works, in contrast to the "scattered" displays of the Indépendants.[11] From 1905 on, both its catalogue and exhibition integrated applied art, ceramics, tapestries, architecture, and works on paper into the same gal-

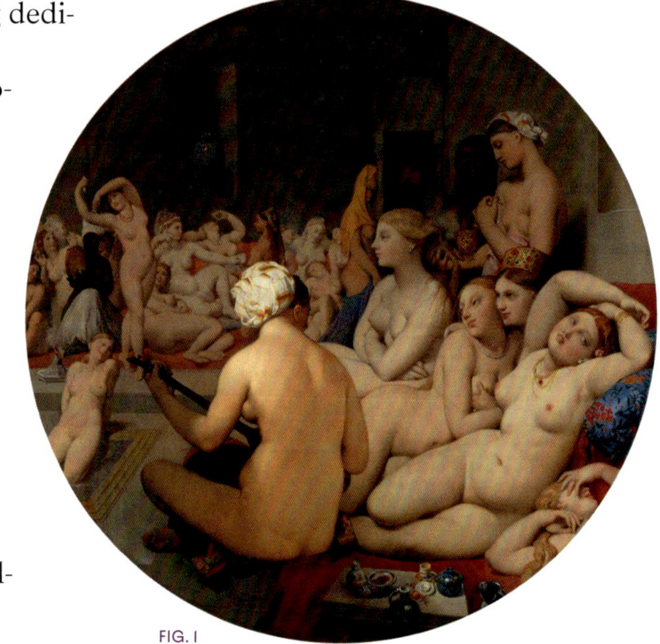

FIG. 1

Jean-Auguste-Dominique
Ingres, *Le bain turc* (The Turkish
Bath), 1862. Oil on canvas
glued on wood, 42½ × 55⅛ in.
(108 × 140 cm). Louvre Museum,
Paris, gift from the Society of
Friends of the Louvre

Édouard Manet, *La musique
aux Tuileries* (Music in
the Tuileries Gardens), 1862.
Oil on canvas, 30 × 46½ in.
(76.2 × 118.1 cm). Sir Hugh Lane
Bequest, 1917, The National
Gallery, London. In partnership
with Hugh Lane Gallery, Dublin

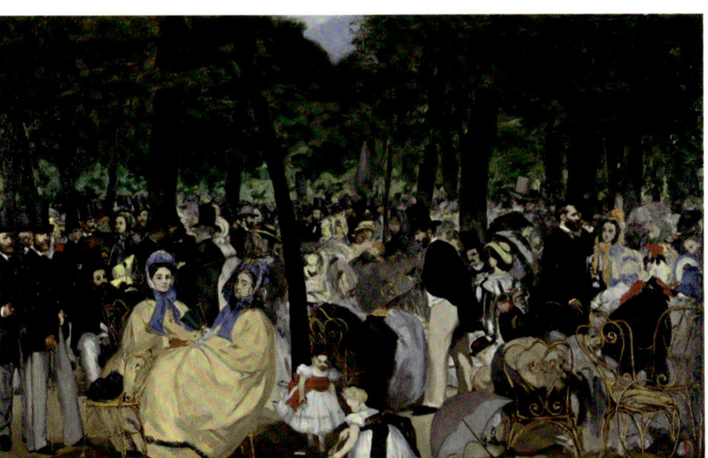

FIG. 2

leries as paintings and sculptures, in nonhierarchical presentations conceived to disrupt the status quo of the turn-of-the-century French art establishment.[12]

Yet the Salon d'Automne's revolutionary approach was balanced with an equally crucial goal of asserting the legitimacy of new art made by young artists to claim and shape French tradition. Among hundreds of newly made works, the 1905 exhibition included a retrospective gallery featuring sixty-eight paintings and drawings by Jean-August-Dominique Ingres, whose centerpiece was *Le bain turc* (The Turkish Bath) of 1862 (fig. 1), and another of thirty-one works by Édouard Manet, featuring his *La musique aux Tuileries* (Music in the Tuileries Gardens, fig. 2), from the same year. The critic Élie Faure explained the logic of including these presentations in his introduction to the salon's catalogue: "Through these retrospective exhibitions, the Salon d'Automne endeavors to demonstrate the ongoing legitimacy of revolutionary effort to rejoin tradition. . . . Ingres and Manet will quietly reaffirm that today's revolutionary is tomorrow's classic."[13] This framing of the salon underscores why the presentation in Gallery VII elicited such passionate controversy. Vauxcelles's review naming Fauvism conjured a resonant image precisely because of the contrast it created between accepted tradition and radical innovation. Yet, it was not intended to be hostile. As the art historian James D. Herbert notes, "Vauxcelles did not place Donatello 'among' (*parmi*) the Fauves; even less 'against' (*contre*) them. . . . Marque was *chez* Matisse and the others, at home with the wild beasts."[14]

The Salon d'Automne was a dizzying enterprise, featuring 1,735 objects, presented in eighteen galleries, representing a wide range of media, scales, and subjects. They were installed in the west wing of the Grand Palais, known as the Palais d'Antin, and although no floor plans of the exhibition survive, reviews note that the Salon d'Automne occupied the same galleries as the Société Nationale des Beaux-Arts exhibition had in the spring. The floor plan for the spring salon, published each year in its accompanying catalogue, offers a sense of how galleries were distributed around the second floor of the building, surrounding the rotunda and the dramatic twin staircases (fig. 3).[15] Gallery VII occupies a relatively small footprint. The American collector Dr. Claribel Cone recollected of her visit to the Salon d'Automne: "Having passed through several of the larger halls, we happened to find ourselves in a small room which had been set apart for the independent group of which Matisse was chief. The walls were covered with canvases—presenting what seemed to me then a riot of color—sharp and startling, drawing crude and uneven, distortions and exaggerations—composition primitive and simple as if done by a child."[16]

Photographs of the interior of the 1904 Salon d'Automne reinforce
this sense of an overwhelming visual experience (fig. 4). Paintings are grouped
by artist and displayed in two rows above a low wooden picture rail. A luxuri-
ous red damask fabric patterned with laurel wreaths covers the walls. Potted
plants interrupt the flow of paintings at various intervals, and benches occupy
the center of the space. The extensive skylights and the galleries' red walls
would have echoed the design of France's national museums, including the
Louvre's "Salles Rouges" (Red Rooms), drawing a direct connection to an

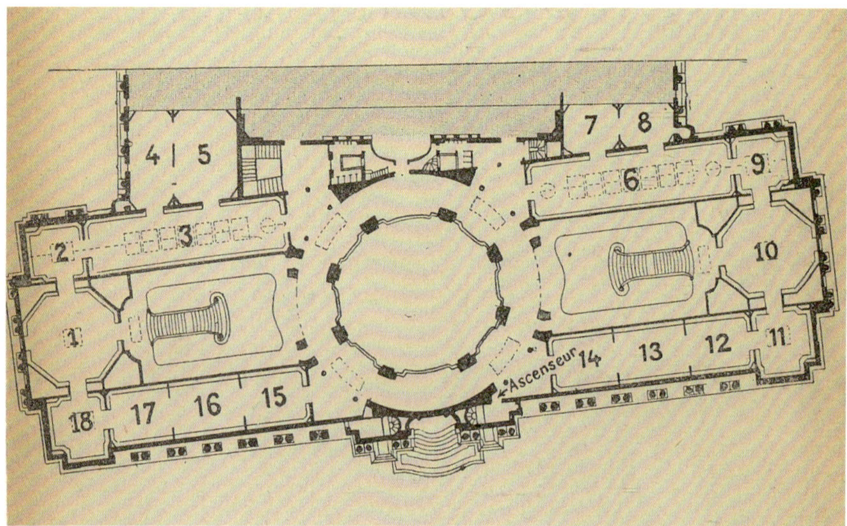

FIG. 3

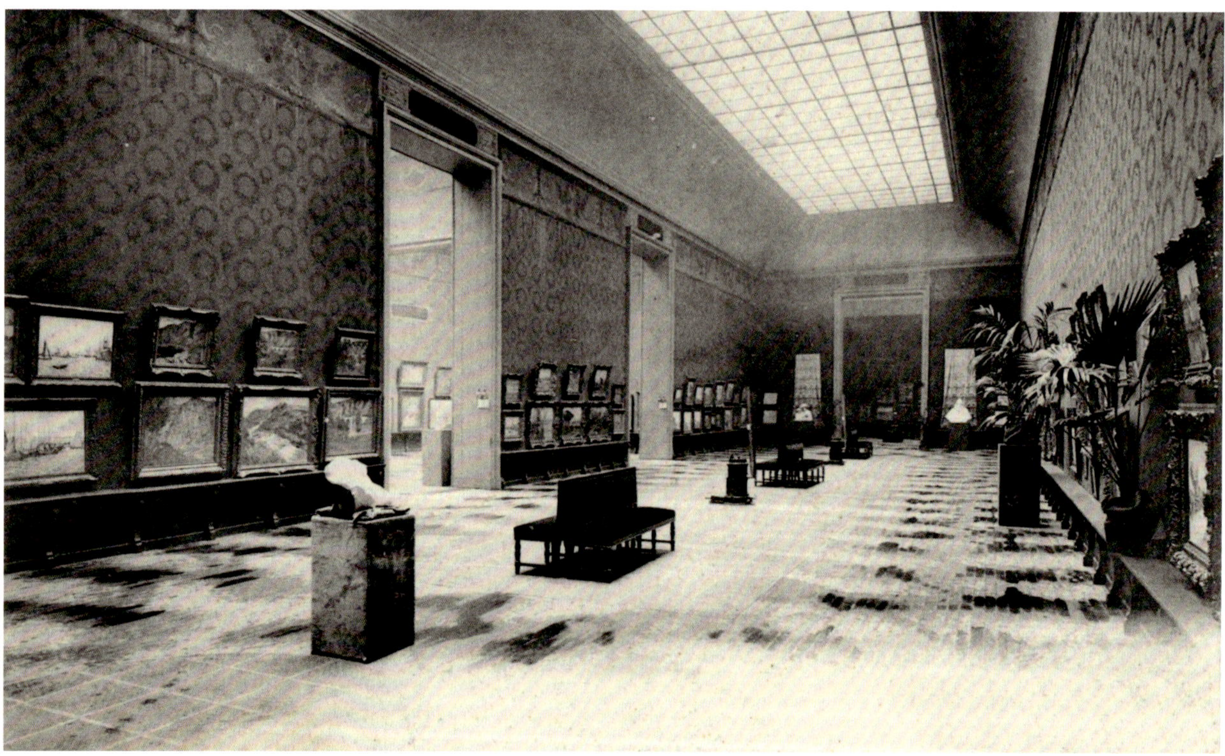

FIG. 4

FIG. 3
Floor plan, Salon of the Société Nationale des Beaux-Arts, published in *Catalogue illustré de la Société nationale des beaux-arts,* 1905. Gallica, Bibliothèque Nationale de France

FIG. 4
View of a gallery at the Grand Palais during the Salon d'Automne, 1904. Private collection

earlier imperial tradition.[17] The Grand Palais's red wall coverings began to be systematically replaced starting in 1903, so it is unclear if the Fauve works were displayed against them. Still, walking through the building to reach Gallery VII would have brought visitors through interiors richly decorated with trompe l'oeil murals executed by young artists such as Matisse and his friend Albert Marquet in 1900.[18] This architectural context, designed to mirror a bygone era, stood in sharp contrast to the unruly and wildly colored works presented in Gallery VII.

As Claudine Grammont observes, after 1900 salons became increasingly theatrical in their staging: "The salon was no longer just a place of aesthetic contemplation but a place of leisure: people went to the salon as they went to the theater…to be entertained."[19] A canny promoter of his young enterprise, Jourdain recognized the shift in the culture of the salon in planning the opening, which took place on Tuesday evening, October 17, 1905: "[It] must be sensational; it must be a social event."[20] Visitor attendance was an important aspect of the new salon's business model; in 1904 it attracted more than twelve thousand viewers for the opening and more than five thousand the following day.[21] In the news, the salon was covered not only by culture critics but also by fashion magazines. By early November, readers of *Vogue* in the United States could enjoy an extensive story describing the gowns and hats seen at the Salon d'Automne's vernissage.[22] This development of the salon into a social event is reflected in the words of a critic for *La Vie Illustré,* who accused the artists in Gallery VII of being preoccupied with "shocking the bourgeois."[23]

WHO WERE THE WILD BEASTS?

The artists who created the fifty-five paintings, sculptures, and works on paper on view in Gallery VII were young, ranging from their mid-twenties to mid-thirties. Some were longtime friends who had exhibited together in the past.[24] Matisse, Manguin, and Marquet had met in the early 1890s, as students at the École des Arts Décoratifs in Paris.[25] They met Camoin in 1898, when all four were enrolled in the studio of Gustave Moreau at the École Nationale des Beaux-Arts. Moreau's students had been known for making avant-garde work since 1895, when Roger Marx described the studio as "a hotbed of militant originality."[26] In 1899, at the Académie Camillo, Matisse and Marquet met Derain, who in turn befriended Vlaminck the following year on a train from Paris to Chatou, the suburb where they both lived and were to share a studio.[27] Matisse's relationship with these younger artists proved to be as productive as the friendships he made at the Beaux-Arts. He later recounted, "To tell the truth, the painting of Derain and Vlaminck did not surprise me, for it was close to the researches that I myself was pursuing. But I was moved that these very young men had certain convictions similar to my own."[28] These six artists were important interlocutors for each other in the summer of 1905 and, excepting Vlaminck, worked side by side on many of the paintings they presented in Gallery VII: Matisse and Derain in Collioure, and Camoin, Manguin, and Marquet in the Côte d'Azur.

The three other painters who showed in Gallery VII—Pierre Girieud, Ramon Pichot, and Jelka Rosen—shared an interest in using vivid colors and had in some cases exhibited together.[29] Once called the "fauve indécis" (the indecisive Fauve), the self-taught Girieud presented five still lifes in Gallery VII, including *Tulipes et vitrail* (Tulips and Stained Glass), *Pivoines et images d'Épinal* (Peonies and Épinal Print; also known as *Legend of Saint Nicholas*), and *Iris sur fond jaune* (Iris on Yellow Background) (pp. 36 and 37).[30] His approach to color and handling of paint, inspired by Van Gogh, were in dialogue with other works in the gallery, particularly Vlaminck's. Pichot's presentation featured landscapes of Catalonia—subjects that aligned with the seascapes presented by the artists who worked in the South of France. Only one of his five salon submissions has been definitively identified—*Sardana (danse populaire)* (Sardana [Popular Dance]), which was illustrated in a review, and whose location is now unknown

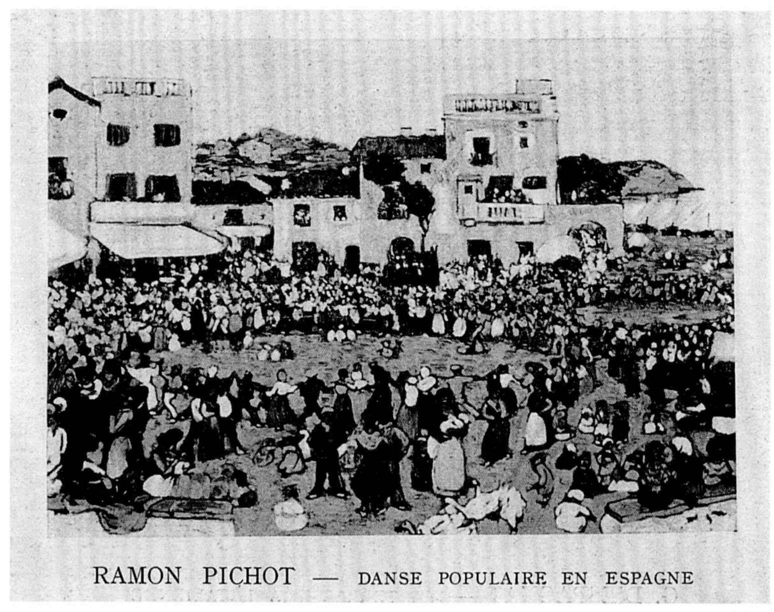

FIG. 5

(fig. 5).[31] On similar themes, Pichot's *Clair de lune (Cadaqués)* (Moonlight [Cadaqués], p. 56) and *Tablao flamenco* (Flamenco Tablao, p. 57) show how, as Vauxcelles notes, he "distinguished himself as a colorist."[32] Jelka Rosen, the only woman artist to be included, actively exhibited in Paris at the turn of the century. There is little evidence of relationships with the other artists in Gallery VII, although she was a friend of Auguste Rodin.[33] Rosen was based in Grez-sur-Loing, just south of Paris, and was recognized for her "understated yet highly effective handling of vibrant color."[34] Few of her works are known today, and none of her four paintings in Gallery VII—views of her garden in Grez from May to August—could be located. *Le pont de Grez* (The Grez Bridge, p. 58) and *Les meules* (Haystacks, p. 59) display her experimentation with pointillism and with a palette that sometimes echoes that of Matisse, which may have brought her compositions into dialogue with those of the Fauves.

THE SAINT-TROPEZ AND AGAY LANDSCAPES

The five paintings that Camoin, Manguin, and Marquet each presented in Gallery VII recorded their travels through the southern coast of France in the summer of that year. Manguin arrived at Saint-Tropez in early May and began painting furiously, as Marquet reported in a June letter to Matisse: "Manguin has his wife pose for him and works nonstop. He doesn't even break for meals but holds his fork in one hand and his pencil in the other, chowing down his food while drawing on the tablecloth. His example fills me with remorse. He's already produced a shitload of works, while my trunk is still full of blank canvases."[35] Marquet had joined Manguin shortly after the latter's arrival and found lodging at the Hotel Sube by early June. By the end of that month, Camoin arrived as well, and departed with Marquet for Agay in mid-July.

Of the paintings Manguin sent for the consideration of the Salon d'Automne's jury in 1905, four feature his wife, Jeanne, on the grounds of the Villa Demière, the house they rented in Saint-Tropez for the summer: *La sieste* (The Nap); *Le pré, Villa Demière* (The Meadow, Villa Demière); *Jeanne sur le bal-con de la Villa Demière* (Jeanne on the Balcony of the Villa Demière); and *Nu sous les arbres, Jeanne* (Nude under the Trees, Jeanne), while the fifth, *Les grands chênes-lièges, Villa Demière* (The Large Cork Oaks, Villa Demière), depicts the surrounding cork oak trees (pp. 38–41).[36] In a letter to Matisse reporting that the canvases submitted by Manguin and Marquet had been admitted by the salon's jury, the artist René Piot remarked, "Manguin has impressed me with his significant leap forward."[37] Vauxcelles echoed the sentiment in his review of the gallery: "Manguin: huge progress."[38] The centerpiece of his presentation, *The Nap,* was featured in *L'Illustration* alongside Matisse's *Femme au chapeau* and *Fenêtre ouverte* (Open Window, Collioure, p. 47) and Derain's *Le séchage des voiles* (Drying of Sails, p. 33), in a sensationalizing illustrated review that brought infamy to the artists in Gallery VII (fig. 6).[39]

Camoin enjoyed broadly positive reception for his landscapes, with one critic noting, for example, his "felicitous understanding of light and its uses," and another setting him apart from the rest of the gallery: "We will abstain from discussing galleries VII and VIII, with the exception of M. Camoin's lumi-nous marine landscapes."[40] He presented four seascapes: *Agay (l'hôtel)* (Agay [The Hotel]), *Agay (bord de mer)* (Agay [Seashore], see p. 31), *Le Port de Cassis*

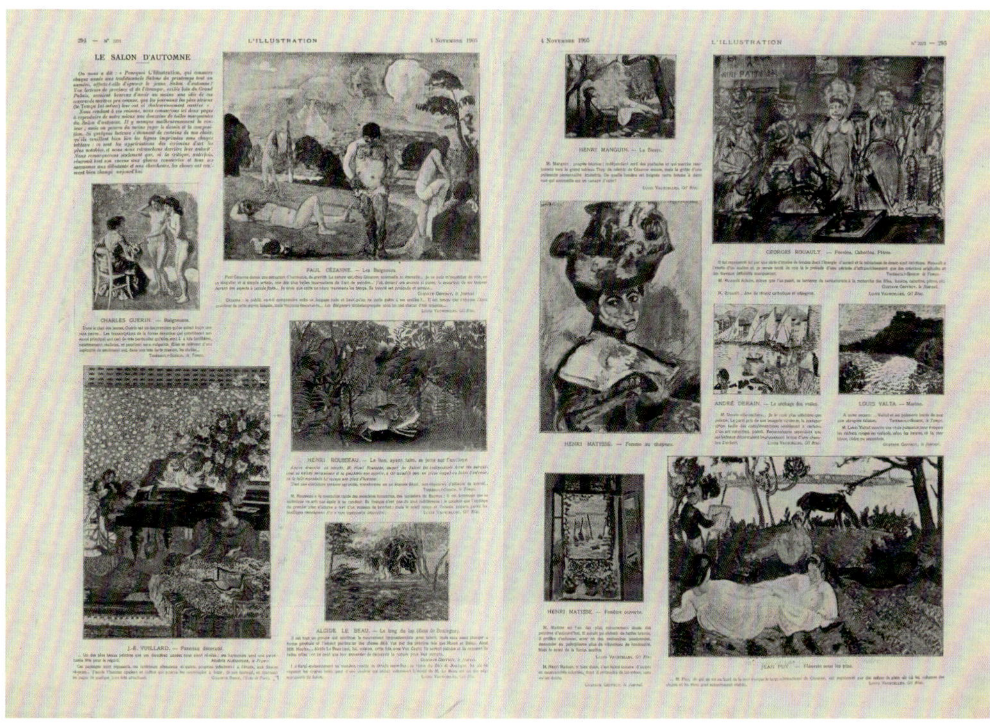

(soleil couchant) (Port of Cassis, Sunset, see p. 30), and *Le Port de Cassis (temps gris)* (The Port of Cassis [Overcast Day]), as well as a portrait, *Madame Yvonne Bouis à l'ombrelle* (Madame Yvonne Bouis with a Parasol, fig. 7).[41]

Marquet showed his *Vue d'Agay* (View of Agay, p. 44), depicting the Mediterranean through verdant vegetation, alongside *Anthéor*—most likely *Anthéor, les roches rouges* (Anthéor, the Red Rocks, p. 45), listed in Druet's collection in the Salon's catalogue; two seascapes from Le Trayas (see p. 45 on the same subject); and *Le Port de Menton* (The Port of Menton).[42] Vauxcelles dedicated significant attention to Marquet's landscapes, praising his joyful colors and original style.[43] While the artists working on the Côte d'Azur were also subject to criticism, their comparatively milder reception points to how the four friends from Moreau's studio diverged over the course of the summer, with Matisse embracing a more abstract approach to color and form. After reconnecting in Paris, Matisse recognized as much when he remarked about their paintings, "I like their work, though truth to tell it is rather the opposite of mine."[44]

COLOR FOR COLOR'S SAKE

Vlaminck stayed in Paris for the summer of 1905, and his five submissions to the salon were small landscapes of the Seine valley near Chatou that stand out for their relatively sober palettes. These included two garden scenes—*La maison de mon père* (My Father's House), a view of his father's home in Chatou, and *Le jardin* (The Garden)—along with the tranquil *L'Étang de Saint-Cucufa* (Saint-Cucufa Pond), a view of the village in *La vallée de Port-Marly* (The Valley at Port-Marly), and a single figure among the trees in *Crépuscule* (Twilight) (pp. 60–65).[45] The bright oranges and reds and loose brushstrokes of the first canvas attracted the most attention, leading a critic to imagine Vlaminck's process as totally random: "Having prepared small balls of color, he threw them any old how at the canvas and called it *My Father's House*. Where is the house? What exactly do these small red cobblestones that fill three-quarters of the painting represent? It's a mystery."[46] Inspired by the expressive brushstrokes of Van Gogh, Vlaminck painted in thick, energetic daubs of contrasting colors, such as the bright reddish-orange foreground of his *Port-Marly* against the green of its rolling hills. A self-identified anarchist, he saw this way of painting as explicitly political: "I wanted to revolutionize habits and contemporary life, to liberate nature, to free it from the authority of old theories and classicism."[47]

In the South of France, Derain had come to "a new conception of light which consists in this: the negation of shadows. Here the light is very strong and the shadows very bright." He describes to Vlaminck having left behind the strict methods of divisionism and letting himself "go with color for color's sake."[48] After a little less than two months of work, he returned to Paris

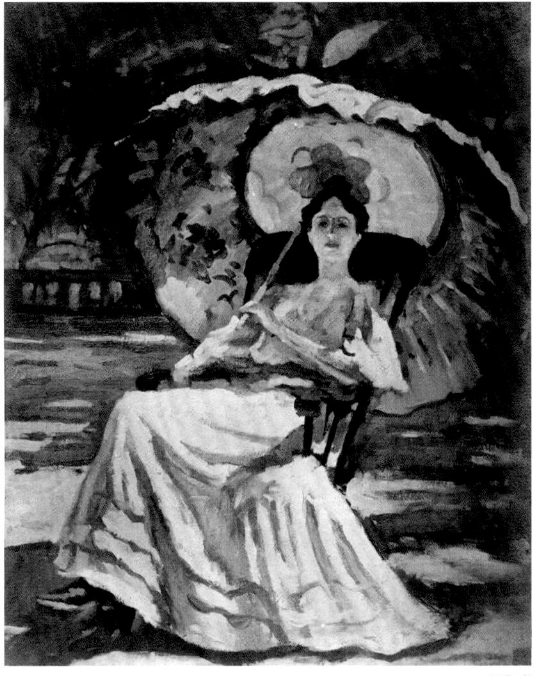

FIG. 7

with "thirty complete canvases, twenty drawings, and some fifty sketches," which he described as "so complex and so different, so unsettling for the critics."[49] Although it seems he had originally planned to submit to the Salon d'Automne at least one canvas made prior to the trip, he ultimately presented five works painted in Collioure. Only one can be definitively identified, *Drying of Sails*, whose image was published immediately next to Matisse's *Femme au chapeau* in *L'Illustration*. The salon's catalogue lists three additional landscapes by Derain: *Chênes-liège* (Cork Oaks), *Vue de Collioures* (*sic*) (View of Collioure), and *Port de pêche* (Fishing Port), as well as a portrait—perhaps of his friend Matisse (p. 34), although Derain executed several others that summer.[50] Such paintings as *Arbres à Collioure* (Trees at Collioure), *Le phare de Collioure* (The Lighthouse of Collioure), and *Barques de pêche à Collioure* (Fishing Boats, Collioure) give a sense of the artist's vivid palette and dramatic experimentation (pp. 32 and 35). Some bits of canvas are left exposed, and luminous contrasting colors—sometimes in concentrated spots, sometimes in broad expanses—float loosely against lighter backgrounds, expressing the flattening effect of Collioure's light that "bears down on all sides with its immense shout of victory."[51]

Derain had reason to be concerned about how his paintings would be received. Even before the salon opened to the public, he faced opposition from the jury. In the same letter in which Piot praised Manguin's progress, he reported to Matisse, "You can count on me for Derain, whom I find very talented. . . . We'll do our best with Rouault and Guerin [who were among that year's jurors], although one senses much greater resistance than last year. I really like [Derain's] submissions but few will perhaps understand this great abstraction."[52] The resistance continued in the press. Even the sympathetic Vauxcelles wrote that his *Boats* "would be just the thing to decorate the walls of a child's bedroom."[53] Derain's landscapes engendered both interest and rejection, yet, as a relatively lesser-known artist working primarily in the genre of landscape, he was not subject to as much attention as Matisse.

Alongside Derain in Collioure, Matisse reported that he completed "forty watercolors, one hundred drawings, and fifteen canvases."[54] He had planned to submit as the centerpiece of his presentation in Gallery VII a large canvas portraying the port of Collioure, *Le Port d'Avall* (The Port of Avall), but he struggled with the composition (fig. 8). On August 19 he wrote to Marquet: "Not happy about my work, large painting is a failure despite its division [technique]."[55] He would miss the deadline for submitting paintings for the consideration of the jury (September 15–17) and, after securing an extension, wrote to his friend Simon Bussy that he was "working on a 1.5 m × 40 cm painting depicting the Collioure port, where I've just spent four months....It's a long process, since I make small dots, and especially as they don't always succeed the first time around."[56] In the end, Matisse decided not to show the work, presumably substituting *Femme au chapeau*, which hung alongside *Open Window, Collioure*,

Jeune femme en robe japonaise au bord de l'eau (also known as *La Japonaise au bord de l'eau* [La Japonaise: Woman beside the Water], p. 49), *Matinée d'été* (Summer Morning), and *Nature morte* (Still Life). While the still life has yet to be identified, *Summer Afternoon* may be the painting now titled *Un beau matin d'été* (A Beautiful Summer Morning, p. 53), rather than the landscape *Les toits de Collioure* (The Roofs of Collioure), as was previously assumed.[57] After a visit to the salon with Matisse, Marcel Sembat's recollections seem to be describing this painting next to *La Japonaise: Woman beside the Water:* "Strange paintings: pink, green, and blue streaks within a white tonality…that depict the ghostly Japanese figure of a woman reading; and the brownish-green little fellow lost among the roses."[58] In addition to these canvases, Matisse also presented five works on paper, including two watercolors, *Baigneuse* (Reclining Bather) and *La promenade* (The Promenade), and drawings titled *Japonaise* (Woman in Japanese Dress), *Marine (pêcheur)* (Seascape [Fisherman]), and *Marine (bateaux)* (Seascape [Boats]) (see pp. 48, 50, 51, 54, and 55).

In contrast to the predominance of landscape painting in Gallery VII, half of the works Matisse presented were focused on figures, all featuring the artist's wife, Amélie. In letters exchanged in late June, referring to Matisse's last public exhibition before the Salon d'Automne, Vauxcelles had praised the "dazzling luminosity and vibration" of his *Tulipes perroquet II* (Parrot Tulips II, fig. 9) and challenged the artist: "But will you achieve similarly successful effects with figures? I do hope so.…Come back, M. Matisse, with an armful of beautiful artworks. Show the most beautiful ones at the Salon d'Automne, and count on me to badmouth them in my publications."[59] Whether or not that exchange influenced Matisse's experiments with the figure in Collioure, he had a willing model in Amélie, whom he depicted in numerous drawings and watercolors and several paintings. In his treatment of her likeness, Matisse was working through challenging formal questions, as he reported in a letter to Signac: "Something I just noticed while executing a life-size decorative

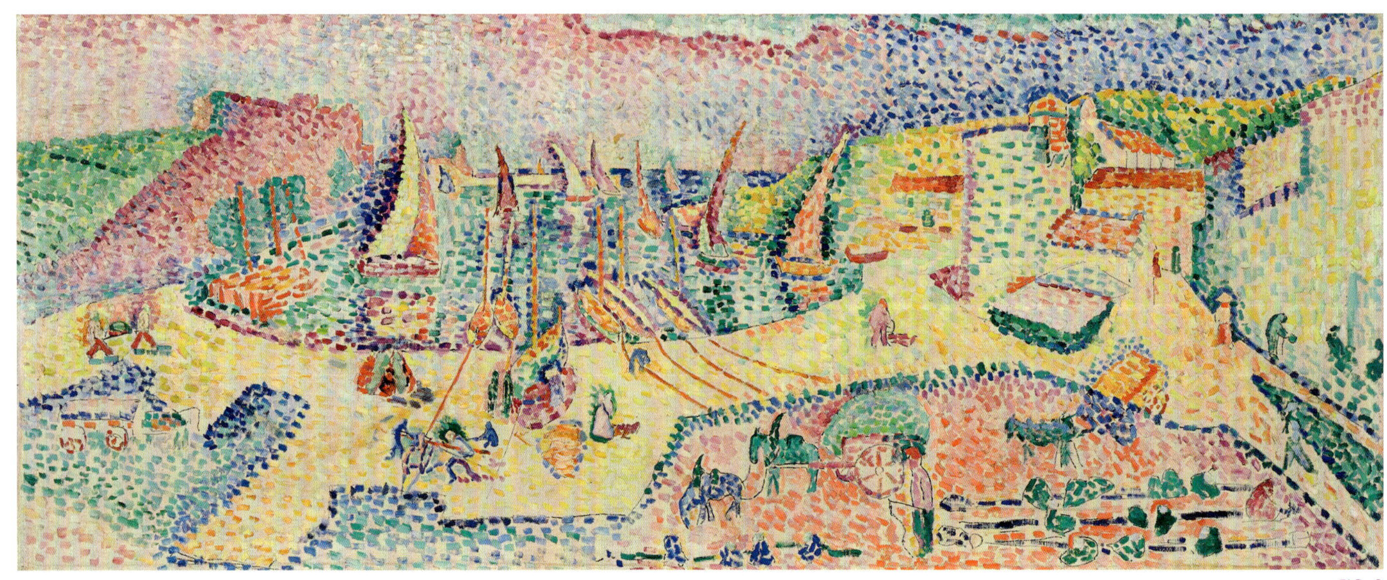

FIG. 8

figure prompts me to ask: have you found in my picture of female bathers, a perfect accord between the character of the drawing and the character of the painting? To me the two seem completely different, even absolutely contradictory…. Result: the painting, especially when applied in small dots, destroys the drawing, *which derives all its eloquence from contours.*"[60] Matisse grappled with this question in works such as *La Japonaise: Woman beside the Water,* in which the figure's form seems to blend into the landscape, loosely defined through an increasingly free approach to color and brushwork. Searching for guidance on resolving the relationship between color and form in his paintings, Matisse asked Signac to send him the following quote by Paul Cézanne on the subject: "Drawing and color aren't distinct from each other. In the process of painting or drawing, as color becomes more finely tuned, drawing gains precision. When color is at its richest, form is at its fullest…. It can all be summarized in this way: experiencing sensations and reading Nature."[61]

Matisse's choice to replace the unfinished *Port of Avall* with *Femme au chapeau,* rather than another of the landscapes from Collioure, marked a breakthrough—as he left behind the strictures of pointillism and sought to deploy color in the service of expression, to capture sensation rather than perception. Despite the failure of his original plan, Matisse reported that "it was the first time in my life I was content to be exhibiting."[62]

From the jury, who Matisse said nearly rejected his submissions, to critics and the public, audiences placed the painting at the center of the "scandal" surrounding Gallery VII, to the artist's great disappointment. Many reviews focused on Matisse's handling of color, likening his efforts to those of a child—"As for Henri Matisse, the author of this portrait of a woman with green shoulders, a green face, and red hair…a strange profligacy of violent colors that appear to owe their juxtaposition to mere chance or child's play."[63] Others found Matisse's painting to be overly cerebral: "It is the product of theories."[64] Perhaps more surprisingly, Matisse's subject also figured

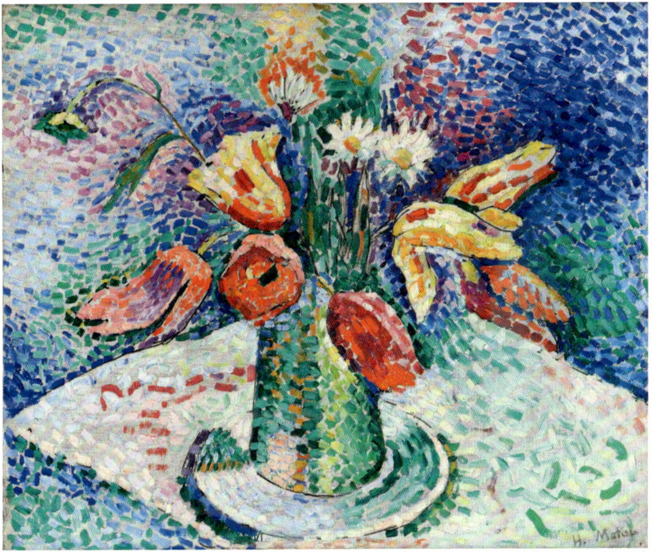

FIG. 9

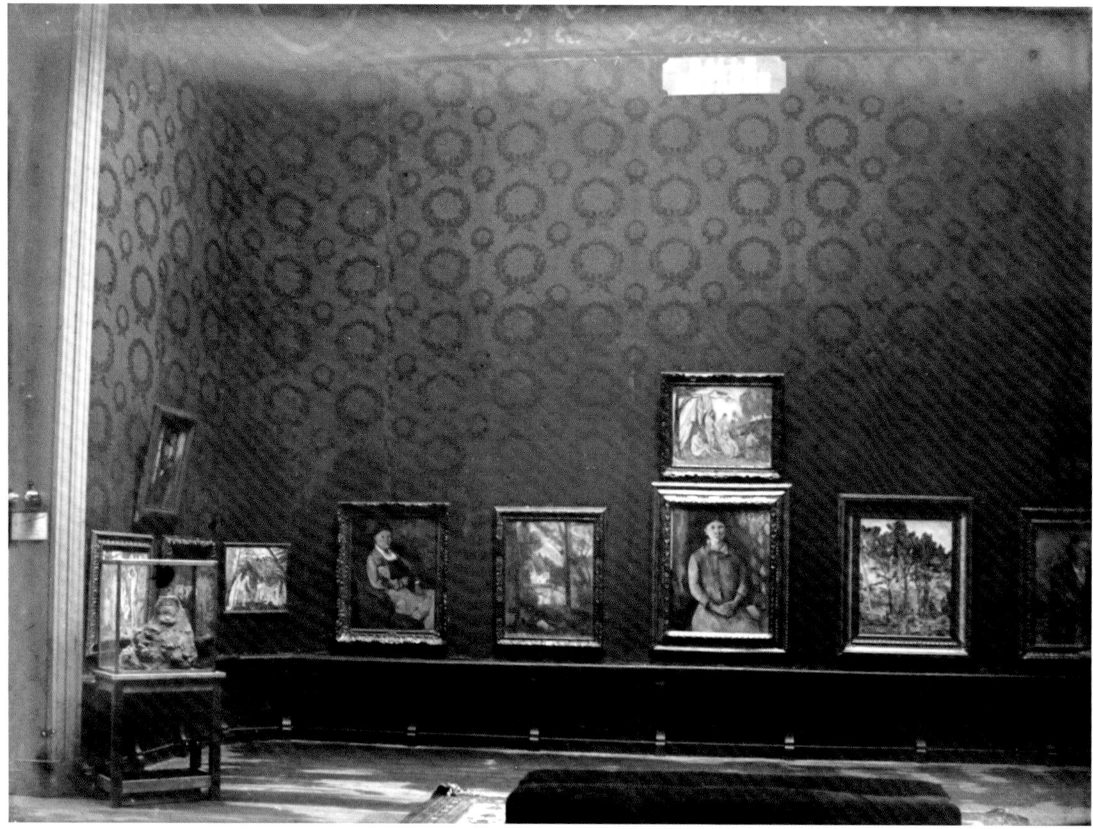

FIG. 10

in sometimes gendered critiques of his depiction of Amélie Matisse's milli-nery: he "occupies himself with coloring monstrous hats" or (later) "This is a modiste's taste; his love of color is no more than a love for rags."[65] As Claudine Grammont proposes in her essay in this volume, the format of *Femme au chapeau* alludes to a well-established portrait tradition, which may have con-tributed to its power to shock—particularly amid dozens of more conserva-tive takes on the trope also on view at the salon.[66] It also surely put Matisse in direct dialogue with Cézanne, whose retrospective at the previous year's Salon d'Automne—to which Matisse lent the Cézanne painting in his personal collection—featured several portraits of Madame Cézanne (fig. 10), including *Madame Cézanne au chapeau vert* (Madame Cézanne with Green Hat, p. 91). Visitors, too, responded to *Femme au chapeau* with unusual passion. As Gertrude Stein recalled, "It infuriated the public. They tried to scratch off the paint"; her brother Leo wrote that it "made everybody laugh except a few who got mad about it."[67]

Yet critics still broadly recognized Matisse's contribution as a leading artist of his generation—"It's Matisse's school that appears most alive, most novel, and most debated"—and called him "most naturally gifted." *Femme au chapeau* was identified as a pivotal work within his oeuvre: "Henri Matisse has a woman's portrait that will be the object of much debate but embodies a new stage in investigations by this tormented artist."[68] It was Matisse's presen-tation at the Salon d'Automne that solidified his reputation as the leader of the Fauves.[69] This was a decisive moment for his career, especially considering that *Femme au chapeau* caught the attention of Leo Stein, who described the work as "the nastiest smear of paint I had ever seen," but who nonetheless appreciated its radicality and made an offer for the painting that provided crucial early support for the artist.[70]

"IN THE DOMAIN OF ABSTRACTION"

As much as the works of the artists featured in Gallery VII engendered confusion and rejection—"Is this art?…We'll let its authors have a good laugh"—they were also understood as charting a new path for painting: "Stepping into the gallery dedicated to [Matisse], one sets off to scrutinize intentions and investigate theories; one feels fully in the domain of abstraction."[71] For many contemporary viewers, these works in the context of the Grand Palais made not only an aesthetic statement but also a political one. Reviews abound with language referring to the artists in Gallery VII as anarchists. André Gide addressed the tension between innovation and tradition at the heart of the 1905 Salon d'Automne when he wrote: "One could maybe tolerate that these young painters, alongside Manet, posed as anarchists; one could accept that they represented something like the far-left of painting; but alongside Ingres, what on earth were they pretending? To represent no longer some excessive paradox of art, but art itself, Art with a capital A?"[72] In presenting his *Femme au chapeau* at the Salon d'Automne, Matisse placed it at the center of contemporary debates about the direction of French art in the twentieth century. His painting not only made radical use of color that proposed a new way of looking at the world but also, in the context of its debut, stood out for embodying the intersection of the established and the avant-garde, looking back in order to chart the future. ❧

1   For "room of incoherents," see J.-C. Holl, "Le Salon d'Automne," *Les Cahiers d'Art et de Littérature,* Nov. 1905, p. 80. For the "gallery of dangerous madmen" label, see Octave Maus, "L'art au Salon d'Automne," *Mercure de France,* Jan. 1, 1907, p. 61. Translations from French-language sources are by Fabienne Adler and Anne Levine unless otherwise indicated.

2   "Au salon," *Le National,* Oct. 21, 1905, p. 4.

3   Published installation views attributed to the 1905 Salon d'Automne have proven to be from other years, most often from 1904—the first year the salon was held in the Grand Palais.

4   Louis Vauxcelles, "Le Salon d'Automne," *Supplément à Gil Blas,* Oct. 17, 1905. The original sculptures Albert Marque presented in Gallery VII, *Portrait de Marthe Lebasque* (Portrait of Marthe Lebasque, marble bust) and *Torse d'enfant* (Torso of a Child, bronze), are now lost. *Torso of a Child* was acquired by the French state out of the Salon d'Automne (Collection du Centre National des Arts Plastiques, FNAC 1745), but its current location is unknown. Thank you to Gaëlle Guerin and Pauline Lucet at CNAP for their assistance with this research.

5   Most other reviewers covered a combination of these artists and some also included Jean Puy in Gallery VII or VIII. Vauxcelles places Puy in Gallery III; see "Le Salon d'Automne." For other mentions of Jean Puy's works, see Pierre Veber, "Le Salon d'Automne passé en par M. Pierre Veber," *The New York Herald,* Oct. 17, 1905, p. 8; Le Masque Rouge, "Notes d'art: Le Salon d'Automne," *L'Action,* Oct. 18, 1905, p. 1; and Etienne Charles, "Le Salon d'Automne," *La Liberté,* Oct. 17, 1905, p. 9.

6   Most recently, see Dita Amory and Ann Dumas, eds., *Vertigo of Color: Matisse, Derain, and the Origins of Fauvism,* exh. cat. (New York: Metropolitan Museum of Art, 2023); and Arthur Fink, Claudine Grammont, and Josef Helfenstein, eds., *Matisse, Derain, and Their Friends: The Parisian Avant-Garde 1904–1908,* exh. cat. (Berlin: Deutscher Kunstverlag; Basel: Kunstsammlung Basel, 2023).

7   Frantz Jourdain and Robert Rey, *Le Salon d'Automne* (Paris: Les Arts et le Livre, 1926), 12.

8   See Fae Brauer, *Rivals and Conspirators: The Paris Salons and the Modern Art*

Centre (Cambridge, UK: Cambridge Scholars Publishing, 2013), 289–95.

9   Jourdain and Rey, Le Salon d'Automne, 8.

10   Catalogue de peinture, dessin, sculpture, gravure, architecture et arts décoratifs (Paris: Cie Française des Papiers-Monnaie, 1905), 200.

11   In his introduction to the 1905 Salon d'Automne catalogue, Élie Faure noted that the curation was an important advantage: "The Salon d'Automne … has the good fortune of gathering young energies of which the Indépendants' overly anxious and scattered beautiful offerings had only granted us a glimpse"; Catalogue de peinture, 18.

12   For Jourdain, the nonhierarchical integration of media was central to his revolutionary ambitions: "We did not believe in the arbitrary separation between what are routinely designated as the major arts and the minor arts"; Jourdain and Rey, Le Salon d'Automne, 28. So too was his claim that participation in the salon required "no passport, no manifesto, no diploma, no commitment"; "Le Salon d'Automne," Excelsior: Journal Illustré Quotidien, Sept. 29, 1911, p. 4.

13   Faure, introduction to Catalogue de peinture, 19.

14   James D. Herbert, Fauve Painting: The Making of Cultural Politics (New Haven, CT: Yale University Press, 1992), 8.

15   Analysis of reviews suggests that the galleries for the Salon d'Automne likely retained the same layout—for instance, one critic remarks that the entrances to Galleries VII and VIII were through Gallery VI, which several accounts clearly identify as one of two long, three-part galleries. See Charles, "Le Salon d'Automne," p. 9.

16   Quoted in Barbara Pollack, The Collectors: Dr. Claribel and Miss Etta Cone (New York: Bobbs-Merrill, 1962), 70. A review by Camille Mauclair also notes the small sizes of Galleries VII and VIII; "Le Salon d'Automne," Revue Politique et Littéraire, Oct. 1905, p. 522.

17   Caroline Dubail, "Le Grand Palais ose la couleur," Les Dossiers Pédagogiques du Grand Palais, no. 10 (Sept. 2023): 29. Dubail, Historian of the Grand Palais, uncovered a piece of the original fabric, confirming the color, pattern, and material.

18   "I was personally obliged to work with Marquet on the decoration of the ceiling of the Grand Palais"; Henri Matisse in "Interview with Jacques Guenne, 1925," in Jack Flam, Matisse on Art (Berkeley: University of California Press, 1995), 81.

19   Claudine Grammont, "L'avant-garde comme stratégie: L'exemple du scandale des Fauves," in Quel scandale, ed. Marie Dollé (Saint-Denis: Presses Universitaires de Vincennes, 2006), 72.

20   "Au Salon d'Automne: L'inauguration d'aujourd'hui," La Presse, Oct. 17, 1905; Jourdain and Rey, Le Salon d'Automne, 13.

21   See "Beaux-Arts," L'Aurore, Oct. 19, 1904, p. 2.

22   "Paris: From Our Own Correspondent," Vogue (New York), Nov. 9, 1905, pp. 598–99.

23   "Au Salon d'Automne," La Vie Illustrée, Oct. 27, 1905.

24   The Galerie Berthe Weill presented works by Marquet and Matisse in a 1902 group show; by Camoin, Manguin, Marquet, and Matisse in 1904; and by those artists as well as Marque in April of 1905. See Berthe Weill: Art Dealer of the Parisian Avant-Garde, exh. cat. (Paris: Flammarion, 2024), 187.

25   See Jean-Pierre Manguin, "Chronologie," in Manguin: La volupté de la couleur, exh. cat., ed. Marina Ferretti Bocquillon (Giverny: Musée des Impressionnismes Giverny, 2017), 140.

26   Quoted in Claudine Grammont, "Chronique d'un scandale annoncé," in Les Fauves et la critique, exh. cat. (Turin: Palazzo Bricherasio; Lodéve: Musée Fleury, 1999), 21. Grammont charts the evolution of these artists' identification with Moreau in the press for over a decade to demonstrate that the shocked critical reactions to the 1905 salon were not wholly genuine, their works having been known to critics for several years.

27   Isabelle Monod-Fontaine, "André Derain: Painting against the Tide," in André Derain: An Outsider in French Art (Copenhagen: Statens Museum for Kunst, 2007), 15.

28   Quoted in Georges Duthuit, The Fauvist Painters (New York: Wittenborn Schultz, 1950), 28.

29   In 1902, Girieud had shown alongside Matisse and Marquet at the Galerie B. Weill in June, and alongside Pichot in November. See list of exhibitions at www.bertheweill.fr/expositions.

30   Louis Vauxcelles, "Le Salon des Indépendants," Gil Blas, March 20, 1907, p. 1.

31   See Isabel Fabregat Marín, Ramon Pichot Gironès: De els Quatre Gats a la Maison Rose, exh. cat. (Barcelona: Museo Nacional d'Art de Catalunya, 2017).

32   Vauxcelles, "Le Salon d'Automne."

33   On Jelka Rosen's relationships with Rodin, see Lionel Carley, "On the Trail of Delius in Paris and Grez," and Elizabeth Ferry, "The 1880s: The Ambience and Artistic Life of Paris," both in The Delius Society Journal 143 (Spring 2008).

34   G. Hidien, "A l'exposition des femmes artistes," L'Oeuvre d'Art, Jan. 20, 1897, p. 15.

35   Albert Marquet to Henri Matisse, Saint-Tropez, June 15, 1905, in Matisse-Marquet: Correspondance, 1898–1947, ed. Claudine Grammont (Lausanne: Bibliothèque des Arts, 2008), 41.

36   For exhibition and provenance histories of these works, see Marie-Caroline Sainsaulieu, Henri Manguin: Catalogue raisonné de l'oeuvre peint (Neuchâtel: Ides et Calendes, 1980), 88–99.

37   René Piot to Henri Matisse, undated (1905), Archives Henri Matisse, Paris.

38   Vauxcelles, "Le Salon d'Automne."

39   For the critical reception of Manguin's work between 1902 and 1905, see Dominique Lobstein, "Manguin parmi les fauves," in Bocquillon, Manguin: La volupté de la couleur, 13–25.

40   Charles, "Le Salon d'Automne," p. 2; Félix d'Anner, "Le Salon d'Automne," L'Intransigeant, Oct. 18, 1905, p. 2.

41   Thanks to Assia Quesnel, Archives Camoin, for her efforts to identify these works.

42   Thank you to Sandrine Canac, director of digital archival projects, and Claude Jacir, consultant, at the Wildenstein Plattner Institute for their assistance with this research.

43   Vauxcelles, "Le Salon d'Automne."

44   Henri Matisse to Paul Signac, Paris, Sept. 14, 1905, in Amory and Dumas, Vertigo of Color, 174.

45   For more on the provenance and exhibition history of these works, see Vlaminck: Critical Catalogue of Fauve Paintings and Ceramics (Paris: Wildenstein Institute, 2008), 88–19.

46   Correspondence Havas, Oct. 22, 1905, translated in Vlaminck: Critical Catalogue, 110.

47   Maurice de Vlaminck, The Dangerous Corner (New York: Abelard-Schuman, 1966), 74.

48   André Derain to Maurice de Vlaminck, Collioure, July 28, 1905, in Amory and Dumas, Vertigo of Color, 164–65.

49   Derain to Vlaminck, Collioure, Aug. 5, 1905, and Derain to Vlaminck, Aug. 1905, in Amory and Dumas, Vertigo of Color, 167–71.

50   The possible identification of Derain's portrait of Matisse is supported by the

recollection of Dr. Claribel Cone: "We stood in front of a portrait—it was that of a man bearded, brooding, tense, fiercely elemental in color with green eyes (if I remember correctly), blue beard, pink and yellow complexion." Pollack, *The Collectors,* 70.

51 Derain to Champenois, Collioure, Aug. 1905, in Amory and Dumas, *Vertigo of Color,* 169–70.

52 René Piot to Henri Matisse, undated (1905), Archives Henri Matisse, Paris.

53 Vauxcelles, "Le Salon d'Automne."

54 Henri Matisse to Paul Signac, Paris, Sept. 14, 1905, in Amory and Dumas, *Vertigo of Color,* 174.

55 Matisse to Marquet, Collioure, Aug. 19, 1905, in Grammont, *Matisse-Marquet,* 43–44.

56 Henri Matisse to Simon Bussy, Sept. 19, 1905, quoted in *Matisse in the Collection of The Museum of Modern Art,* ed. John Elderfield, exh. cat. (New York: Museum of Modern Art, 1978), 180.

57 One clue to its identity can be found in a review by Gustave Kahn: "a particularly exquisite [still life] where the gold of fruit and the snow of tablecloth form a union at once intimate and shimmering." "Le Salon d'Automne," *La Revue Illustrée,* Nov. 1, 1905, p. 17.

58 Michel Sembat, Oct. 29, 1905, in *Matisse-Sembat correspondance: Une amitié artistique et politique, 1904–1922* (Lausanne: La Bibliothèque des Arts, 2004), 164–65. Thank you to Anne Théry for her assistance with this identification.

59 Louis Vauxcelles to Henri Matisse, Paris, June 27, 1905, Archives Henri Matisse, Paris. The exhibition Vauxcelles refers to was a group show at the Galerie Pierrefort in June 1905. See Vauxcelles's review, "La vie artistique," *Gil Blas,* June 14, 1905, p. 1.

60 Matisse to Signac, Collioure, July 14, 1905, in Amory and Dumas, *Vertigo of Color,* 161.

61 Quoted in Émile Bernard, "Paul Cézanne," *L'Occident,* July 1, 1904, p. 24.

62 Matisse to Signac, Paris, Sept. 28, 1905, in Amory and Dumas, *Vertigo of Color,* 175.

63 Charles, "Le Salon d'Automne," p. 3.

64 André Gide, "Promenade au Salon d'Automne," *Gazette des Beaux-Arts,* Dec. 1, 1905, p. 483.

65 René Wisner, "Le Salon d'Automne," *Écrit pour l'Art,* Dec. 15, 1905, p. 488; André Salmon, *La jeune peinture française* (Paris: Société des Trente, 1912), 19.

66 See also John Klein, "When Worlds Collide: Matisse's *Femme au chapeau* and the Politics of the Portrait," in *Matisse and Other Modern Masters: The Elise S. Haas Collection,* exh. cat. (San Francisco: San Francisco Museum of Modern Art, 1993).

67 Gertrude Stein, *The Autobiography of Alice B. Toklas* (1933; repr. New York: Vintage Books, 1990), 34; Leo Stein to Mabel Weeks, Nov. 29, 1905, quoted in Rebecca Rabinow, "Discovering Modern Art: The Steins' Early Years in Paris, 1903–1907," in *The Steins Collect: Matisse, Picasso, and the Parisian Avant-Garde,* ed. Janet Bishop, Cécile Debray, and Rebecca Rabinow, exh. cat. (San Francisco: San Francisco Museum of Modern Art; New Haven, CT: Yale University Press, 2011), 35.

68 Maurice Denis, "La peinture," *L'Ermitage,* Oct. 15, 1905, p. 317; Gide, "Promenade au Salon d'Automne," p. 483; Le Masque Rouge, "Le Salon d'Automne."

69 Even in his famous review, Vauxcelles refers to the artists in Gallery VII as "Marquet and company." See Grammont, "Chronique d'un scandale annoncé," 25.

70 Leo Stein, *Appreciation: Painting, Poetry, and Prose* (New York: Crown, 1947), 158.

71 Maurice Denis, "La peinture," *L'Ermitage,* Nov. 15, 1905, p. 317.

72 Gide, "Promenade au Salon d'Automne," p. 476.

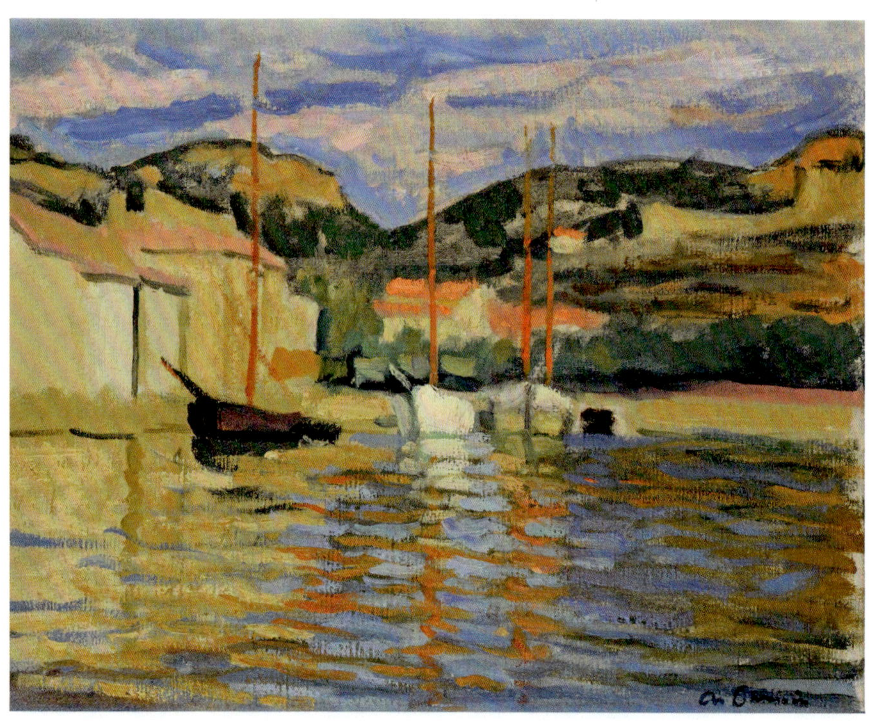

Charles Camoin, *Le Port de Cassis à la tartane noire* (The Port of Cassis with the Black Tartane), 1904. Oil on canvas, 13 × 16¼ in. (33 × 41 cm). Private collection

Possibly Salon d'Automne cat. no. 286, *Le Port de Cassis (soleil couchant)*

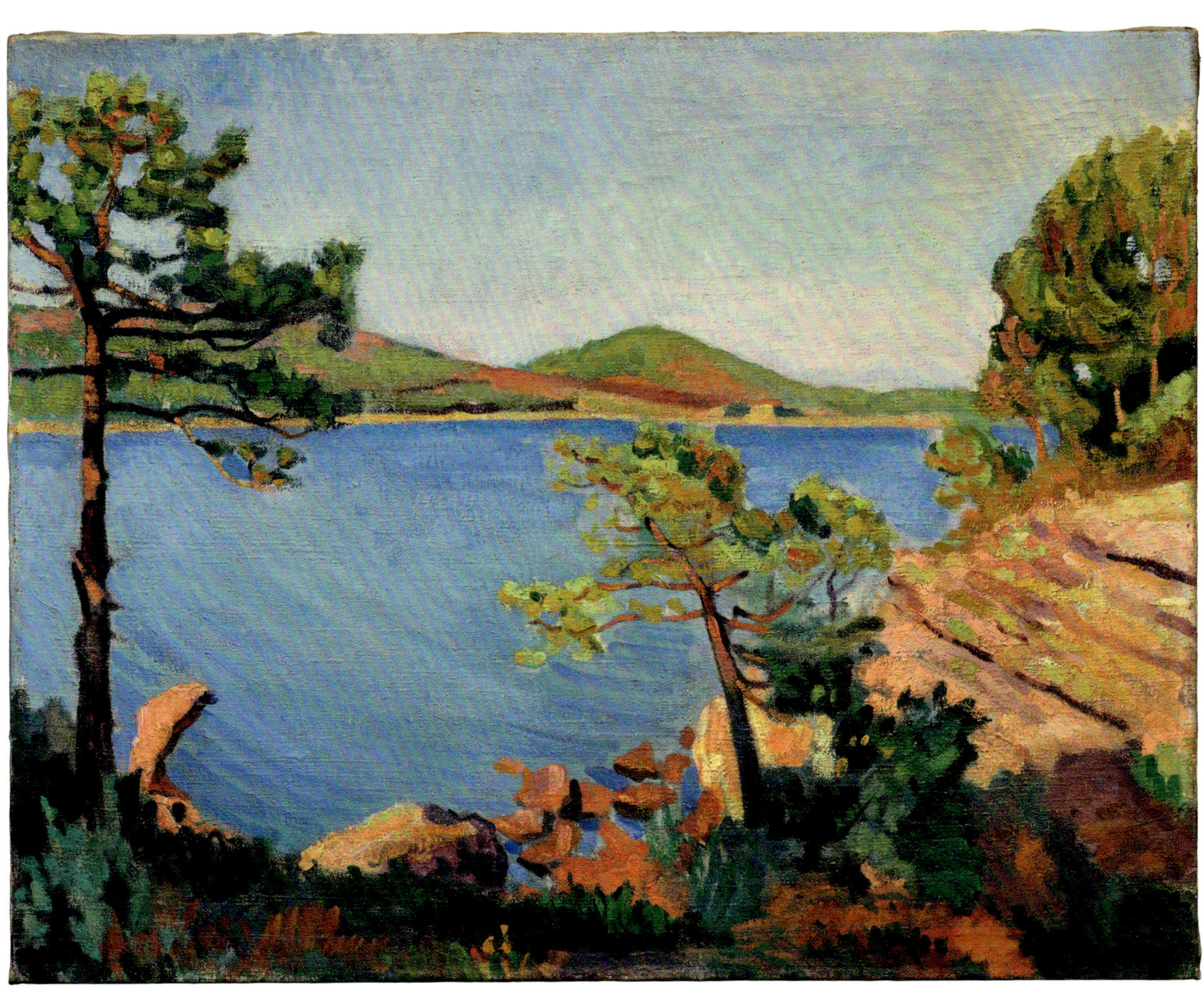

Charles Camoin, *Bord de mer à Agay* (Seashore at Agay), 1905. Oil on canvas,
25⅝ × 32 in. (65 × 81.3 cm). Private collection

Possibly Salon d'Automne cat. no. 285, *Agay (bord de mer)*

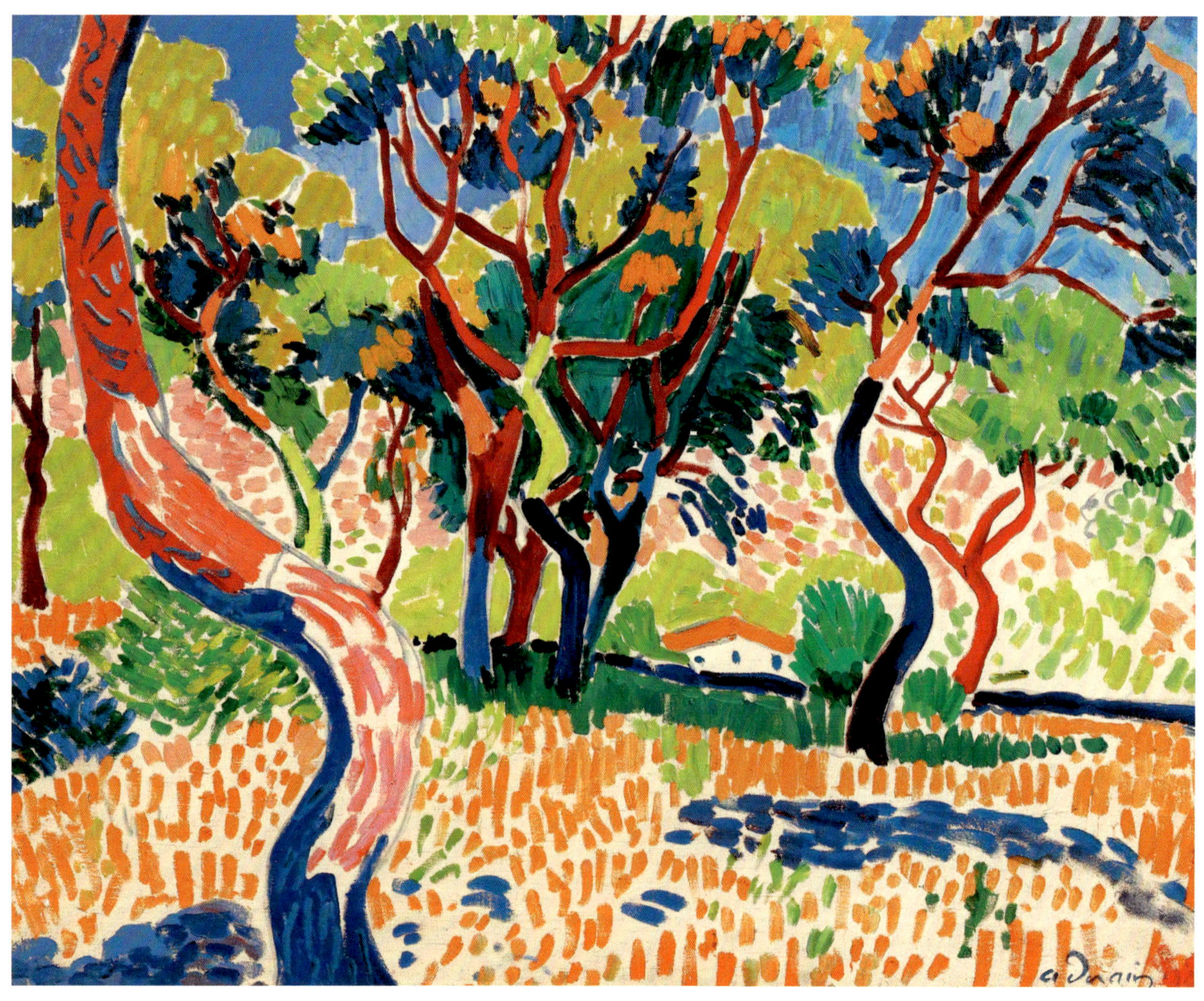

André Derain, *Arbres à Collioure* (Trees at Collioure), 1905. Oil on canvas,
25⅝ × 31⅞ in. (65 × 81 cm). Private collection

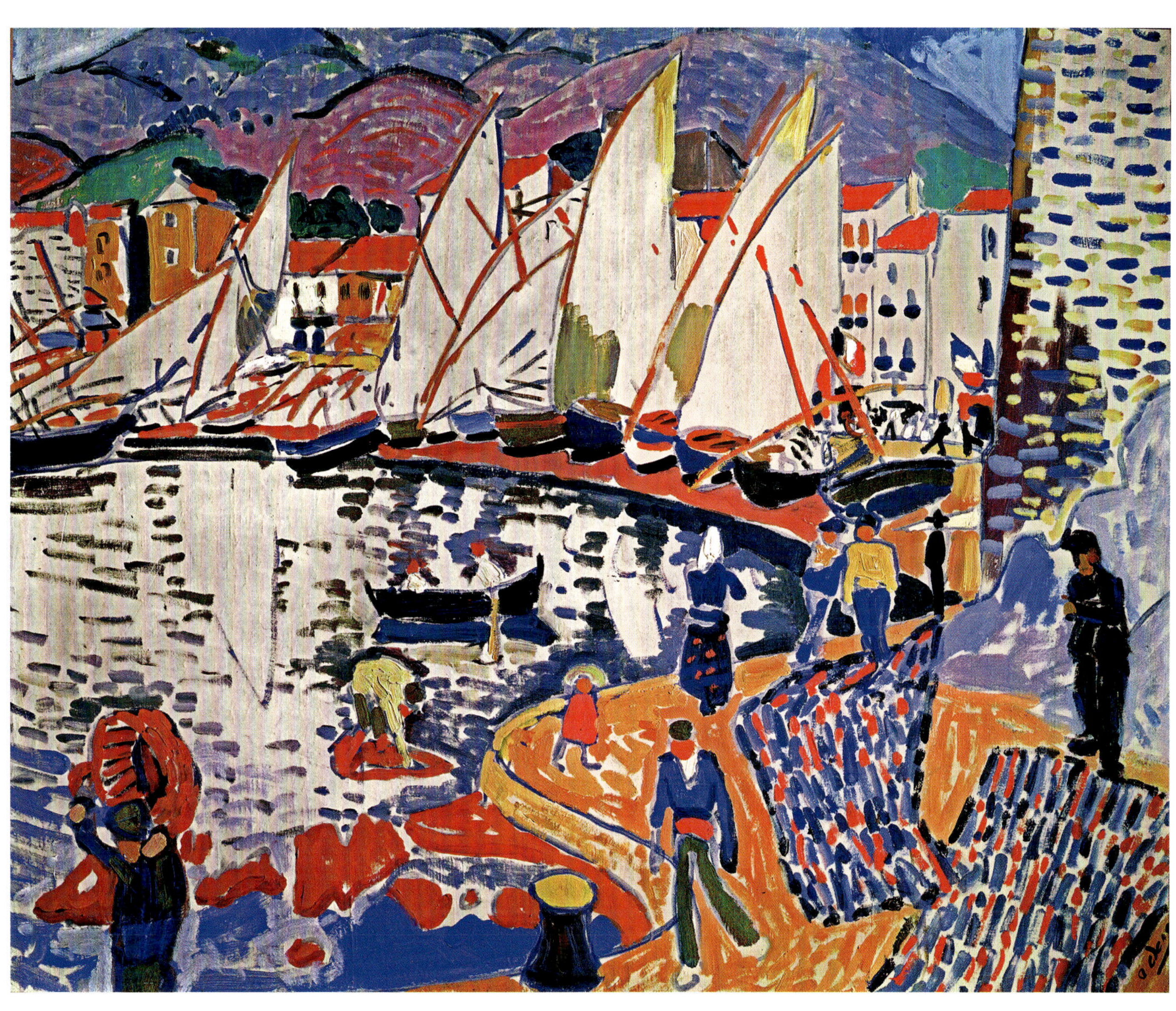

André Derain, *Le séchage des voiles* (Drying of Sails), 1905. Oil on canvas,
32¼ × 39¾ in. (82 × 101 cm). The Pushkin State Museum of Fine Arts, Moscow
Salon d'Automne cat. no. 440, *Le séchage des voiles*

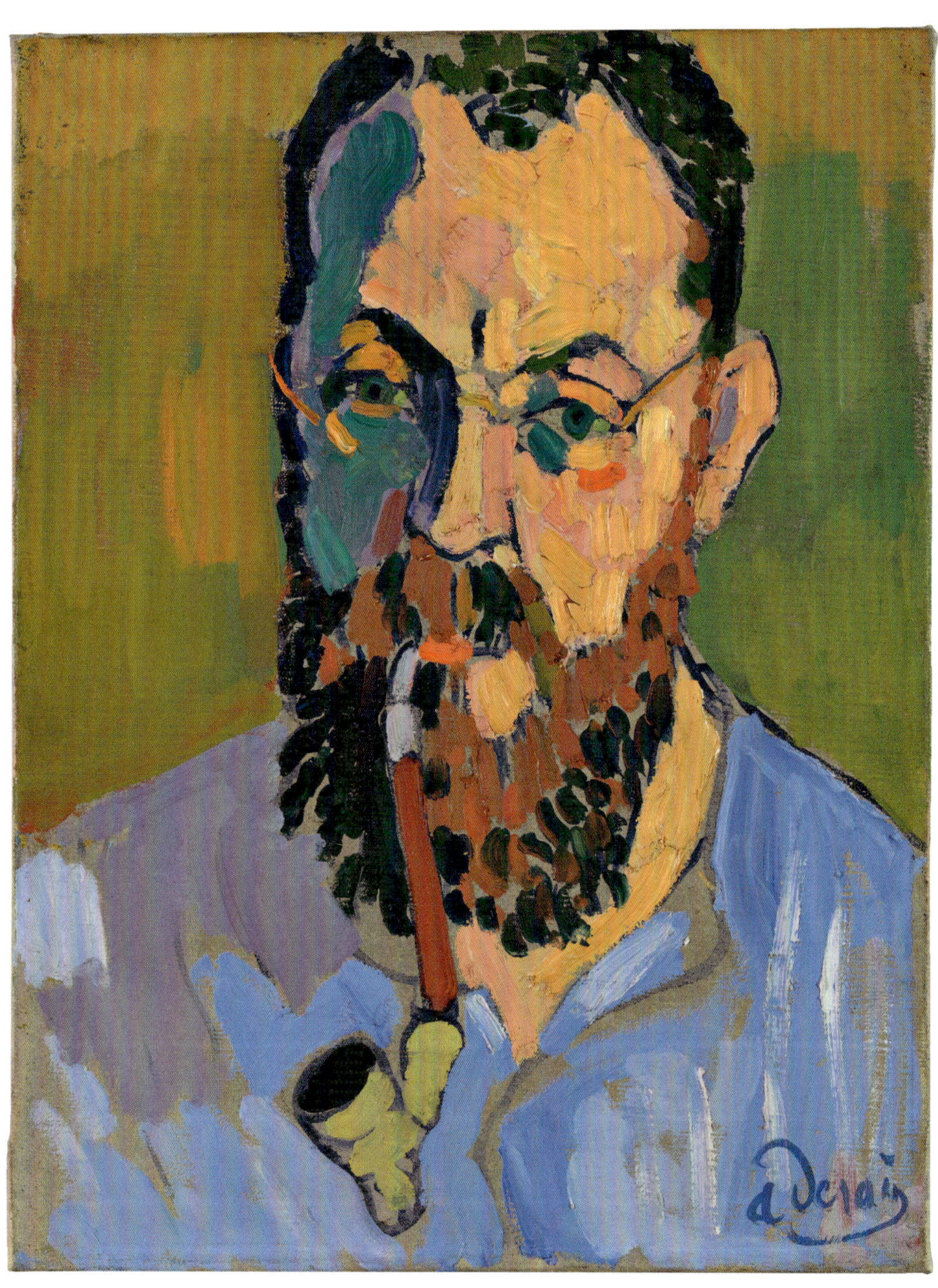

André Derain, *Henri Matisse,* 1905. Oil on canvas, 18⅛ × 13¾ in. (46 × 34.9 cm).
Tate, purchased 1958

Possibly Salon d'Automne cat. no. 436, *Portrait*

34

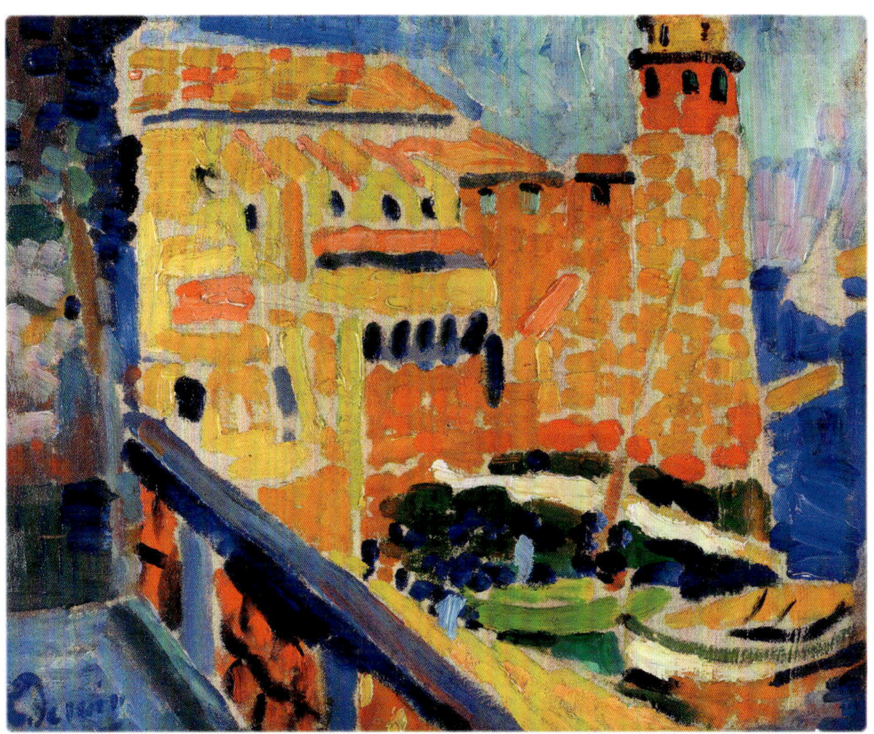

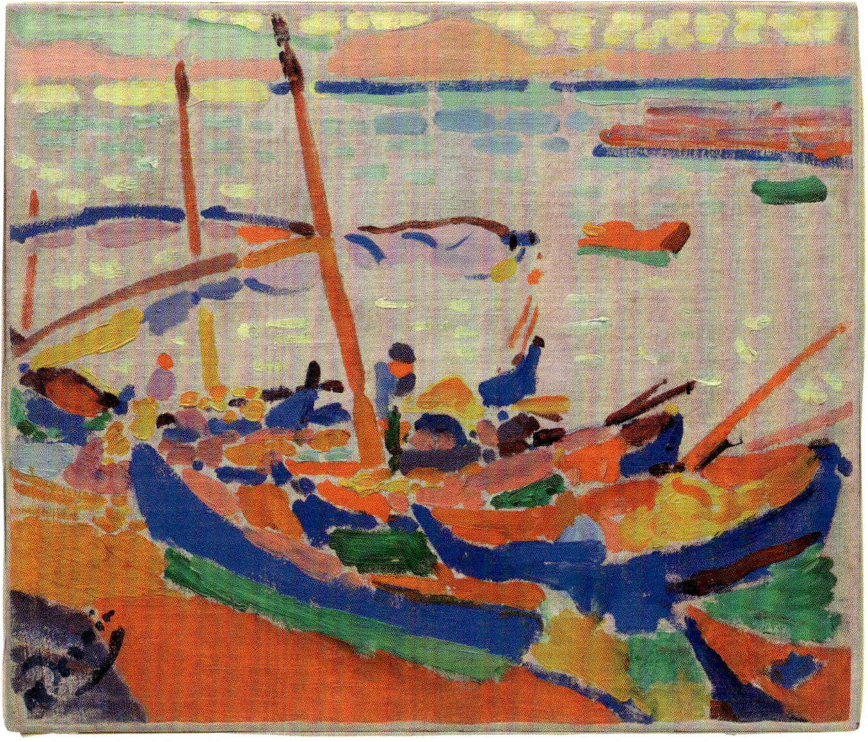

André Derain, *Le phare de Collioure* (The Lighthouse of Collioure), 1905. Oil on canvas,
12¹³⁄₁₆ × 15¹⁵⁄₁₆ in. (32.5 × 40.5 cm). Musée d'Art Moderne de Paris, donation Henry-Thomas, 1984
Representative of Salon d'Automne cat. no. 438, *Vue de Collioures*

André Derain, *Barques de pêche à Collioure* (Fishing Boats, Collioure), 1905.
Oil on canvas, 14¹⁵⁄₁₆ × 17¹⁵⁄₁₆ in. (38 × 45.5 cm). The Museum of Modern Art, New York,
the Philip L. Goodwin Collection, 1958
Representative of Salon d'Automne cat. no. 439, *Port de pêche*

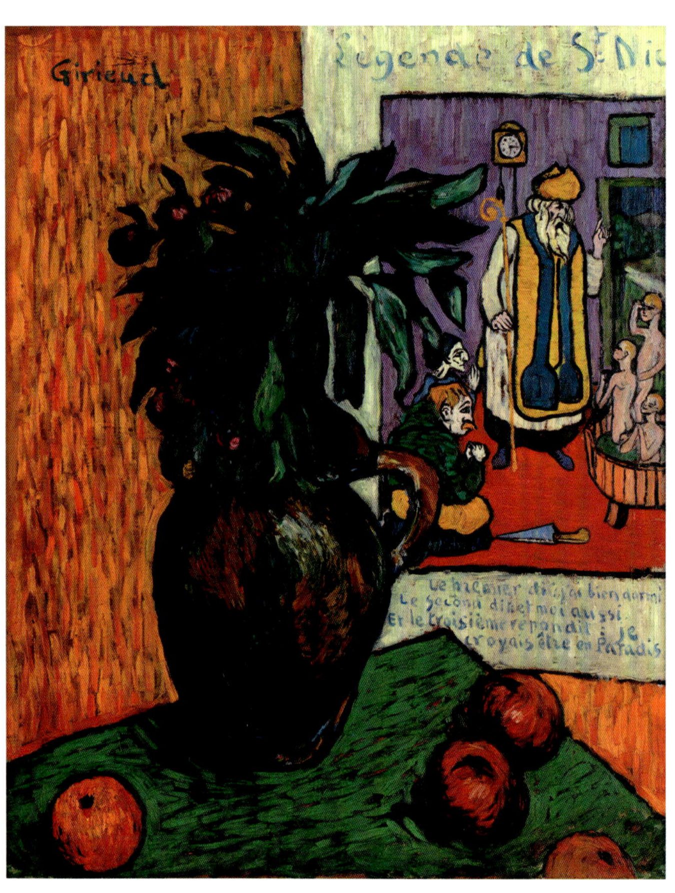

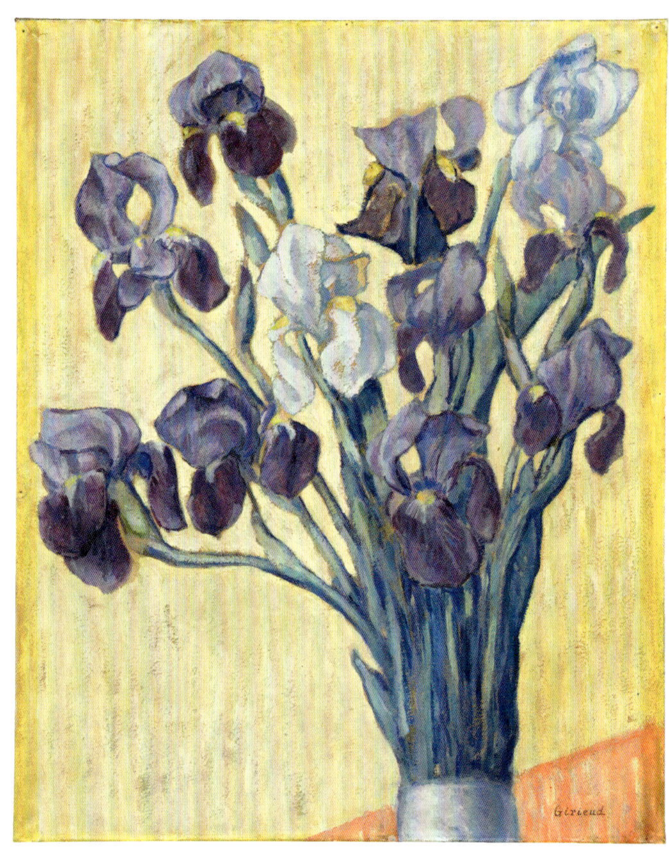

Pierre Girieud, *Légende de Saint Nicolas* (Legend of Saint Nicholas), 1905.
Oil on canvas, 31⅞ × 25⅟₁₆ in. (81 × 64 cm). Private collection

❧ Salon d'Automne cat. no. 632, *Pivoines et images d'Épinal*

Pierre Girieud, *Iris sur fond jaune* (Iris on Yellow Background), 1905. Oil on
paper mounted on canvas, 24 × 19⅝ in. (61 × 49 cm). Museum Wiesbaden, donation
from a private collection, 2018

❧ Salon d'Automne cat. no. 634, *Iris*

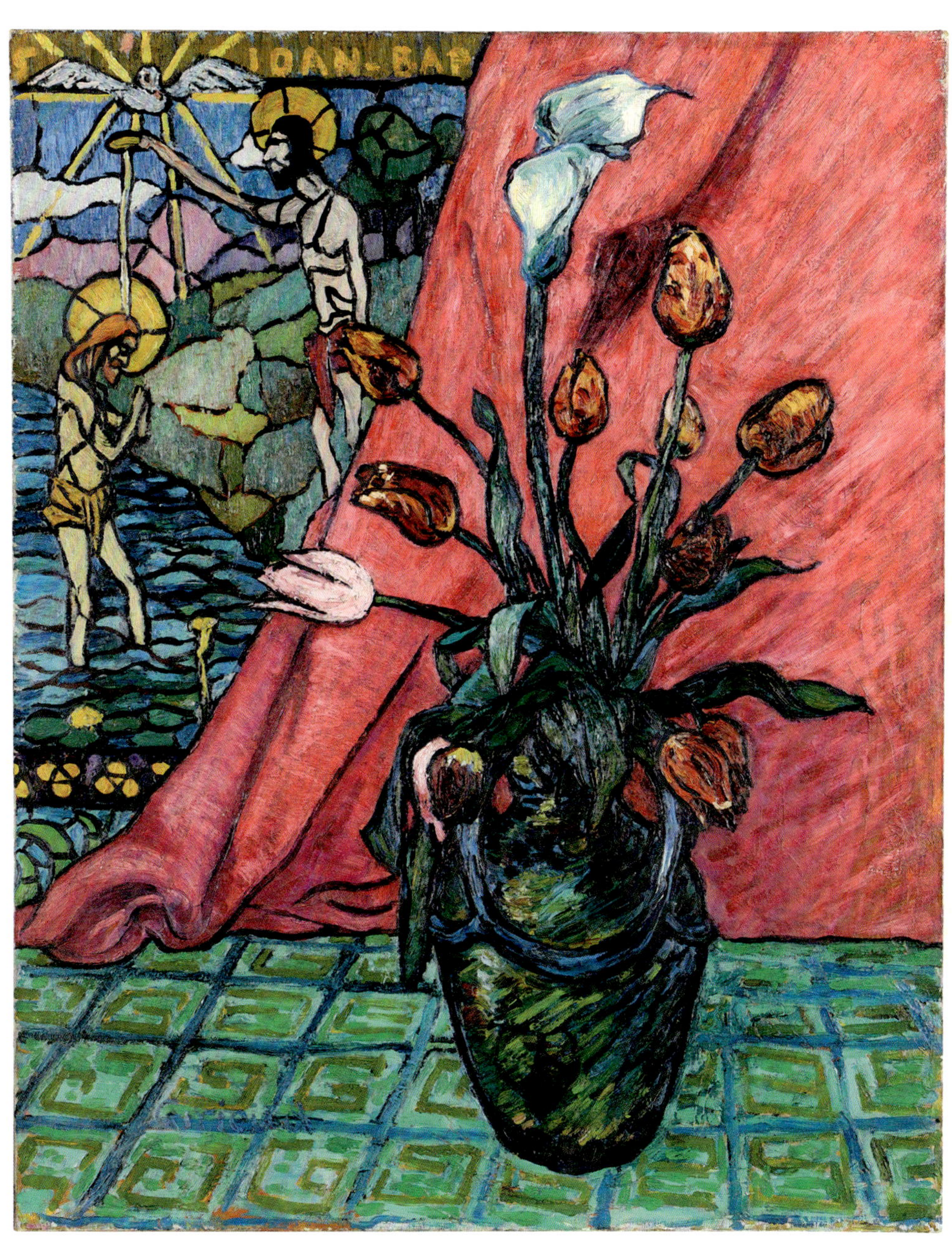

Pierre Girieud, *Tulipes et vitrail* (Tulips and Stained Glass), 1905. Oil on canvas, 32 × 25½ in. (81.3 × 64.8 cm). Collection of Michel Giraud, France

Salon d'Automne cat. no. 631, *Tulipes et Vitrail*

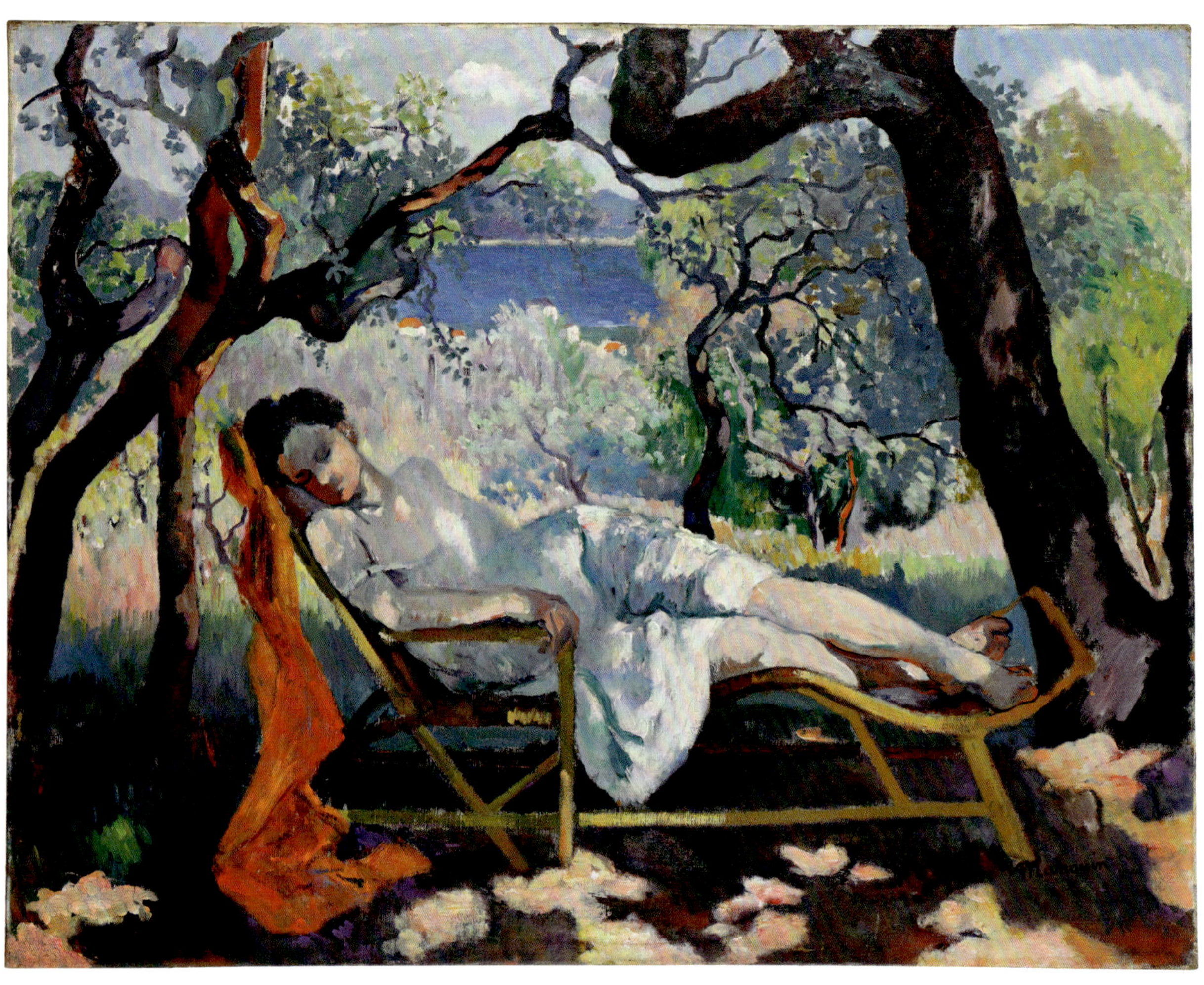

Henri Manguin, *La sieste* (The Nap), 1905. Oil on canvas, 35⅟₁₆ × 46⅟₁₆ in. (89 × 117 cm). Kunst Museum Winterthur, Hahnloser/Jaeggli Collection

Salon d'Automne cat. no. 1014, *La sieste*

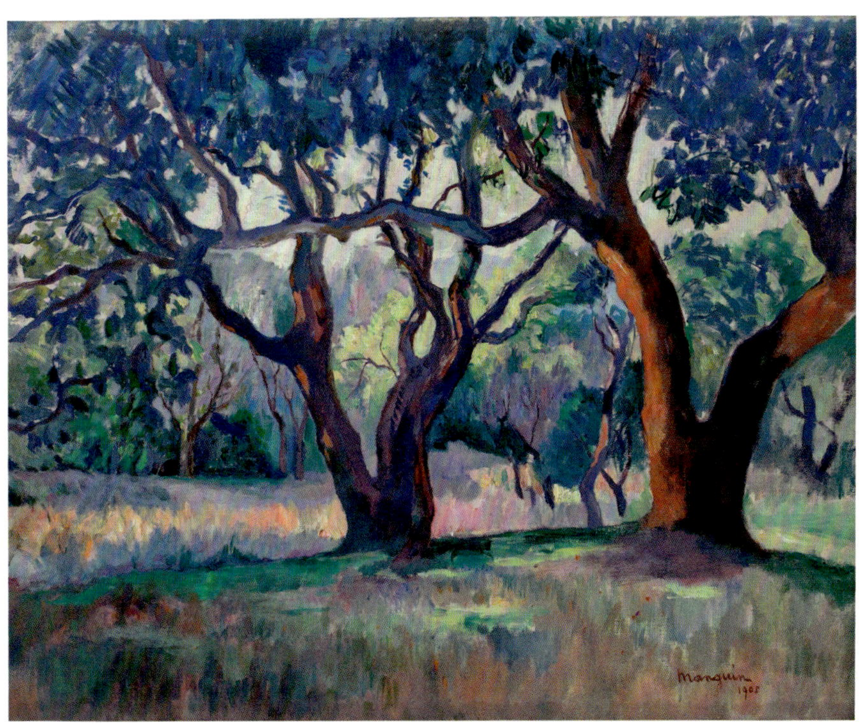

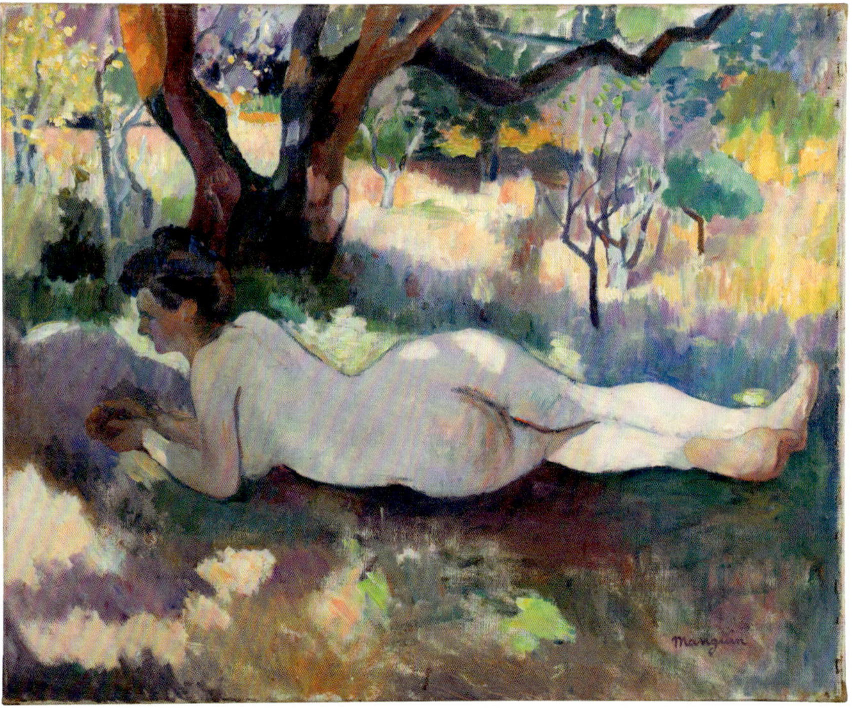

Henri Manguin, *Les grands chênes-lièges, Villa Demière* (The Large Cork Oaks, Villa Demière), 1905. Oil on canvas, 32 × 39 in. (81.3 × 100.1 cm). Private collection

❧❧❧ Salon d'Automne cat. no. 1017, *Les chênes-lièges*

Henri Manguin, *Nu sous les arbres, Jeanne* (Nude under the Trees, Jeanne), 1905. Oil on canvas, 25⁹⁄₁₆ × 31⅞ in. (65 × 81 cm). Private collection

❧❧❧ Salon d'Automne cat. no. 1016, *Sous les arbres*

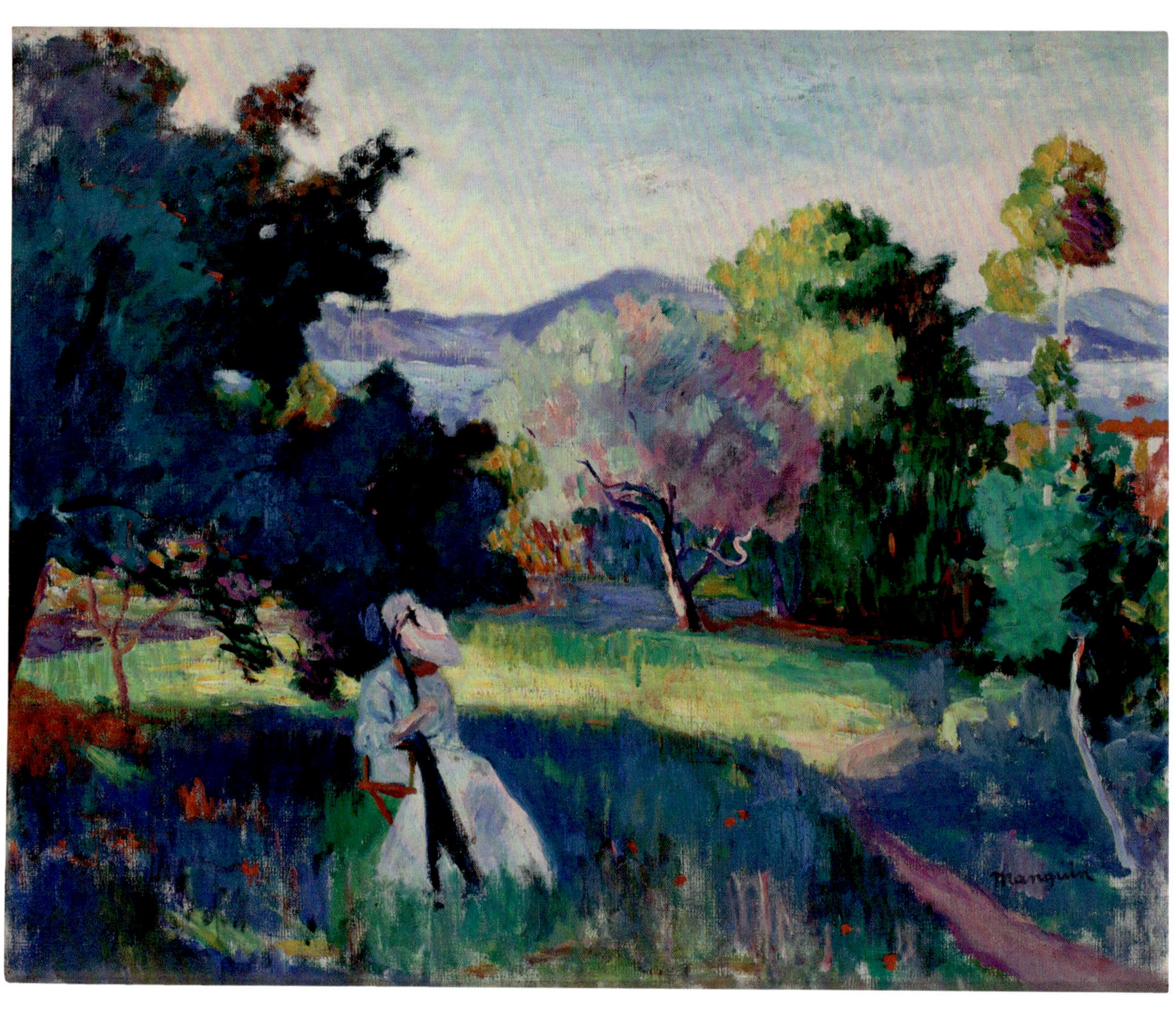

Henri Manguin, *Le pré, Villa Demière* (The Meadow, Villa Demière), 1905.
Oil on canvas, 23⅝ × 31⅞ in. (60 × 81 cm). Private collection

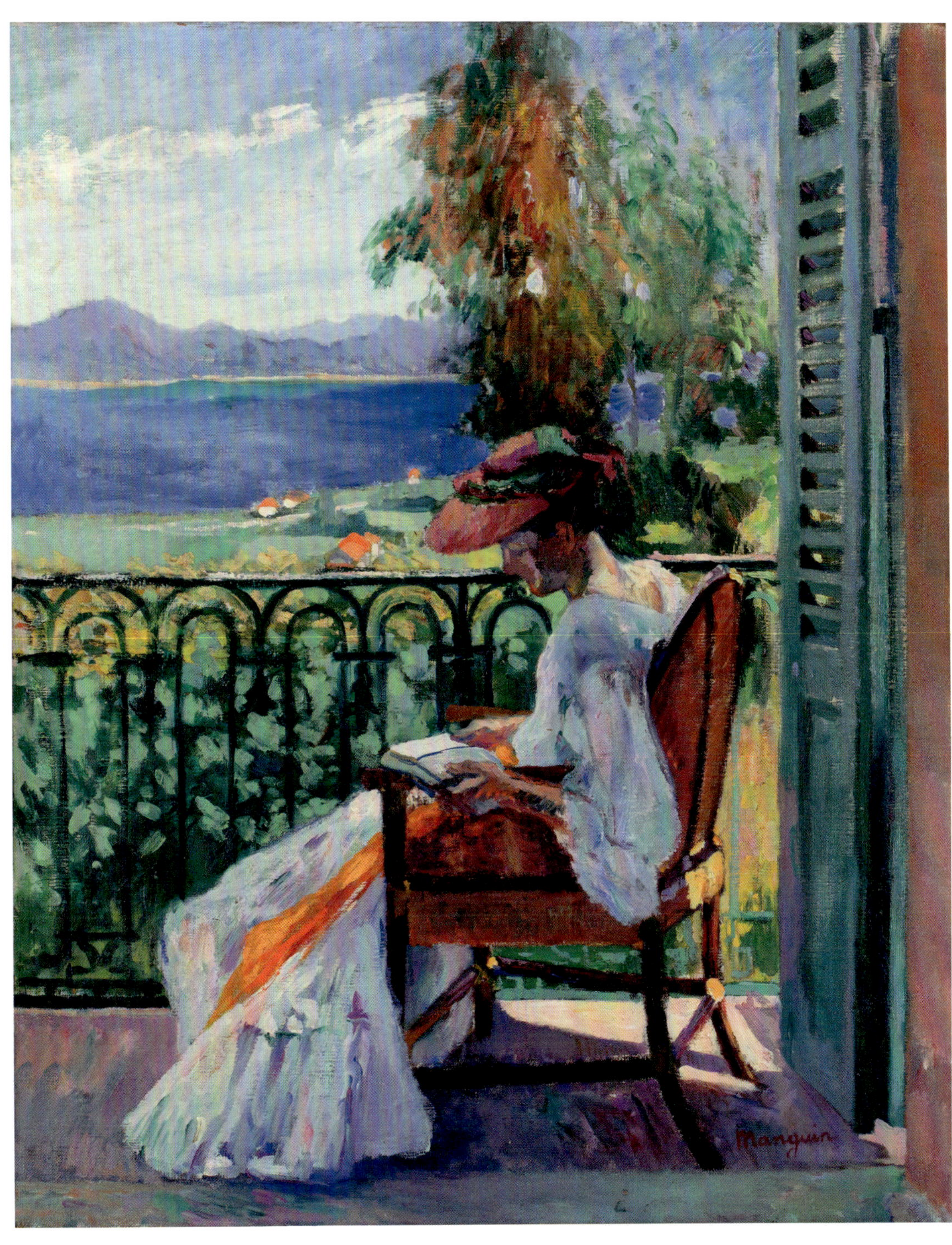

Henri Manguin, *Jeanne sur le balcon de la Villa Demière* (Jeanne on the Balcony of the
Villa Demière), 1905. Oil on canvas, 32 × 25½ in. (81 × 65 cm). Private collection

Salon d'Automne cat. no. 1015, *Sur le balcon*

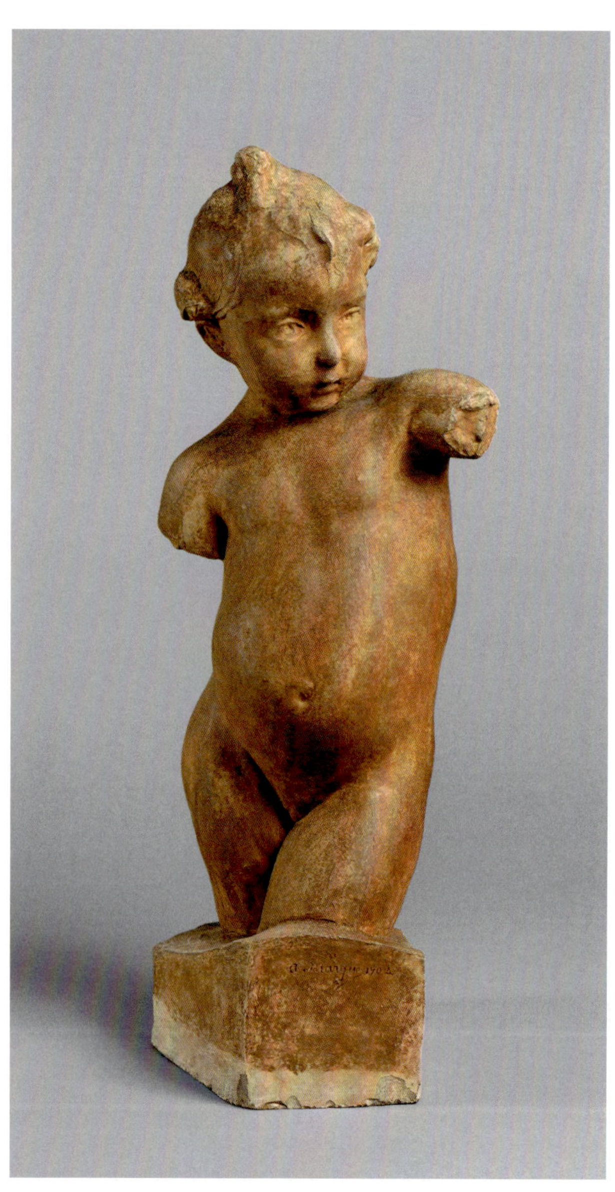

Albert Henri Marque, *Torse d'enfant* (Bust of a Child), 1904. Patinated plaster,
18⅛ × 6 ½ × 7½ in. (46 × 16.5 × 19 cm). Lyon, Musée des Beaux-Arts

Representative of Salon d'Automne cat. no. 1042, *Portrait de Marthe Lebasque*

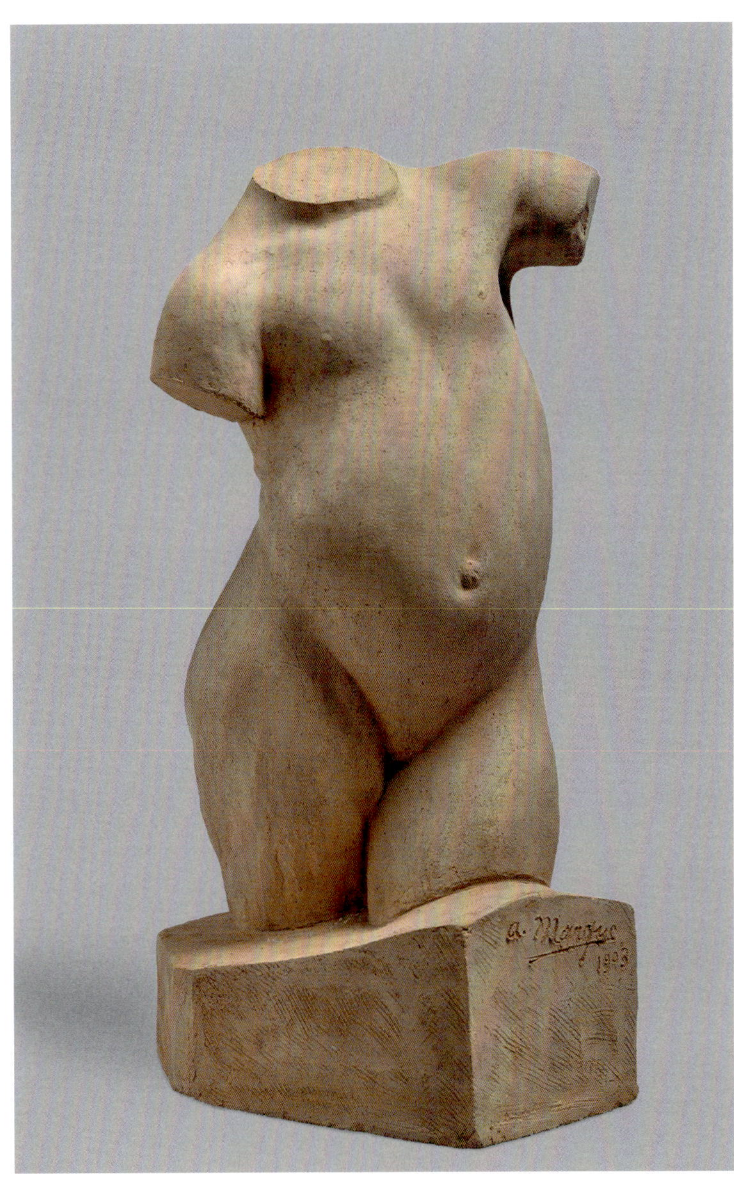

Albert Henri Marque, *Buste d'enfant* (Bust of a Child), 1903. Terracotta,
13 × 6⁵⁄₁₆ × 6¹¹⁄₁₆ in. (33 × 16 × 17 cm). Musée de Grenoble, Agutte-Sembat bequest, 1923
Representative of Salon d'Automne cat. no. 1043, *Torse d'enfant*

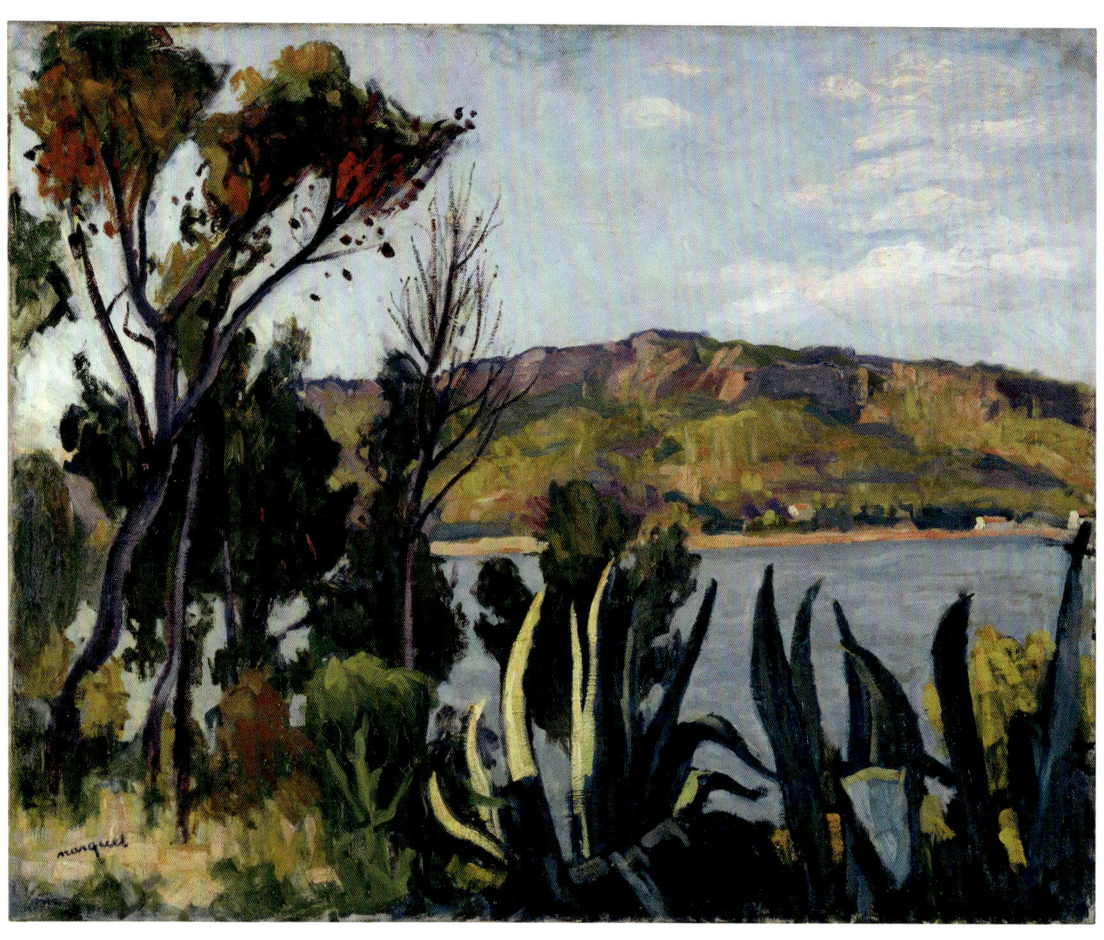

Albert Marquet, *Vue d'Agay* (View of Agay), ca. 1905. Oil on canvas, 25⅜ × 31½ in. (64.5×80.7 cm). Musée National d'Art Moderne / Centre Georges Pompidou, Paris, bequest of M. Gaston Migeon, 1931

Salon d'Automne cat. no. 1046, *Agay*

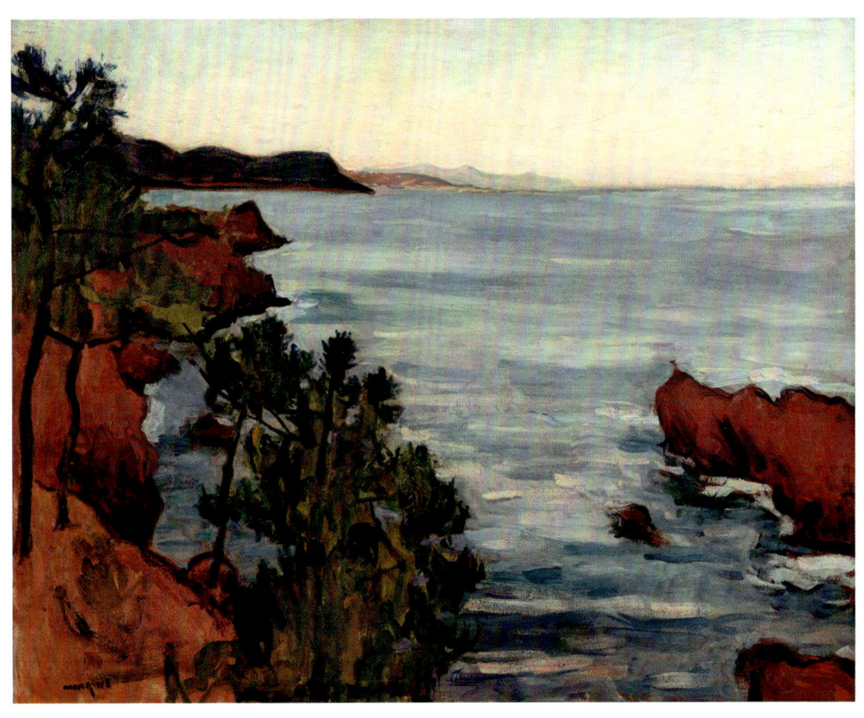

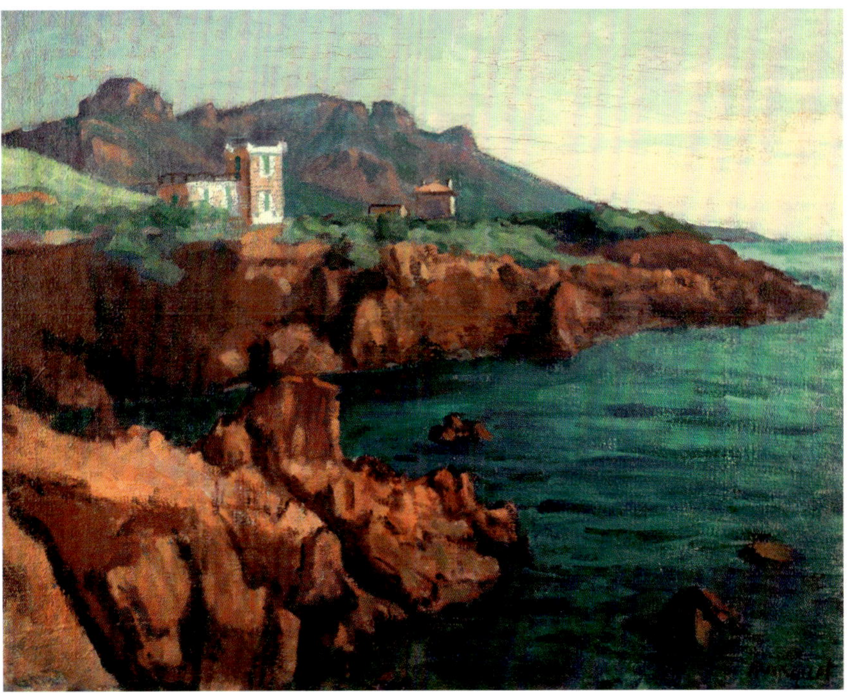

Albert Marquet, *Le Trayas, calanques roches rouges* (Le Trayas, Red Rocks, Calanques), 1905. Oil on canvas, 25⅝ × 31⅞ in. (65 × 80.9 cm). Private collection
❧❧❧ Representative of Salon d'Automne cat. no. 1047, *Le Trayas*

Albert Marquet, *Anthéor, les roches rouges* (Anthéor, the Red Rocks), 1905. Oil on canvas, 25¹¹⁄₁₆ × 31⅞ in. (65.2 × 81 cm). Private collection, courtesy Galerie MASUREL
❧❧❧ Possibly Salon d'Automne cat. no. 1045, *Anthéor*

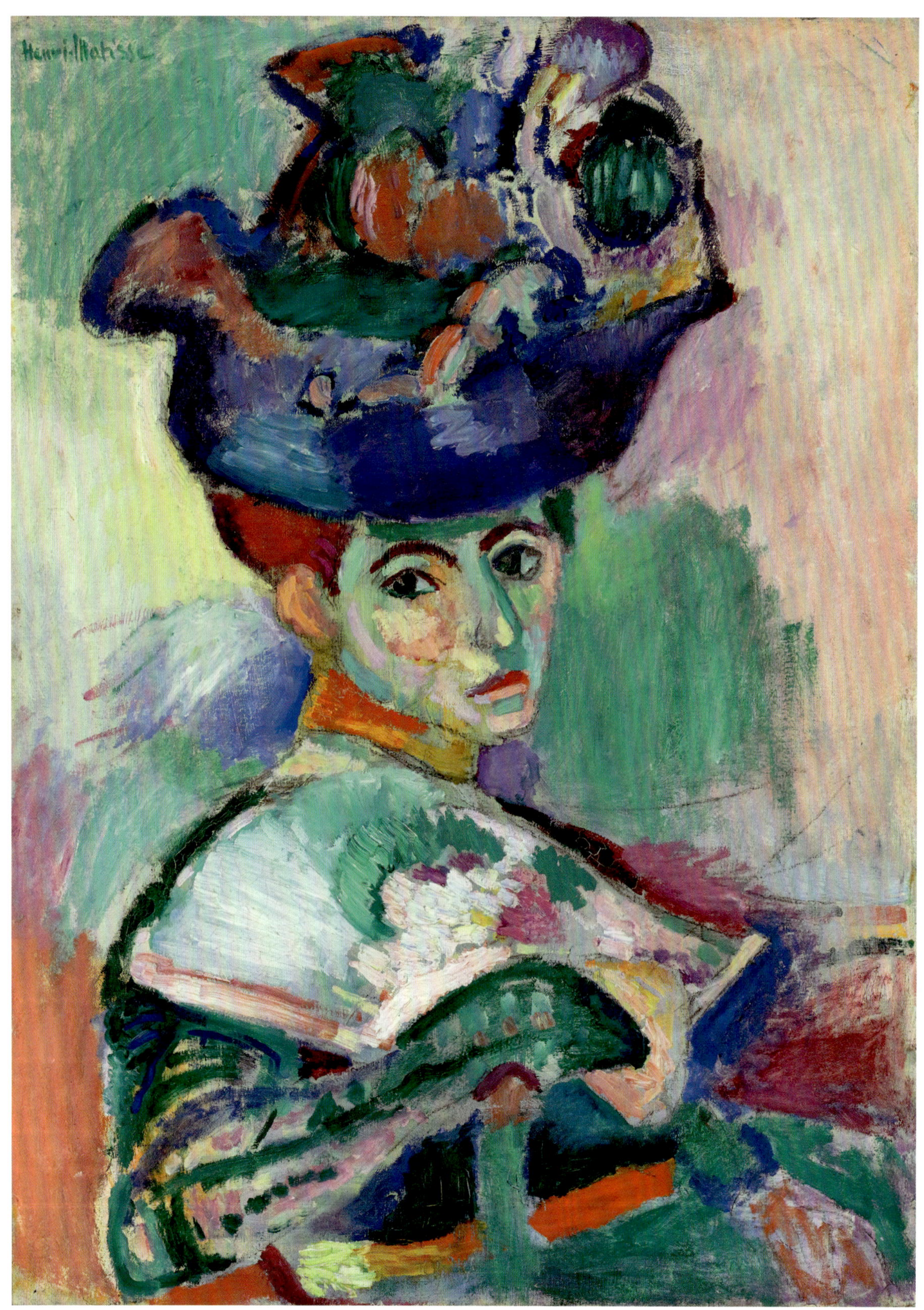

Henri Matisse, *Femme au chapeau* (Woman with a Hat), 1905. Oil on canvas,
31¾ in. × 23½ in. (80.7 × 59.7 cm). San Francisco Museum of Modern Art, bequest of
Elise S. Haas, 1991

Salon d'Automne cat. no. 718, *Femme au chapeau*

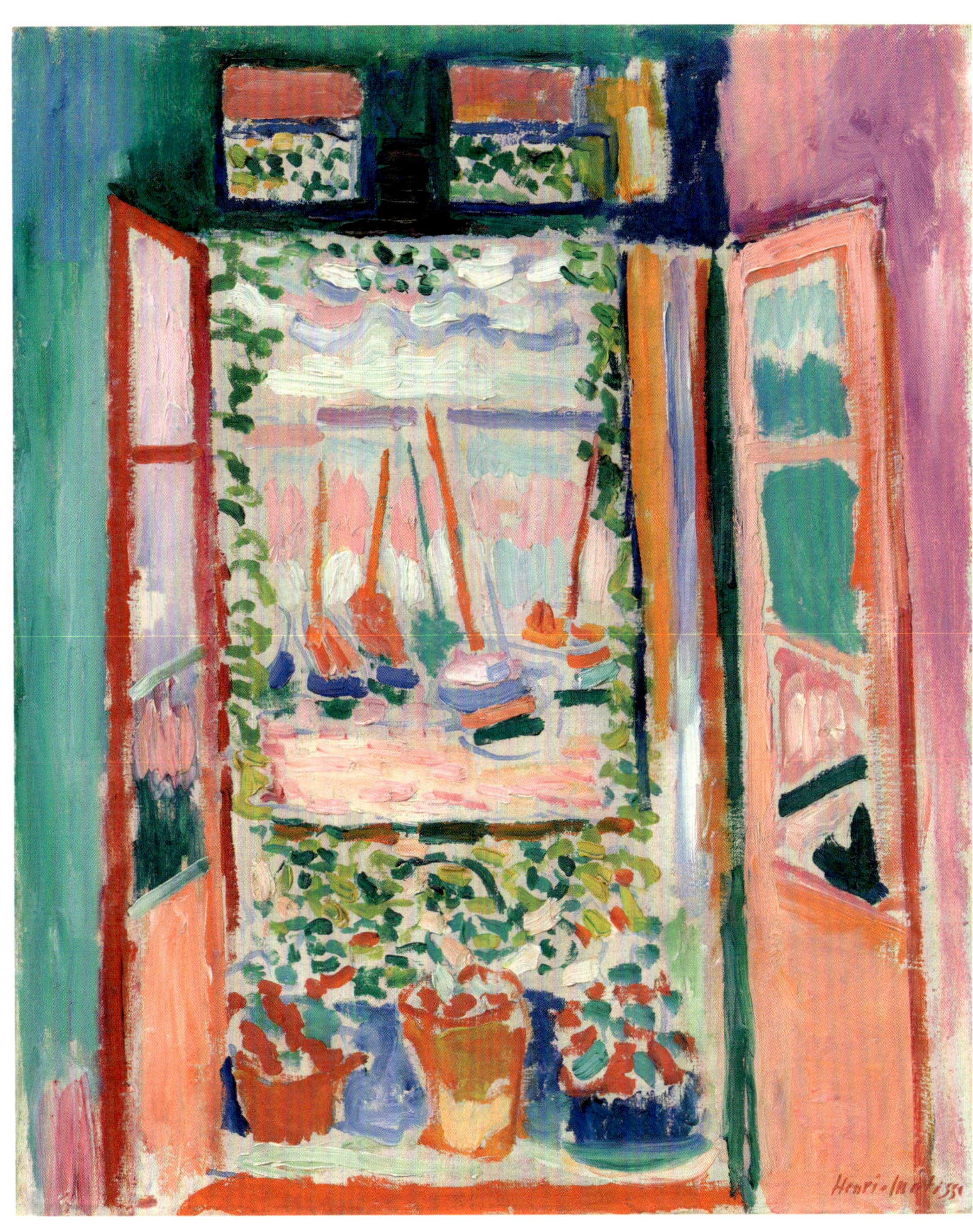

Henri Matisse, *Fenêtre ouverte* (Open Window, Collioure), 1905. Oil on canvas,
21¾ × 18⅛ in. (55.3 × 46 cm). National Gallery of Art, Washington, DC, collection of
Mr. and Mrs. John Hay Whitney, 1998.74.7
 Salon d'Automne cat. no. 715, *Fenêtre ouverte*

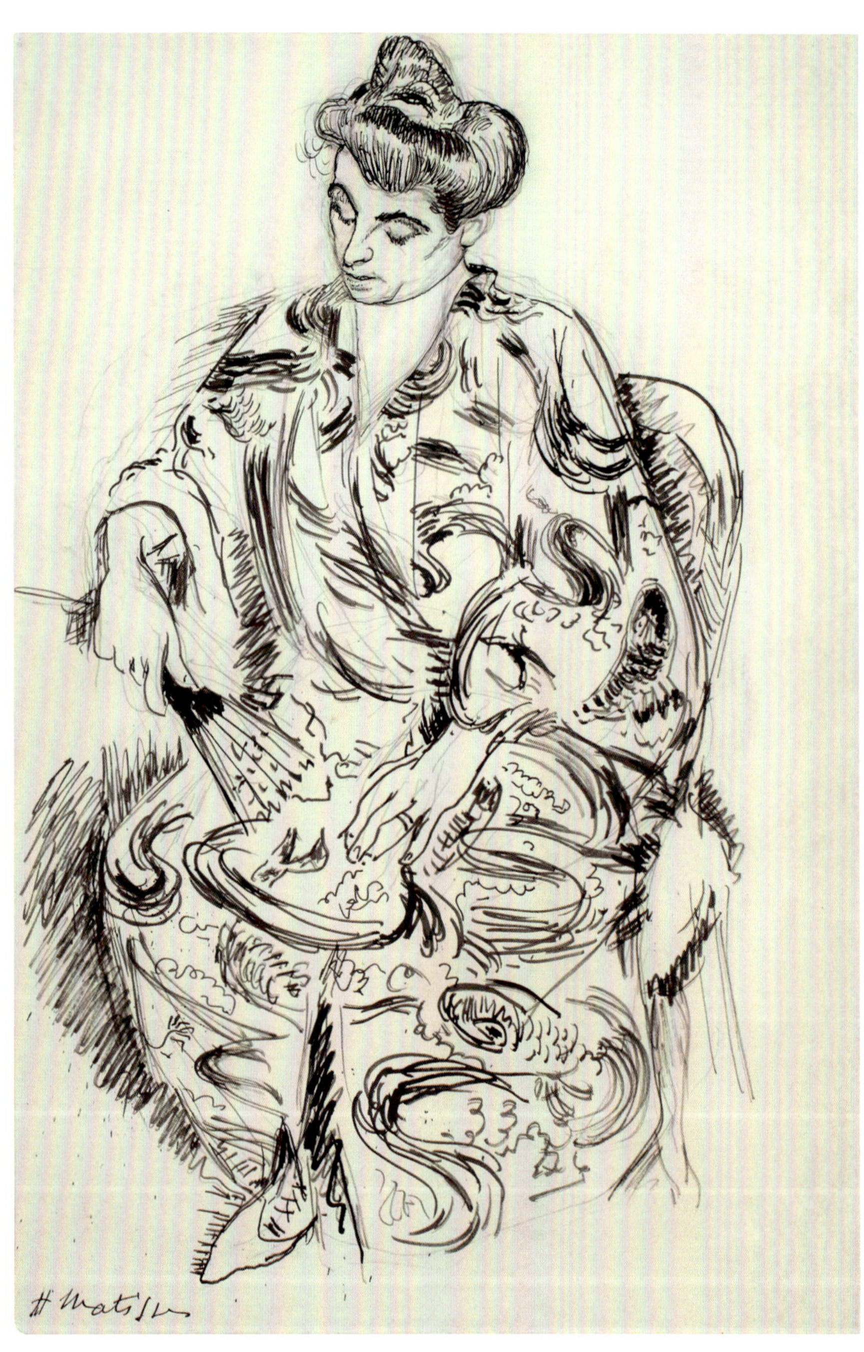

Henri Matisse, *Madame Matisse au kimono* (Madame Matisse in a Kimono), 1905.
Pen and ink on paper, 18 × 11¹⁵⁄₁₆ in. (45.5 × 30.3 cm). Private collection

Possibly Salon d'Automne cat. no. 719, *Japonaise*

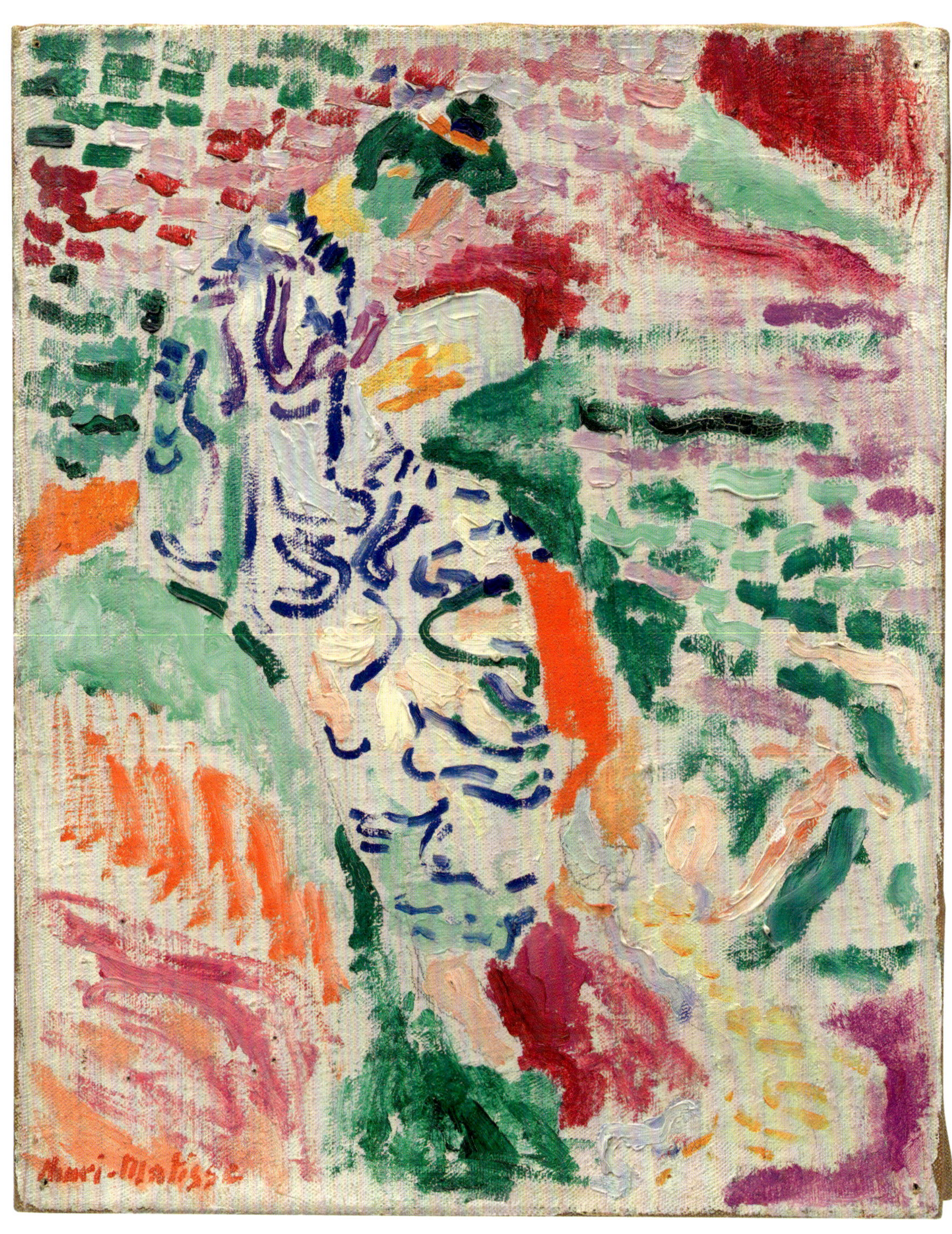

Henri Matisse, *La Japonaise au bord de l'eau* (La Japonaise: Woman beside the Water), 1905. Oil and graphite on canvas, 13¾ × 11 in. (35 × 28 cm). The Museum of Modern Art, New York, purchase and anonymous gift, 1983

❧❧❧ Salon d'Automne cat. no. 714, *Jeune femme en robe japonaise au bord de l'eau*

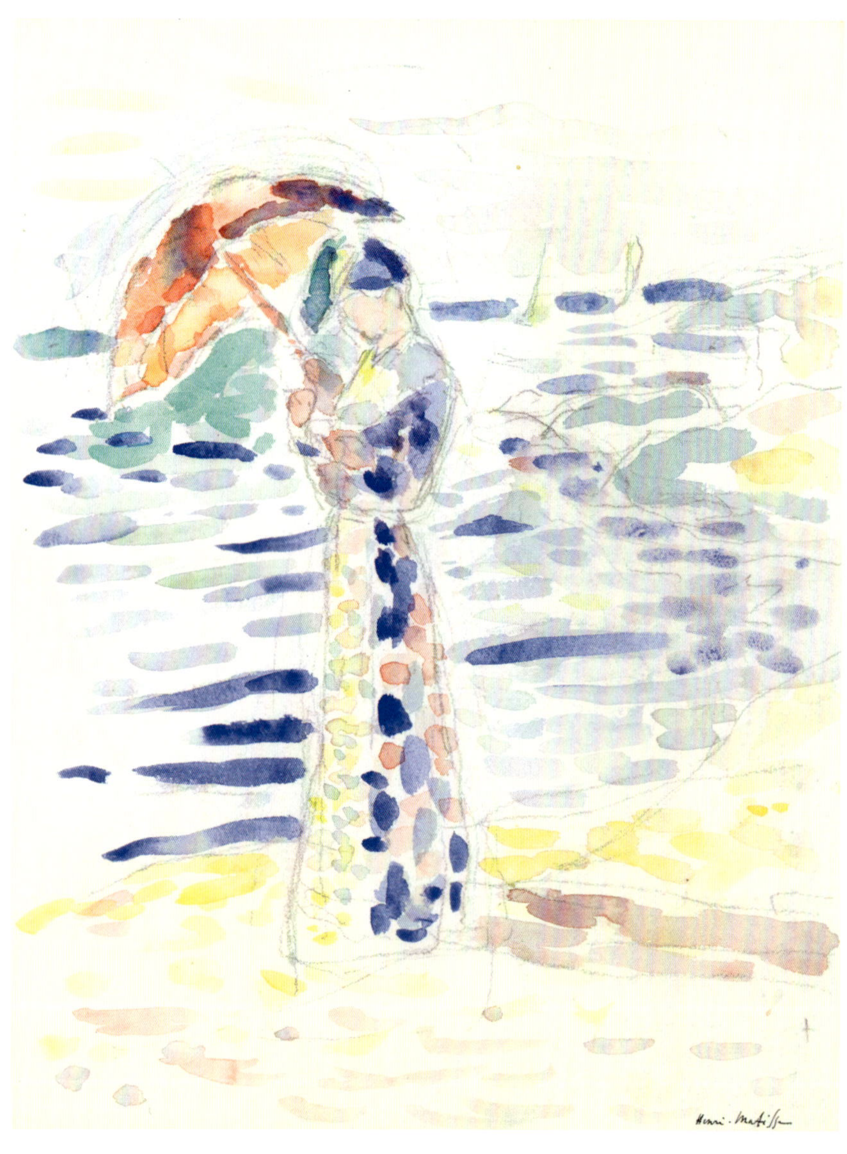

Henri Matisse, *Femme avec ombrelle en bord de mer* (Woman with an Umbrella at the Seashore), 1905. Watercolor and charcoal on paper, 10⅝ × 8¼ in. (27 × 21 cm). The Metropolitan Museum of Art, New York, Alfred Stieglitz Collection, 1949

Possibly Salon d'Automne cat. no. 713, *La Promenade*

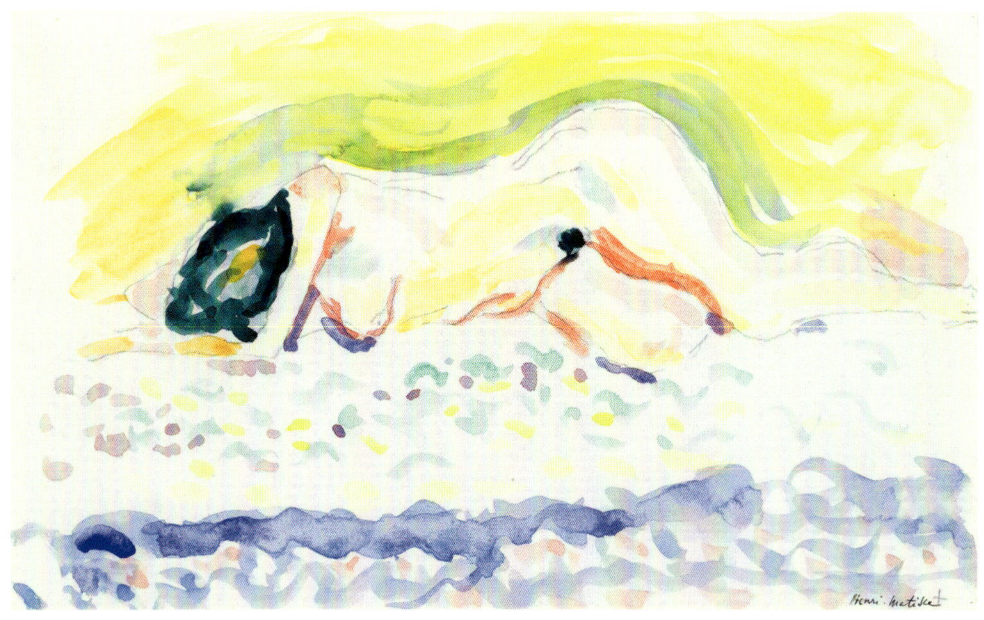

Henri Matisse, *Baigneuse* (Reclining Bather), 1905. Watercolor and graphite on paper, 5¾ × 9½ in. (14.6 × 24 cm). The Metropolitan Museum of Art, New York, Alfred Stieglitz Collection, 1949

Possibly Salon d'Automne cat. no. 722, *Baigneuse*

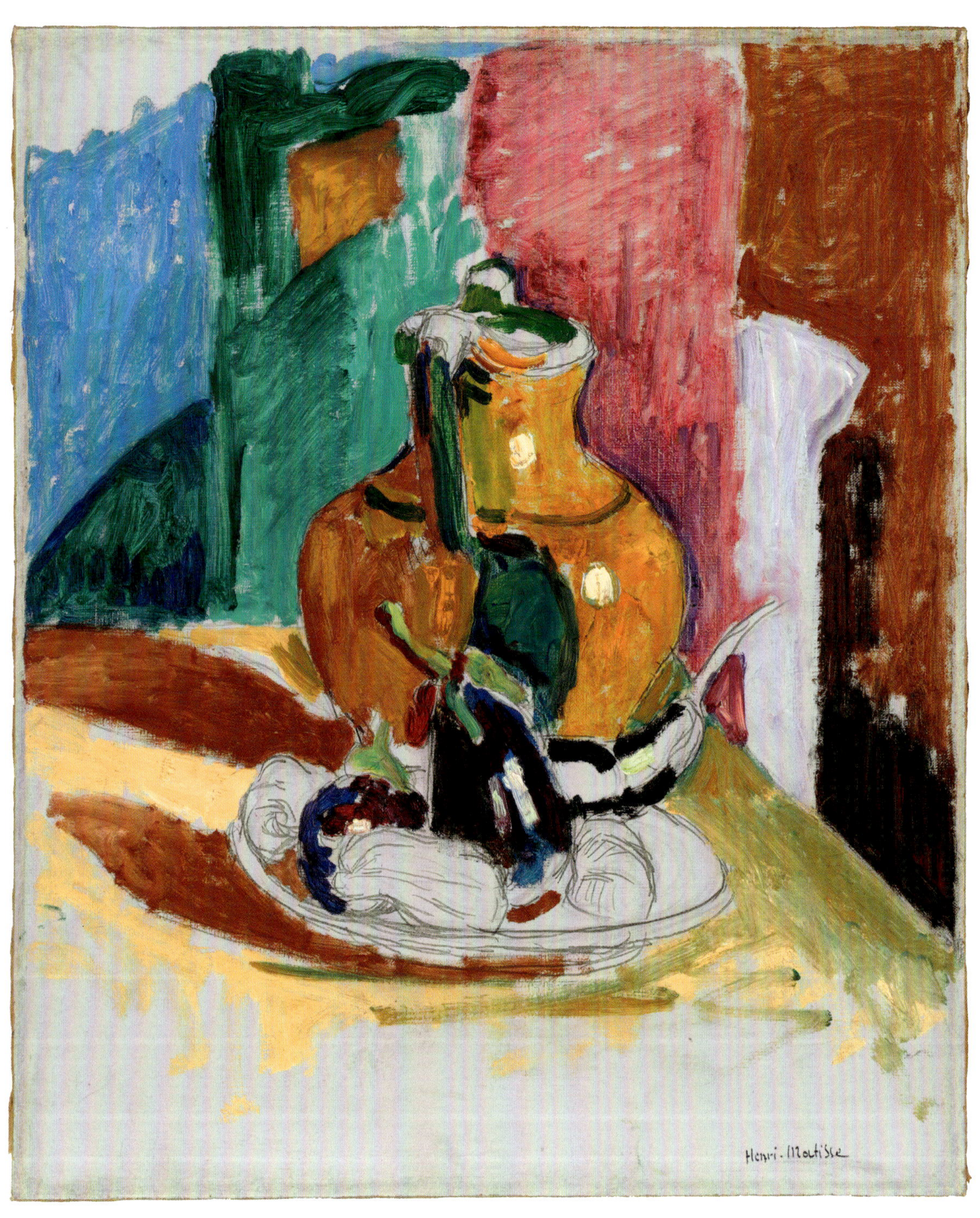

Henri Matisse, *Nature morte* (Still Life), also titled *Yellow Pottery from Provence,* 1905.
Oil on canvas, 21⅞ × 18⅜ in. (55.6 × 46.7 cm). Baltimore Museum of Art, The Cone
Collection, formed by Dr. Claribel Cone and Miss Etta Cone of Baltimore, Maryland

Representative of Salon d'Automne cat. no. 716, *Nature morte*

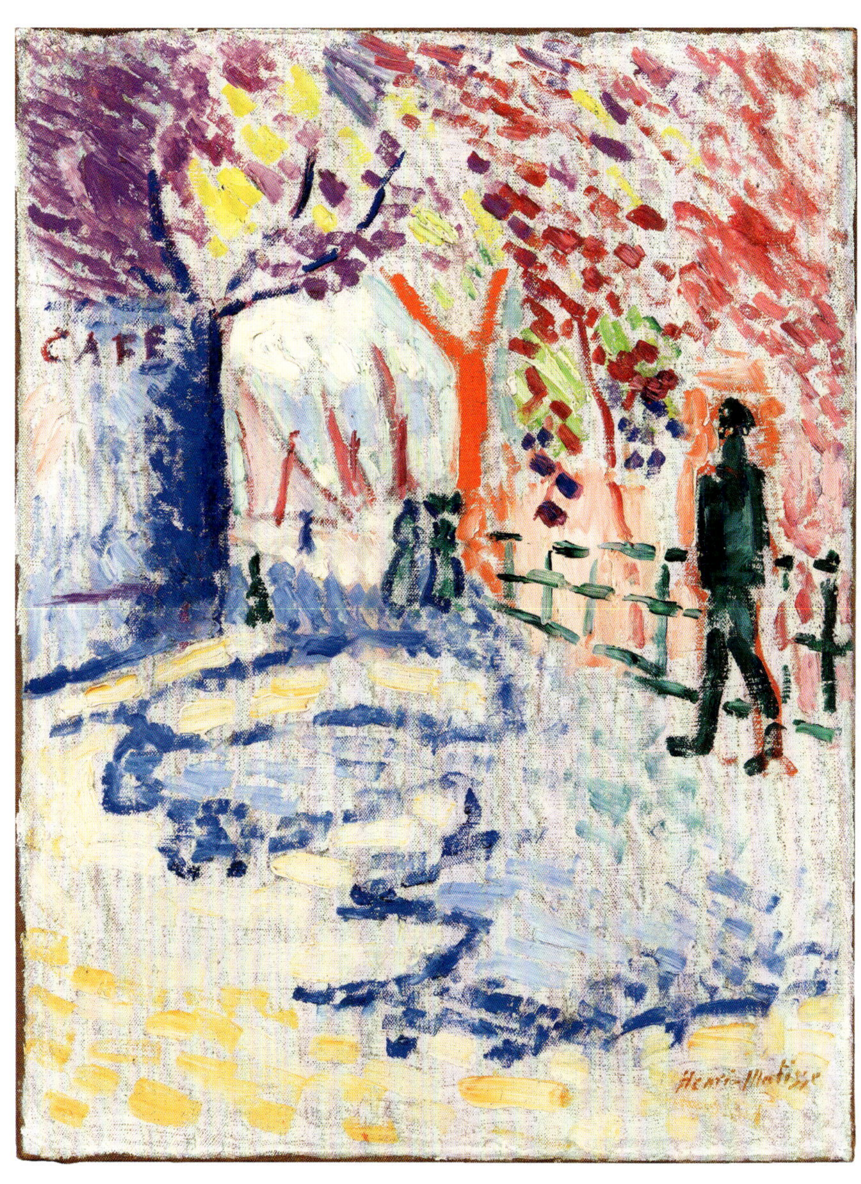

Henri Matisse, *Un beau matin d'été* (A Beautiful Summer Morning), 1905.
Oil on canvas, 16 × 12¾ in. (40.5 × 32.4 cm). M. S. Rau Art and Antiques, New Orleans
❧❧❧ Possibly Salon d'Automne cat. no. 717, *Matinée d'été*

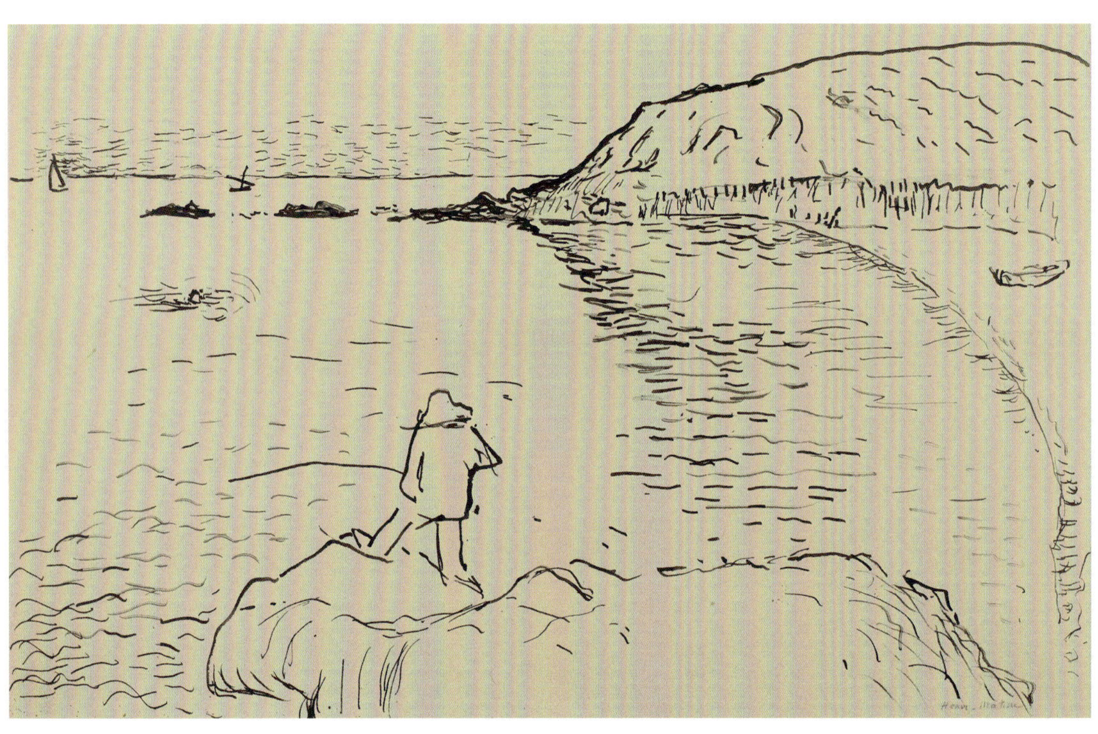

Henri Matisse, *Le pêcheur* (The Fisherman), 1905. Pen and ink on paper, 11⅞ × 19⅛ in. (30.2 × 48.6 cm). The Pushkin State Museum of Fine Arts, Moscow
Possibly Salon d'Automne cat. no. 720, *Marine (pêcheur)*

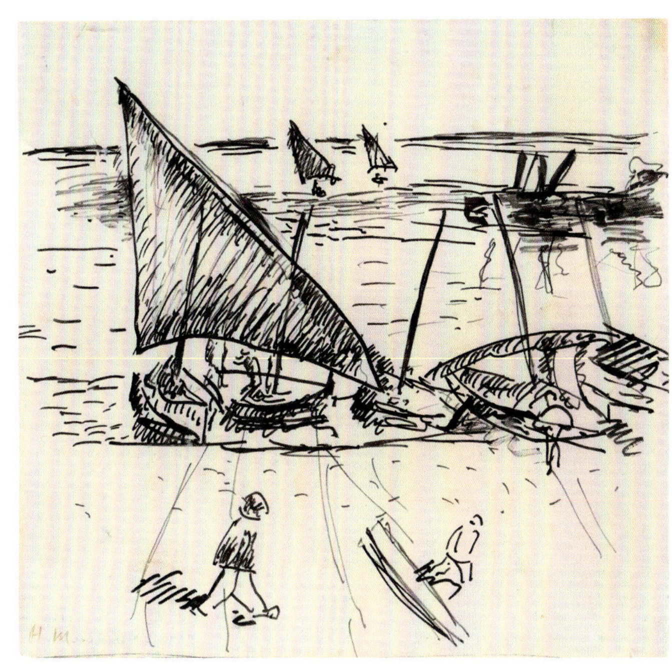

Henri Matisse, *Barques à Collioure* (Boats in Collioure), 1905. Ink on paper, 7³⁄₁₆ × 7½ in. (18.2 × 19 cm). Musée d'Art Moderne de Céret

Representative of Salon d'Automne cat. no. 721, *Marine (bateaux)*

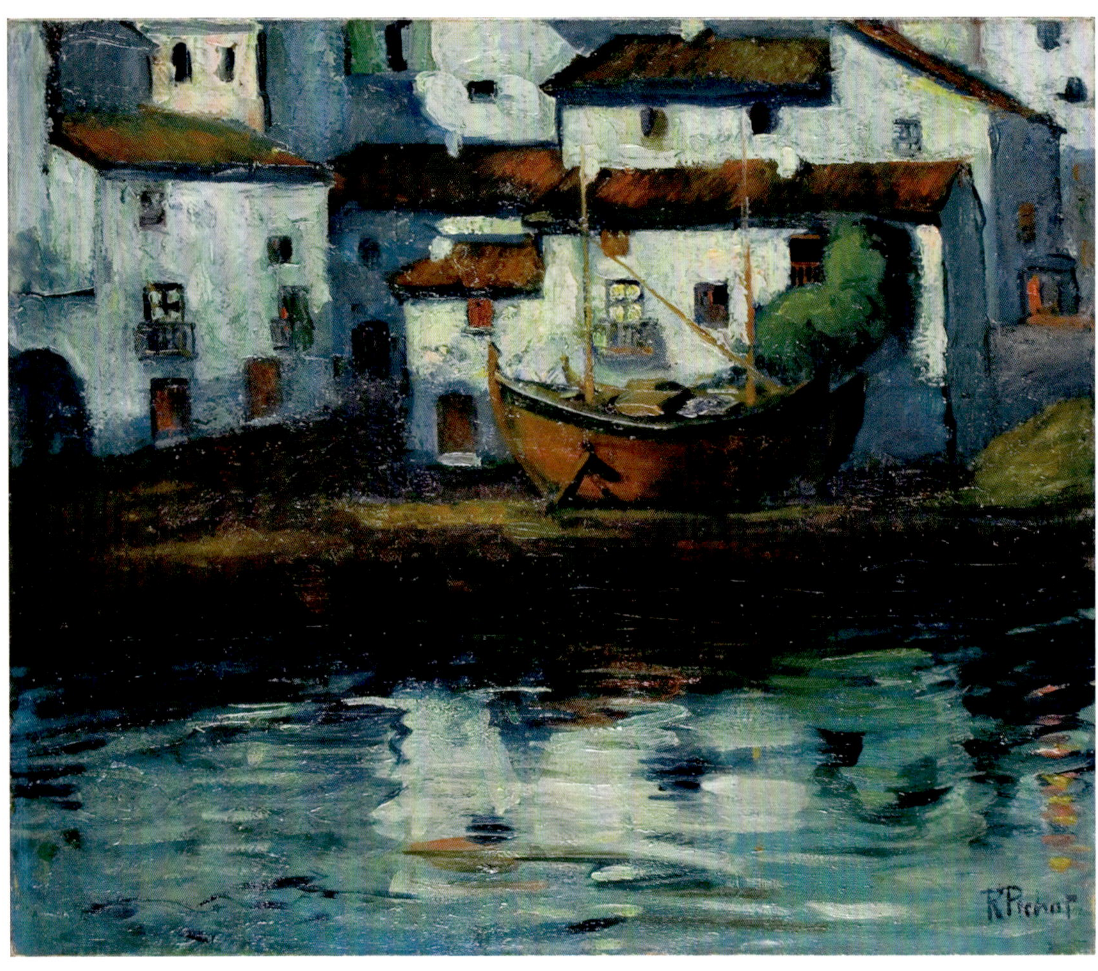

Ramon Pichot, *Clair de lune (Cadaqués)* (Moonlight [Cadaqués]), ca. 1905–11.
Oil on canvas, 18 × 21¾ in. (45.7 × 55.4 cm). Artur Ramon Art, Barcelona
❧❧❧ Representative of Salon d'Automne cat. no. 1244, *Clair de lune*

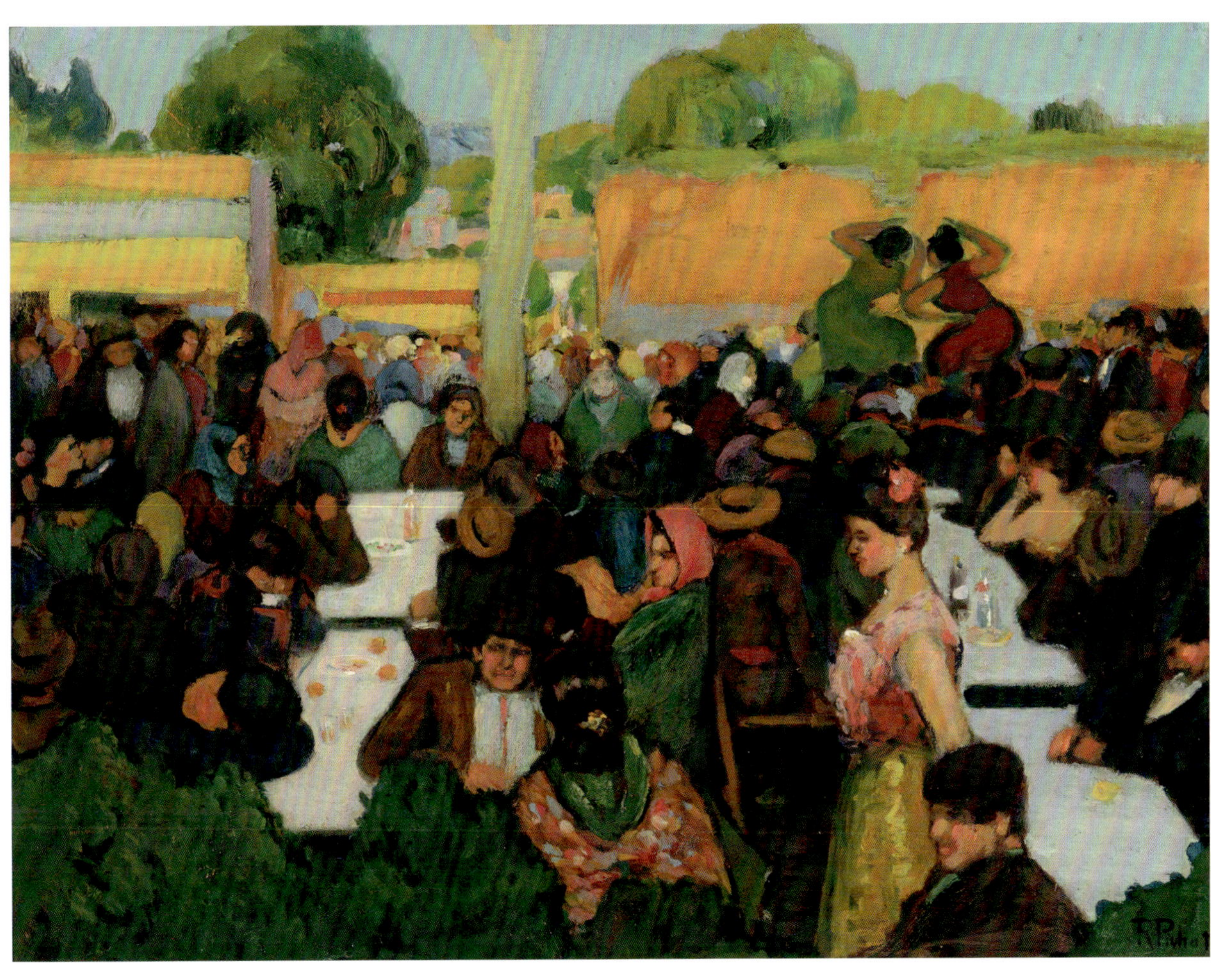

Ramon Pichot, *Tablao flamenco* (Flamenco Tablao), ca. 1905–10. Oil on cardboard,
18¼ × 24 in. (46.5 × 61 cm). Artur Ramon Art, Barcelona

Representative of Salon d'Automne cat. no. 1243, *Sardana (danse populaire)*

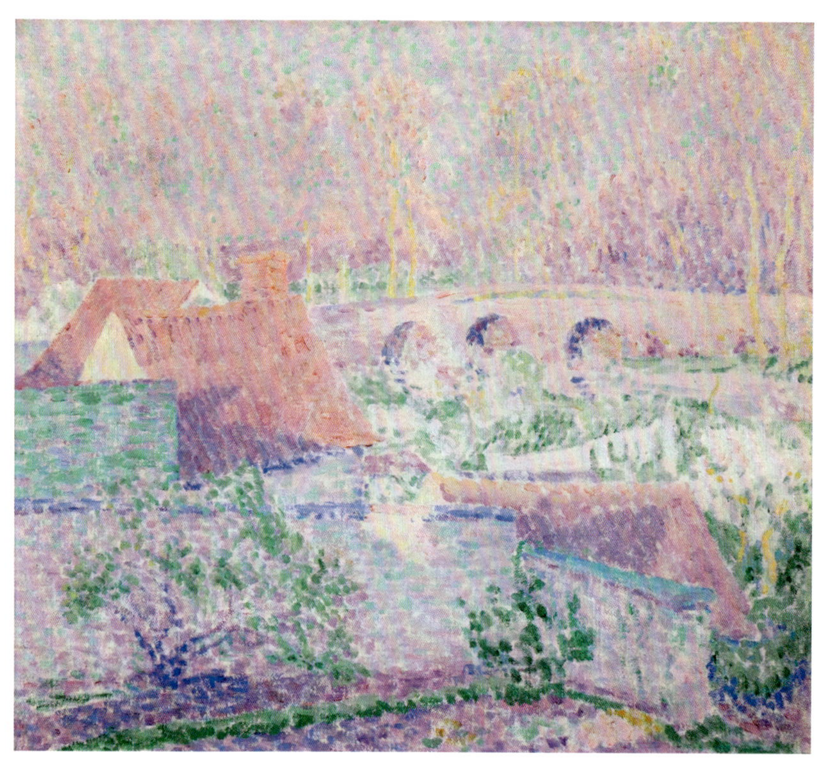

Jelka Rosen, *Le pont de Grez* (The Grez Bridge), n.d. Oil on canvas, 32⁵⁄₁₆ × 35³⁄₈ in.
(82 × 90 cm). Mairie-Musée de Grez-sur-Loing, France

Representative of Salon d'Automne cat. nos. 777–780, *Jardin fleuri*

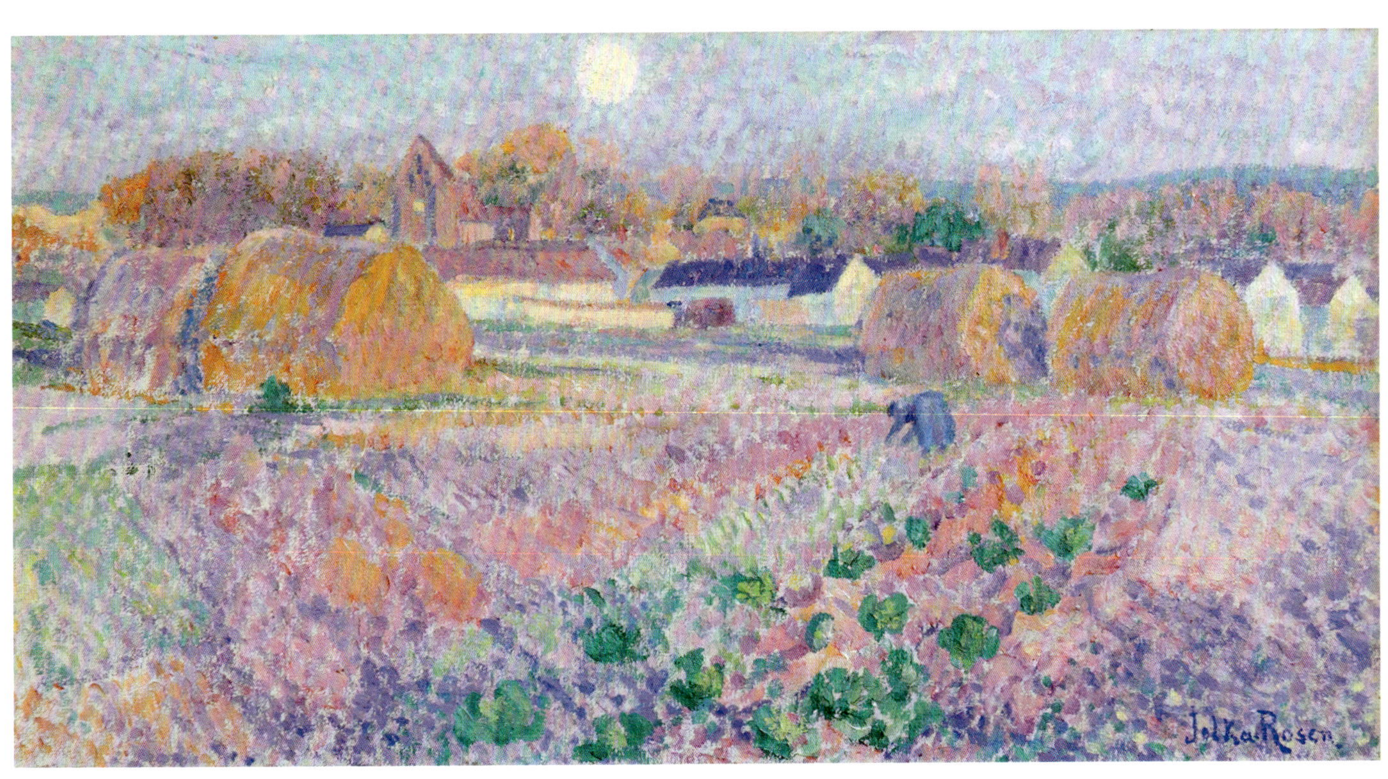

Jelka Rosen, *Les meules* (Haystacks), n.d. Oil on canvas, 27⅝ × 46½ in. (70 × 118 cm).
Mairie-Musée de Grez-sur-Loing, France

Representative of Salon d'Automne cat. nos. 777–80, *Jardin fleuri*

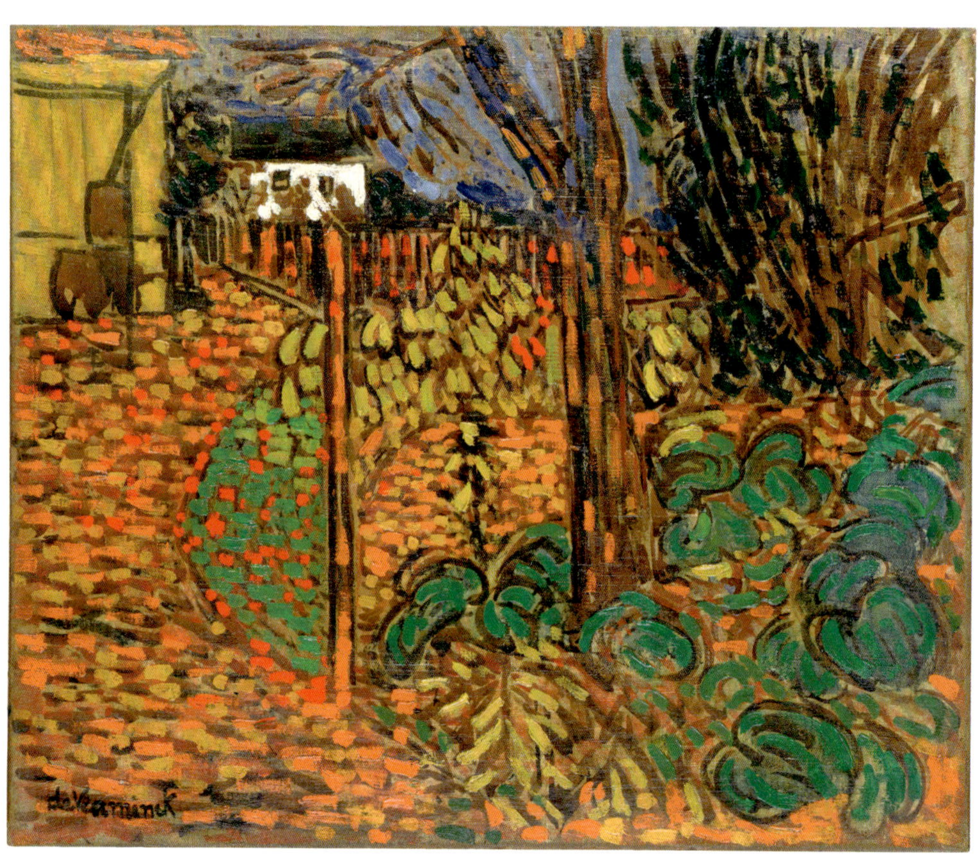

Maurice de Vlaminck, *La maison de mon père* (My Father's House), 1905. Oil on canvas, 21¼ × 25¾ in (54 × 65 cm). Pola Museum of Art, Pola Art Foundation, Hakone, Japan

Salon d'Automne cat. no. 1577, *La maison de mon père*

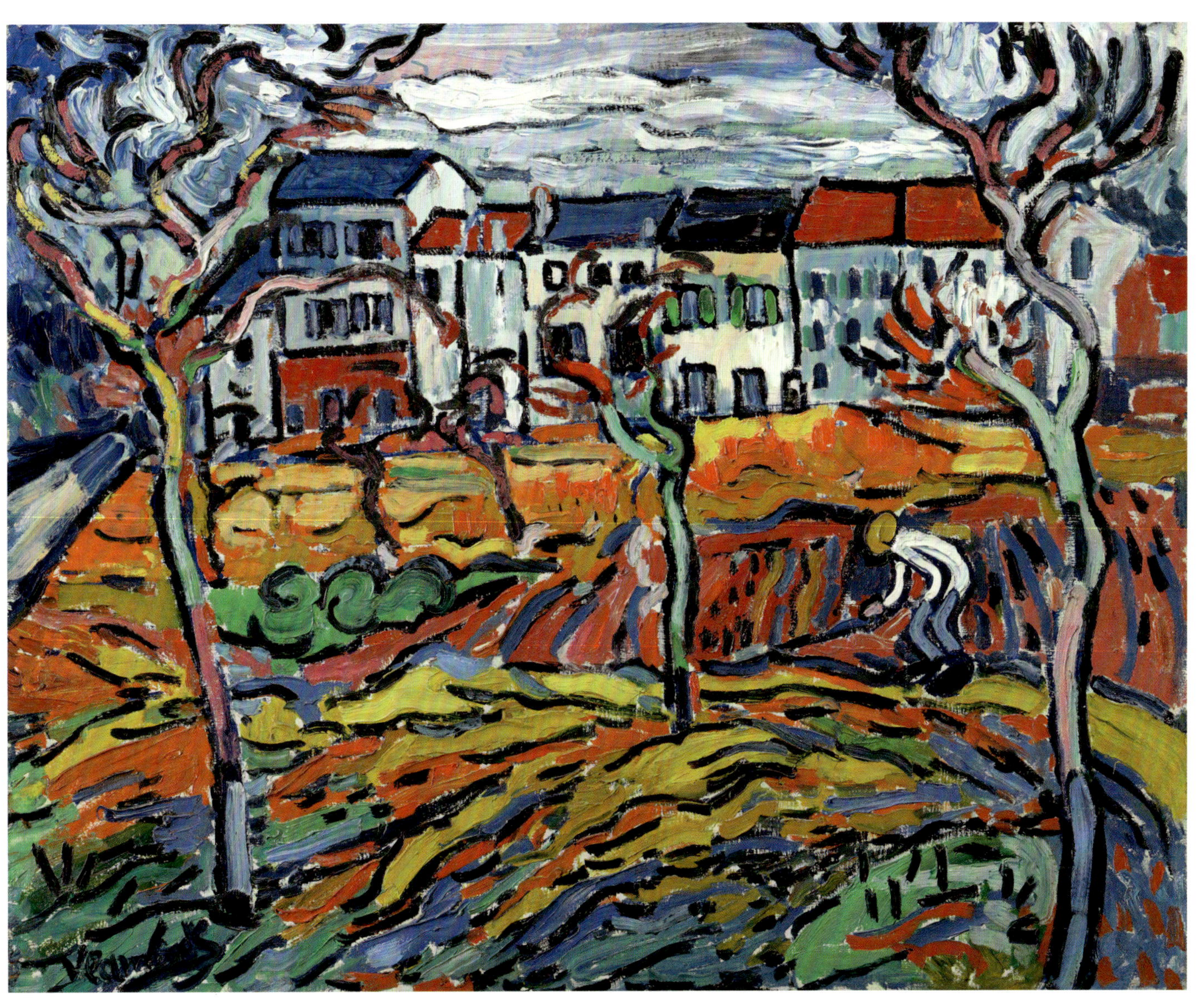

Maurice de Vlaminck, *Maisons à Chatou* (Houses at Chatou), ca. 1905. Oil on canvas, 32 × 40 in. (81.3 × 101 cm). The Art Institute of Chicago, gift of Mr. and Mrs. Maurice E. Culberg, 1951.19

Representative of cat. no. 1577, *La maison de mon père*, and cat. no. 1576, *La vallée de la Seine à Marly*

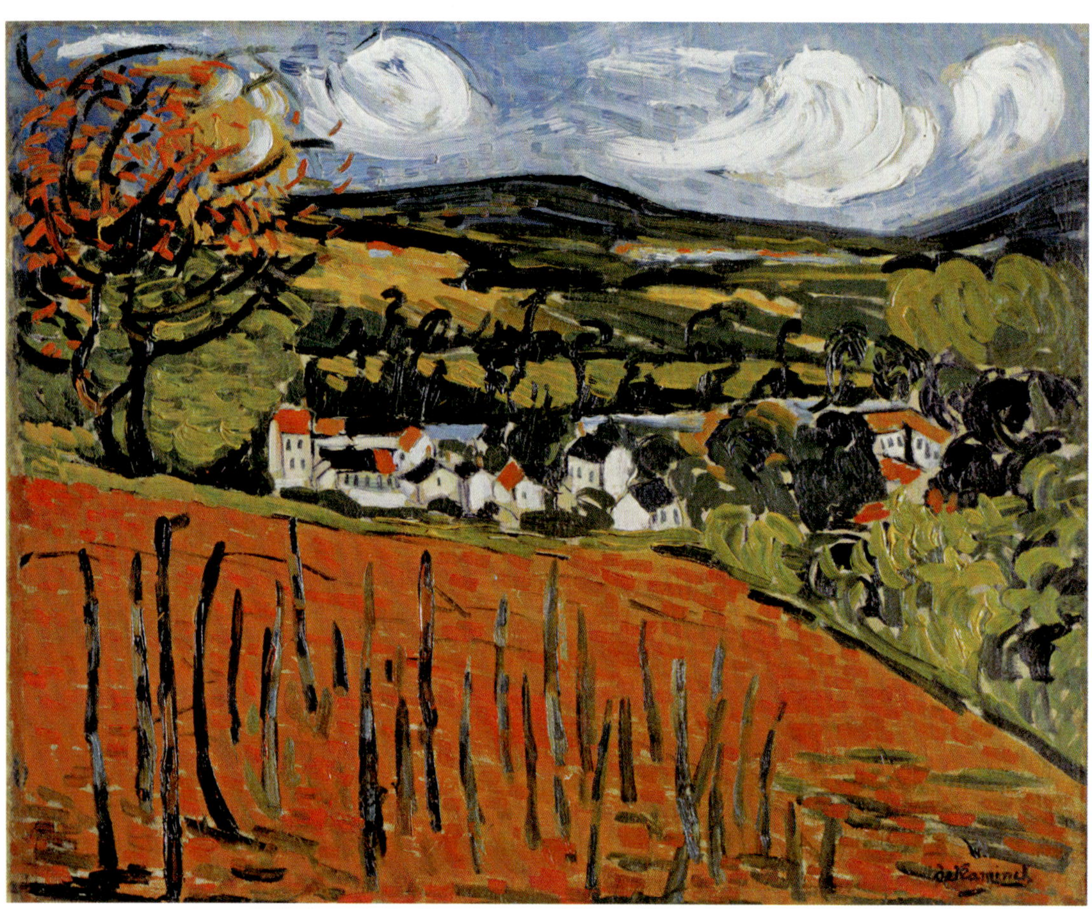

Maurice de Vlaminck, *La vallée de Port-Marly* (The Valley at Port-Marly), 1904–5.
Oil on canvas, 25½ × 31½ in. (65 × 80 cm). Private collection
❧❧❧ Salon d'Automne cat. no. 1576, *La vallée de la Seine à Marly*

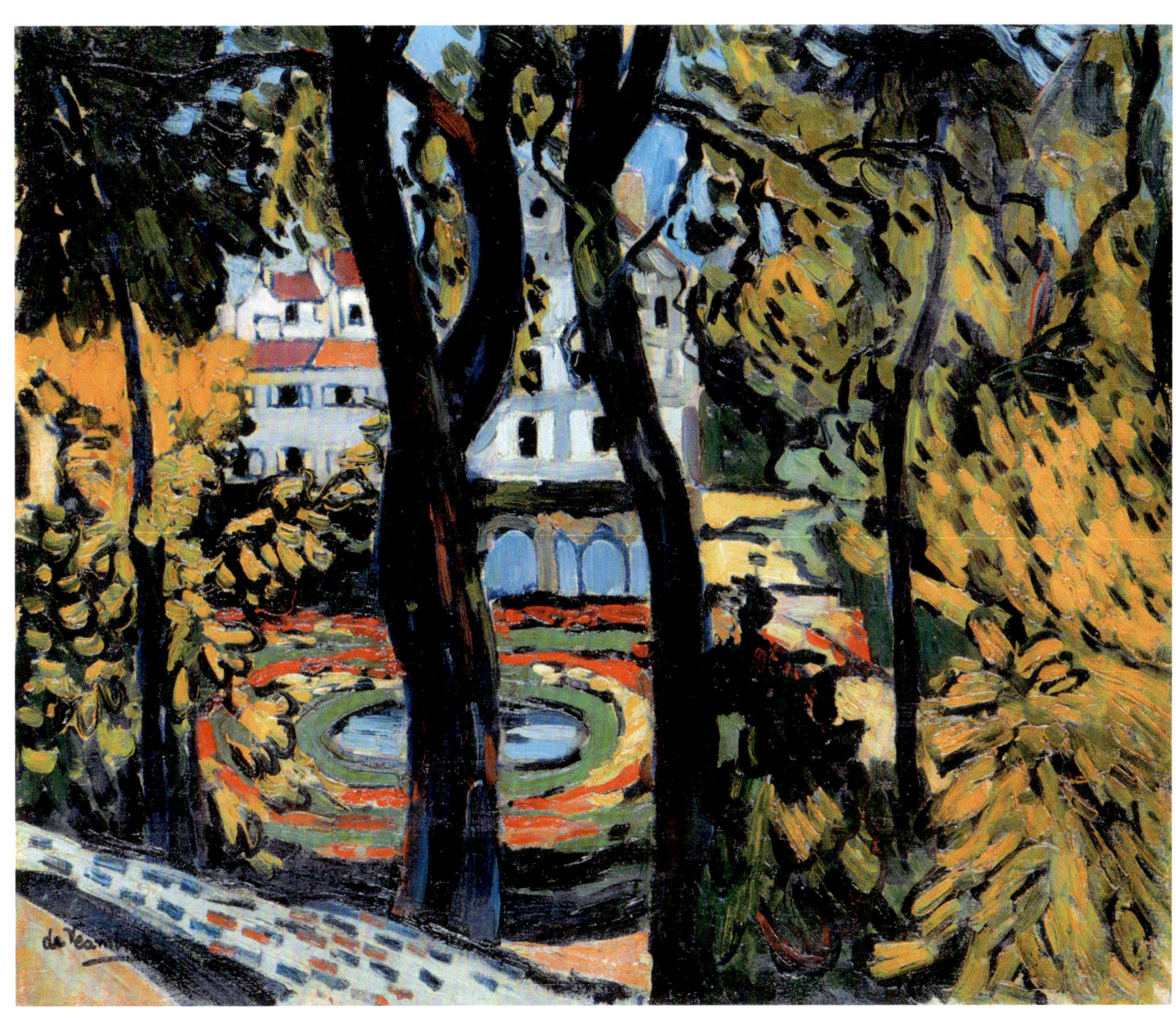

Maurice de Vlaminck, *Le jardin* (The Garden), also titled *Jardin public à Carrières-Saint-Denis* (Park at Carrières-Saint-Denis), 1905. Oil on canvas, 21⁵⁄₁₆ × 24¹³⁄₁₆ in. (54 × 62.9 cm). Private collection

Salon d'Automne cat. no. 1579, *Le jardin*

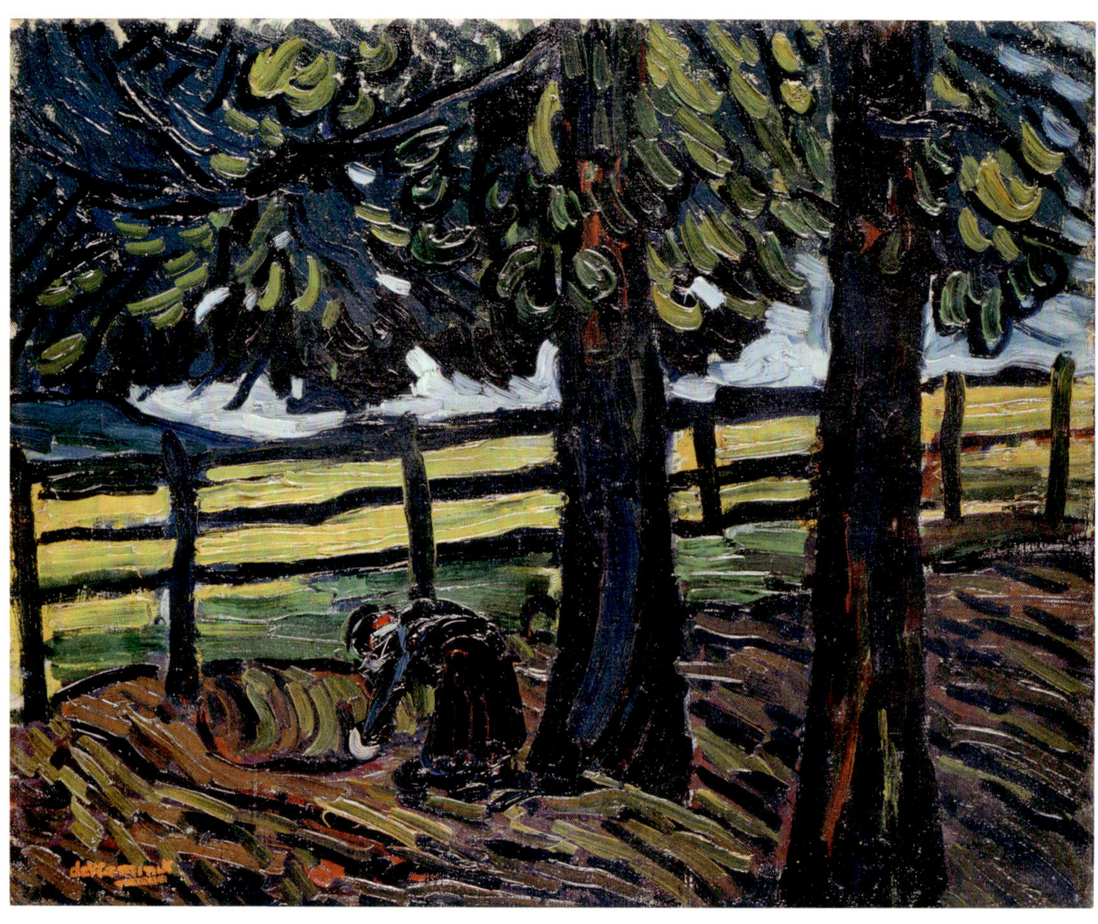

Maurice de Vlaminck, *Crépuscule* (Twilight), 1904–5. Oil on canvas, 21¼ × 25¹³⁄₁₆ in.
(54 × 65.5 cm). Tel Aviv Museum of Art, Max Bodner Bequest

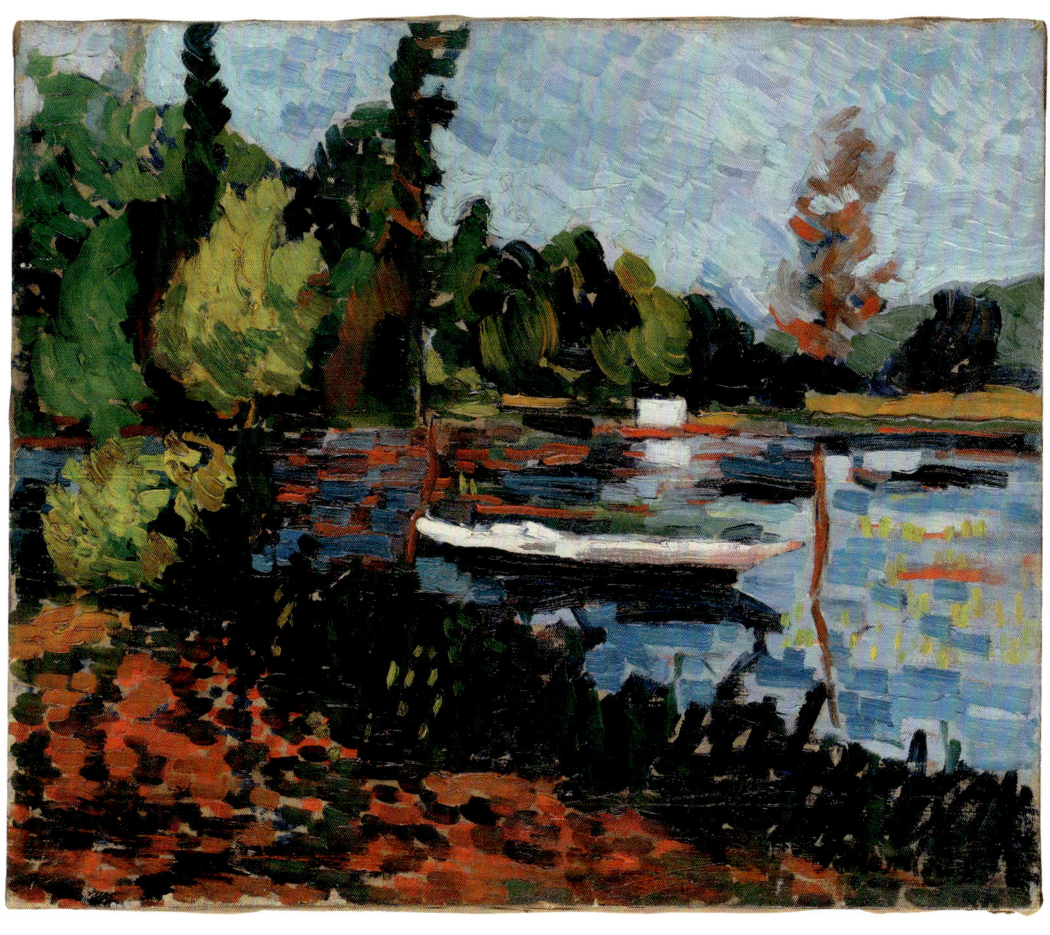

Maurice de Vlaminck, *L'Étang de Saint-Cucufa* (Saint-Cucufa Pond), 1905.
Oil on canvas, 21¼ × 25⅝ in. (54 × 65 cm). Private collection
❧❧❧ Salon d'Automne cat. no. 1580, *L'Etang de Saint-Cucufa*

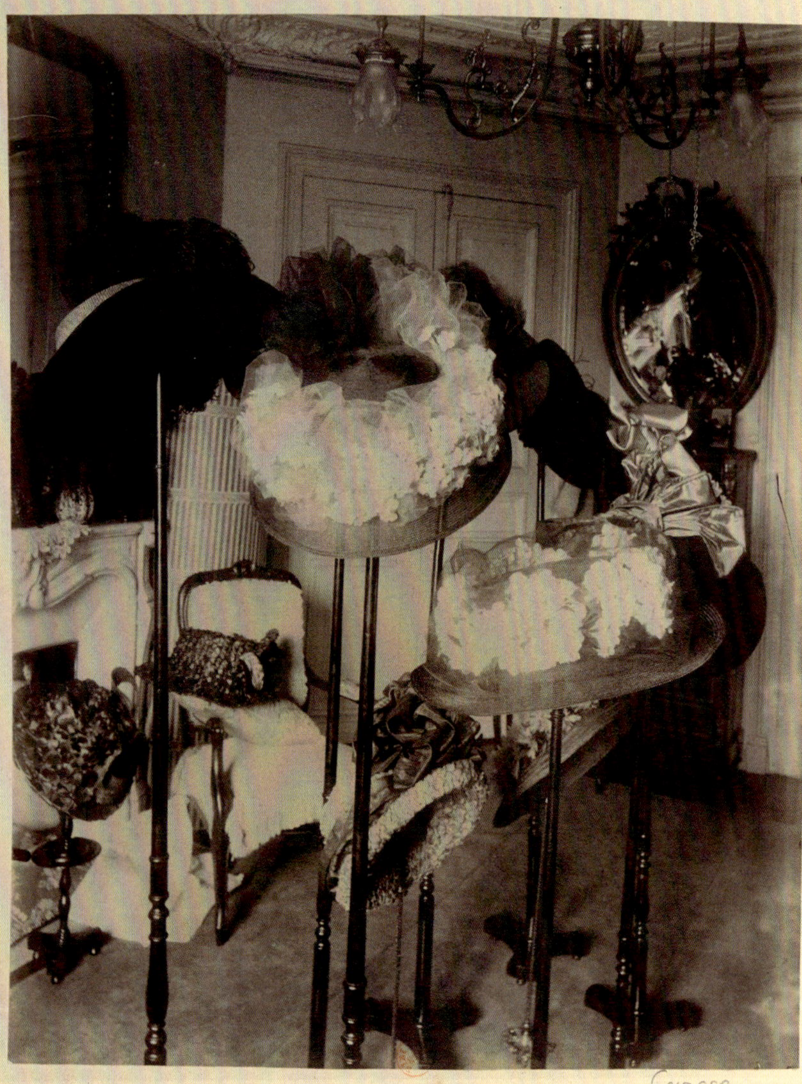

Eugène Atget, *Le salon de Madame C., modiste, place St André des arts* (The Salon of Mrs. C., Milliner, Place St-André-des-Arts), ca. 1910. Albumen print mounted on paper with ink inscription. Gallica, Bibliothèque Nationale de France

A Woman and a Hat

CLAUDINE GRAMMONT

By virtue of the scandal generated during its presentation at the 1905 Salon d'Automne, and its colorful assault on the aesthetic conventions and bourgeois values of its time, *Femme au chapeau* (Woman with a Hat) stands as one of the most emblematic works of Fauvism. The painting's mythical status reflects the narrative of the avant-garde, but it also clouds the historical context of the Belle Époque in which the painting originated—and in particular the ways in which the work registers against the well-established, highly codified subject of "woman with a hat." With this portrait, Matisse recharges the figure with an iconic power. This material presence also reflects in significant ways the nature of the painter's relationship with his wife, Amélie.

She is depicted in the painting from the waist up, in a three-quarter pose, her face turned toward the viewer. She wears a sizable hat and rests an open fan on her shoulder, which extends the roundness of her bust and echoes the curves of her hat. The background remains indistinct. Leo Stein, who would purchase the painting with his sister Gertrude, remembers that at first sight the work seemed like "the nastiest smear of paint I had ever seen."[1] Yet the painter's touch, neither tentative nor clumsy, finds expression in a complex mingling of unexpected colors that purposely get in the way of a literal reading of the figure. Matisse builds the face's architecture by alternating touches of cool colors (green, blue) and warm ones (the red and pink of the mouth), while a touch of yellow lands on the nose as if to highlight its apex. The masterful arrangement is topped by the sharp accents of the deep purple eyebrows set over the sitter's intensely piercing gaze. Background colors form a shapeless halo around the figure, inscribing it in a spatial frame that is abstract yet dynamic. The background functions as the setting of a

FIG. I
"Le Salon d'Automne," *Le Monde Illustré,* July I, 1905, p. 696. Gallica, Bibliothèque Nationale de France

FIG. 2
Les Modes, no. 58, Oct. I, 1905. Gallica, Bibliothèque Nationale de France

ring does, allowing the stones to shine brightly. Three interrelated yet distinct tiers emerge: the bottom section, in which the fan draws the viewer's gaze into the painting, and which, through its thick applications of colors, introduces the work's modus operandi; the mid-section, featuring the sitter's face; and the upper part—much like a mountain's summit—complete with hat and Matisse's signature. Preliminary drawing marks appear here and there, as the artist chose not to overpaint them fully. The work operates via these three zones, offering three reading steps for the gaze, three worlds at once distinct and united in the composition's overarching coherence. This sense of unity is essentially drawn from Paul Cézanne's example, and is achieved here through the relation between contrasting colors. All the while, the canvas embraces a deliberately "unfinished" appearance.

Here, Matisse tackles the pictorial and social registers of bourgeois portraiture. A 1905 review of the Salon d'Automne in the magazine *Le Monde Illustré* featured several specimens across the bottom of its first page: Guirand de Scévola's *Harmonie Argentée*, Abel Faivre's *Printemps* (Spring), and a portrait by "Bunny" (fig. 1).[2] In these and portraits on the pages that follow, women appear in full length or at half-length, dressed in their finest attire, with or without a hat. Each artist seeks to depict the sitter, who is obviously fashion-conscious and luxuriously clad in frothy, sophisticated clothes, in the most flattering terms. Such depictions highlight the distance and freedom claimed by Matisse in a painting that radically moves away from the superficial resemblance of these worldly portraits.

During the Belle Époque, the hat became a feminine accessory of the highest importance and a social marker of both taste and means. Women were loath to be seen outside their homes *en cheveux* (in their hair, or hatless), and each type of occasion—a stroll in the woods, a theater performance, an automobile ride—called for a specific type of hat. Wealthy women had bespoke hats tailored to their measurements, and the milliner's creation was born from careful study of the outfit it was meant to complement. By 1900, the fashionable hat had grown increasingly tall and extravagant. It was frequently pinned atop a high chignon, itself often constructed with a hair extension that added further height to the display (fig. 2). The large hat came into fashion together with the skirt suit and sought to balance the silhouette defined by the new bell skirt. While the basic hat shape was somewhat set, added trimmings turned it into the most striking of displays. Feathers, flowers, fruits, and actual (taxidermied) birds all added volume and color to the hat, turning it into an elaborate production. The hatpin, which secured the hat to a woman's hair, became an indispensable and increasingly sophisticated accessory, with the most refined pins being made of silver and adorned with precious stones (some of these were exhibited in the decorative arts section of the Salon d'Automne).

The connection between hats and couture dates back to the couturier Charles Frederick Worth and his collaboration with the milliner Madame Virot in the 1890s. At the turn of the century, the most famous milliners were Caroline Reboux (see p. 84), Lucienne Rebaté, the Legroux sisters, Madame Blanchot, Madame Deffontaine, and Marie Alphonsine. Each season saw the

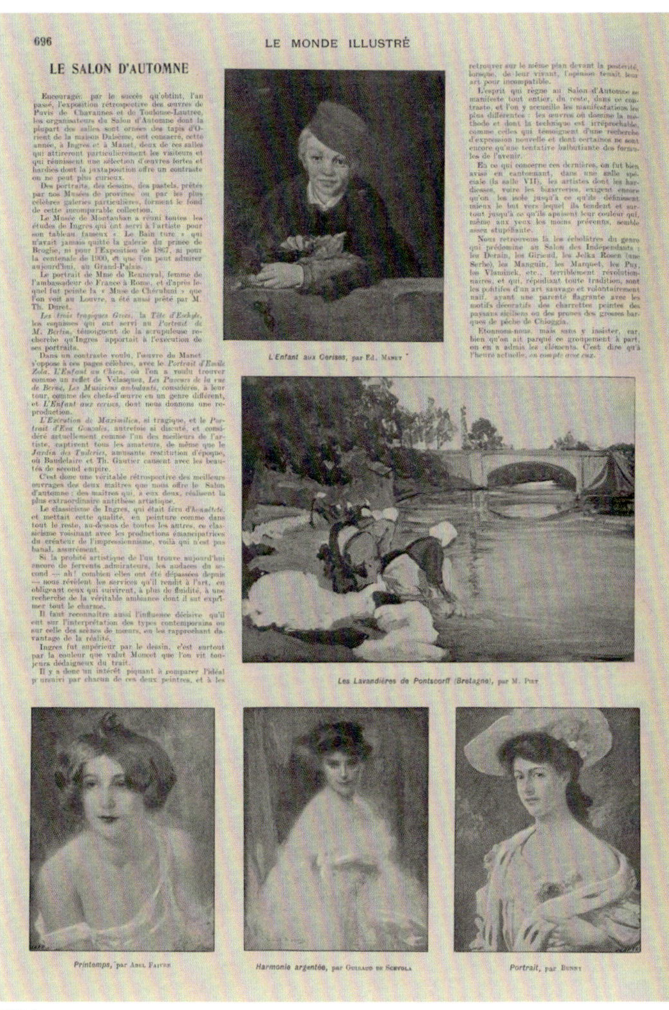

FIG. 1

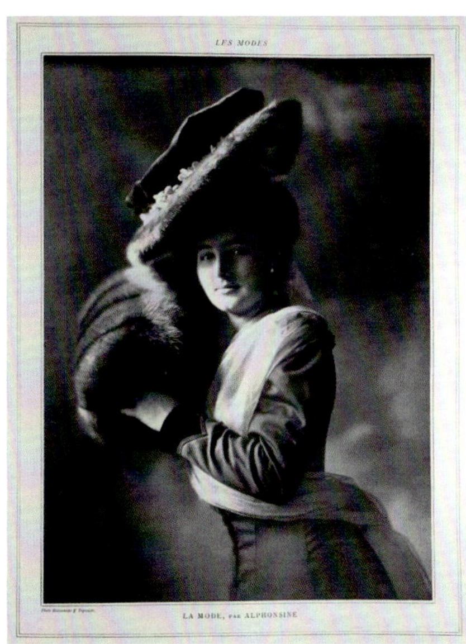

FIG. 2

emergence of new trends: In 1905, for instance, a toque designed by Madame Deffontaine especially for automobile rides was all the rage.[3] An October 1905 issue of *Le Figaro* noted that fashion now required that hats be worn tipped over one ear. Trendy embellishments included "old-fashioned pink tones evocative of the past's most exquisite hues, birds of all kinds, plenty of gouras [crowned pigeons] and korokoros [trogons], and especially velvet birds [birds-of-paradise], more beautiful even than they are in nature as they are dyed and made up. To achieve the look of feathers 'a la colonelle' [colonel style], straight and flexible, ostrich feathers are best used."[4]

In a 1905 article in the literary periodical *Gil Blas*, Louis Vauxcelles suggested that Matisse "must be quite brave, since he knowingly sent to the salon a work doomed to meet the destiny of the Christian virgin thrown to the circus lions."[5] Gertrude Stein reported that Matisse was so vexed by the derisive public reception of his work that he stopped attending the salon, sending Amélie in his place.[6] One wonders whether the painter or the model exhibited greater courage. Was Amélie merely a passive sitter? A deeper investigation into the couple's relationship holds the key to new readings of the painting. Like other famous artists' wives, Amélie Matisse long lingered in her husband's shadow. Little was known about her, save for a handful of accounts, until the publication of Hilary Spurling's biography in 1998.[7] Access to further evidence since then allows for a more nuanced reading of this seminal moment in the history of art, outside traditional readings through the lens of the male artistic genius.

Amélie was thirty-three when Henri painted this portrait. They had met eight years earlier, in October 1897, at a wedding in Neuilly-sur-Seine in which she was a maid of honor. Although Matisse was then living with Camille

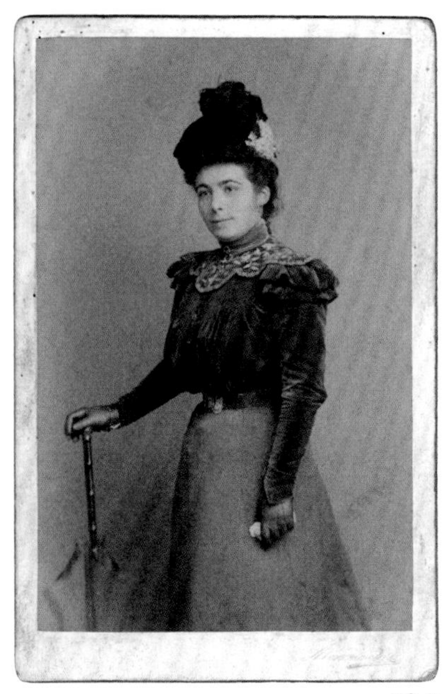

FIG. 3

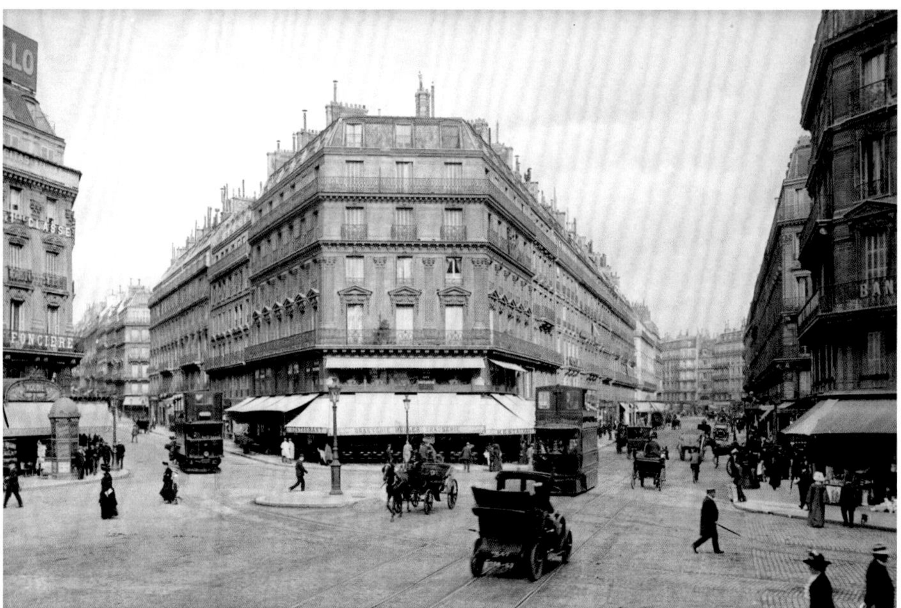

FIG. 4

Joblaud, with whom he shared a daughter, Marguerite, he fell for the pretty young brunette with a regal bearing who knew her own mind (fig. 3). Amélie Parayre was born in Beauzelle, near Toulouse, where her father, Armand, was a schoolteacher. The Parayres were close friends of Gustave Humbert, a republican deputy to the French parliament who rose to the rank of Keeper of the Seals (a position equivalent to today's Minister of Justice). Amélie's father eventually collaborated with Humbert's son, Frédéric, who hired him to take the helm of the radical newspaper of the city of Melun, *L'Avenir de Seine-et-Marne*. Unlike her sister Berthe, known to be studious and well behaved, Amélie spent her youth in a state of constant rebellion. When Amélie's parents left Toulouse for Paris, where they administered Humbert's prosperous financial affairs and his lending bank, Berthe stayed behind to graduate from high school and become a teacher and Amélie joined her parents in the capital. In Paris, she worked as a modiste (a maker of fashionable women's clothing and hats) for her aunt, Nine Boutiq, who headed a successful retail and wholesale hat outlet, La Grande Maison des Modes, on the Boulevard Saint-Denis. Her occupation placed Amélie in the social group known as *midinettes,* or young shopgirls.[8] This growing segment of Parisian society (an estimated 65,000 to 100,000 lived in the capital in 1906) distinguished itself from the rest of the working class by earning a decent income.[9] The midinette was young, as well as financially and socially independent, and became a natural target of puritanical criticism. The fashion district bordered the neighborhood in which many of the era's daily newspapers had their headquarters, and naturally the midinette soon became a media sensation, as well as a key figure within the male erotic imaginary at the turn of the century.

Amélie's life as an independent blue-collar worker came to an end three months after she met Matisse, when the two married. The religious ceremony took place on January 10, 1898, in the very respectable 16th arrondissement Church of Saint-Honoré-d'Eylau, with Frédéric Humbert serving as a witness. Amélie's wedding attire, a wedding gift from Humbert's wife, Thérèse, was a couture dress by Worth. Amélie agreed to raise Matisse's daughter, Marguerite, and the young family soon grew with the birth of a son, Jean, in 1899, followed by that of a second boy, Pierre, the following year. Henri struggled to make a living, and in 1899 Amélie decided to open her own millinery boutique. With help from her aunt, she secured an associate, Marguerite Dameron, and a storefront at 25 rue de Chateaudun, in one of the most exclusive shopping districts of the city (fig. 4). The future looked bright for Amélie, who benefited from Thérèse Humbert's patronage. Thérèse was known for her sophisticated attire and showstopping, extravagantly decorated hats—complete with fruit, flowers, and peacock feathers—which turned heads on the Parisian street. Her annual expenses at Madame Reboux, her favorite modiste, were rumored to reach 20,000 francs.[10] During these years, which Matisse would later describe as "la purée" (the mash), Matisse sold few works, and those at low prices. He managed to sell a copy of a painting from the Louvre to the French state for 300 francs, and a handful of paintings to occasional collectors for 100 francs apiece. He also left a few paintings on consignment at Berthe Weill's small gallery on rue Victor Massé, where one sold in April 1902 for 130 francs. For a time, Matisse had to hire himself out as a decorative painter, producing sets for the 1900 World's Fair for a pitiful one franc and twenty-five cents an hour.[11] Amélie's business was therefore essential in meeting the family's financial obligations. The children spent much of their time with their grandparents in Bohain and their aunt Berthe in Toulouse. Matisse split his time between the free academies, where he drew and painted from live models, and his studio across from Notre-Dame Cathedral at 19 quai Saint-Michel, while Amélie worked as a modiste in her shop.

This neat division of labor—the artist devoted to his work, his wife hard at work as a shopkeeper—is deceiving. The work of the milliner was not merely that of a saleswoman but that of a creator in tune with fashion trends and with the intimate desires of her clients. In his 1902 study devoted to those he elegantly calls "the queens of the needle," the writer and art critic Arsène Alexandre underscores the deeply artistic dimension of these professions, going so far as to suggest that "a great couturier or a great modiste is superior to most of today's artists."[12] The very words that couturiers and modistes use to describe their work, he points out, are directly borrowed from the vocabulary of the fine arts: "line, outline, modelé, blur, etc." Like the couturier, the modiste is very much an artist, whose creative process Alexandre fleshes out: First, "the fashionable customer *explains* her dress to the modiste, and the latter exercises her imagination upon these still fluctuating facts, until, amid often lengthy discussions and tentative fittings, a flash of insight strikes. At the start of each season, the fashion artist must simply feel and know what is in the air." After the client's agreement on the design, three to four hours of work were required to complete the hat's creation. It is impossible to know with certainty, between Amélie and Madame Dameron, who did what in the boutique on the Rue de Chateaudun. In the steps of the hat-making process, the

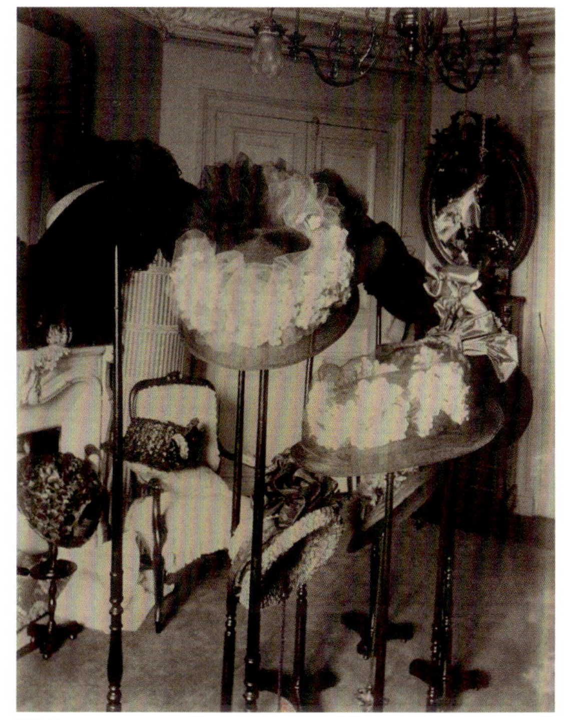

FIG. 5

former (*formière*) built the general structure, determining the hat's shape and movement. The preparer (*apprêteuse*) prepared the hat's ground using materials that Alexandre found "unlikely," and finally the trimmer (*garnisseuse*) created a composition of her own invention (fig. 5). This last step, he explains, was essential, since "a woman's expression depends entirely upon the trimmer's virtuosity." There are "threatening hats, promising hats, ironic hats, and even faithful hats." As he narrates the "hatching of the hat," it becomes clear that the modiste must be seen as an accomplished artist. A great modiste "composes her hat as an artist does his painting. She begins with broad strokes, and finishes with meticulous care."[13] Madame Matisse, the "Woman with a Hat," was a creator in her own right, and not merely the painter's wife—the "remarkable lady of the house" and the "exceptional cook" who "shops at the market and poses for all of her husband's paintings."[14]

In 1902 Amélie's parents were severely affected by a political, legal, and financial scandal that brought the downfall of the Humberts.[15] The Humberts' significant fortune turned out to be entirely fictional, based on a Ponzi scheme implicating most of the family's lenders. As their shady dealings came to light, the Humberts attempted to flee the authorities, before being captured in Spain (fig. 6). Matisse's studio was searched by the police, as was Amélie's boutique. Her father, charged with complicity in the fraud, was eventually acquitted, but the young couple was caught in the scandal engulfing the family and deprived of financial support from Amélie's parents. At the end of 1902, Amélie had no choice but to close her shop and follow her husband and children to Bohain. The following year, she returned to Paris and to her former position in her aunt's establishment. Amélie was gifted in needlework, and her skills extended beyond millinery and into tapestry; she showed a tap-

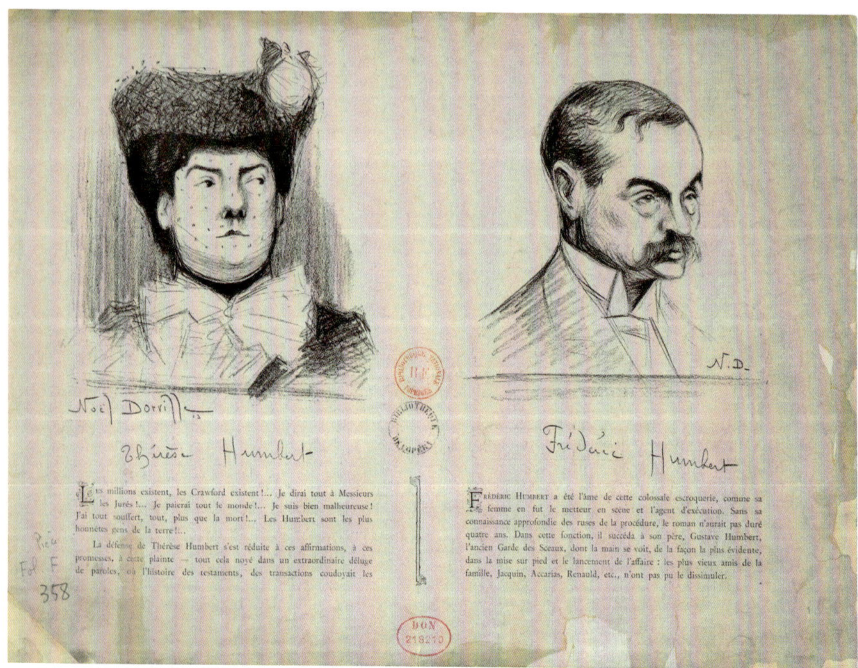

Thérèse Humbert

Les millions existent, les Crawford existent !... Je dirai tout à Messieurs les Jurés !... Je paierai tout le monde !... Je suis bien malheureuse ! J'ai tout souffert, tout, plus que la mort !... Les Humbert sont les plus honnêtes gens de la terre !...

La défense de Thérèse Humbert s'est réduite à ces affirmations, à ces promesses, à cette plainte — tout cela noyé dans un extraordinaire déluge de paroles, où l'histoire des testaments, des transactions coudoyait les

Frédéric Humbert

Frédéric Humbert a été l'âme de cette colossale escroquerie, comme sa femme en fut le metteur en scène et l'agent d'exécution. Sans sa connaissance approfondie des ruses de la procédure, le roman n'aurait pas duré quatre ans. Dans cette fonction, il succéda à son père, Gustave Humbert, l'ancien Garde des Sceaux, dont la main se voit, de la façon la plus évidente, dans la mise sur pied et le lancement de l'affaire : les plus vieux amis de la famille, Jacquin, Accarias, Renauld, etc., n'ont pas pu le dissimuler.

FIG. 6

estry screen of her own making, based on a cartoon by Derain, at the Salon des Indépendants in 1905.[16] Charles Camoin and Albert Marquet painted her at work on the screen, in the studio on Quai Saint-Michel (p. 76), shortly before the exhibition, dressed in the Japanese robe in which she had posed the previous summer in Saint-Tropez (p. 77).

Femme au chapeau has been interpreted as Matisse's homage to Amélie for the sacrifices she endured in order to support his artistic endeavors.[17] The art historian T. J. Clark, for instance, has argued that the wife's bravery is here matched by the painter's courage as he embraces the very literal presence of color and of paint's materiality.[18] This interpretation fails to see the part Amélie herself played in the creation of the work: Who but she would have crafted the very hat she proudly wears, which has kept critics talking ever since? It features at the heart of the work as much as she does, even though the painter's deliberately quick rendering omits details we are left to imagine—fruits, certainly, and perhaps also feathers and birds aptly perched on the upward-tilted, winged creation. If, as Alexandre suggested, each of a modiste's creations conveys its own personality, then let us call Amélie's a "rebellious hat," matching in its character the audacity of Henri's painted manifesto. This work of art is the result of a collaboration between a painting artist and a hat-making one. Amélie ceases to be merely the wife and model devoted to the cause of painting, and becomes, through the portrait, a fully fleshed-out woman. ❀

1   Leo Stein, *Appreciation: Painting, Poetry and Prose* (New York: Crown, 1947), 158.

2   "Le Salon d'Automne," *Le Monde Illustré,* Oct. 28, 1905, pp. 696–97.

3   *Les Modes,* Oct. 1, 1905.

4   Claire de Chancenay, "Coulisses de la mode," *Le Figaro,* Oct. 17, 1905.

5   Louis Vauxcelles, "Le Salon d'Automne," *Supplément à Gil Blas,* Paris, Oct. 17, 1905.

6   Gertrude Stein, *The Autobiography of Alice B. Toklas* (New York: The Literary Guild, 1933), 48.

7   Hilary Spurling, *The Unknown Matisse: A Life of Matisse, Volume I: 1869–1908* (London: Hamish Hamilton, 1998). Many areas of Amélie Matisse's life remain difficult to know, particularly following her divorce from Henri in 1939.

8   On this subject, see Anaïs Albert, "Les midinettes parisiennes à la Belle-Époque: Bon goût ou mauvais genre?" *Histoire, Économie & Société* 3 (2013): 61–74.

9   Fénelon Gibon, *Employées et ouvrières* (Lyon: E. Vitte, 1906).

10   Spurling, *Unknown Matisse,* 183.

11   See Henri Matisse, *Bavardages: Les entretiens égarés—Propos recueillis par Pierre Courthion* (Paris: Skira, 2017), 61. For the copies, see Berthe Weill, *Pan! dans l'œil, ou trente ans dans les coulisses de la peinture contemporaine, 1900–1930* (Paris: L'Echelle de Jacob, 2009), 41, 85.

12   Arsène Alexandre, *Les reines de l'aiguille: Modistes et couturières* (Paris: Théophile Belin, 1902), 68.

13   Alexandre, *Les reines de l'aiguille,* 72, 130, 143, 149.

14   See Stein, *Autobiography of Alice B. Toklas,* 43.

15   See Spurling, *Unknown Matisse,* chap. 8, "Paris and Bohain," 236–70.

16   In the exhibition catalogue that lists artists in alphabetical order, she appears before her husband, under her married name: "Matisse (Mrs. Henri), born in Beauzelle (Haute-Garonne), 19, quai Saint-Michel, Paris, 2770, Tapestry screen after a cartoon by André Derain." See Spurling, *Unknown Matisse,* 319.

17   See, for example, Spurling, *Unknown Matisse,* 335.

18   T. J. Clark, "Madame Matisse's Hat," *London Review of Books,* Aug. 14, 2008, pp. 29–32.

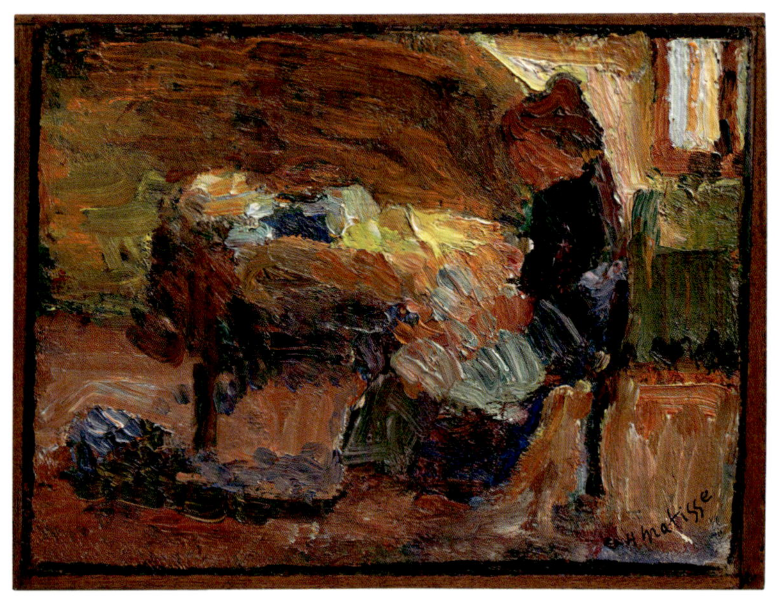

Henri Matisse, *Madame Matisse cousant* (Madame Matisse Sewing), ca. 1899. Oil on cardboard mounted on wood panel with border, 6¹¹⁄₁₆ × 9⅛ in. (17 × 23 cm). Private collection

Albert Marquet, *Portrait de Madame Matisse* (Portrait of Madame Matisse), ca. 1900. Oil on canvas, 51³⁄₁₆ × 38³⁄₁₆ in. (130 × 97 cm). Musée Matisse, Nice, gift of Madame Henri Matisse, 1960

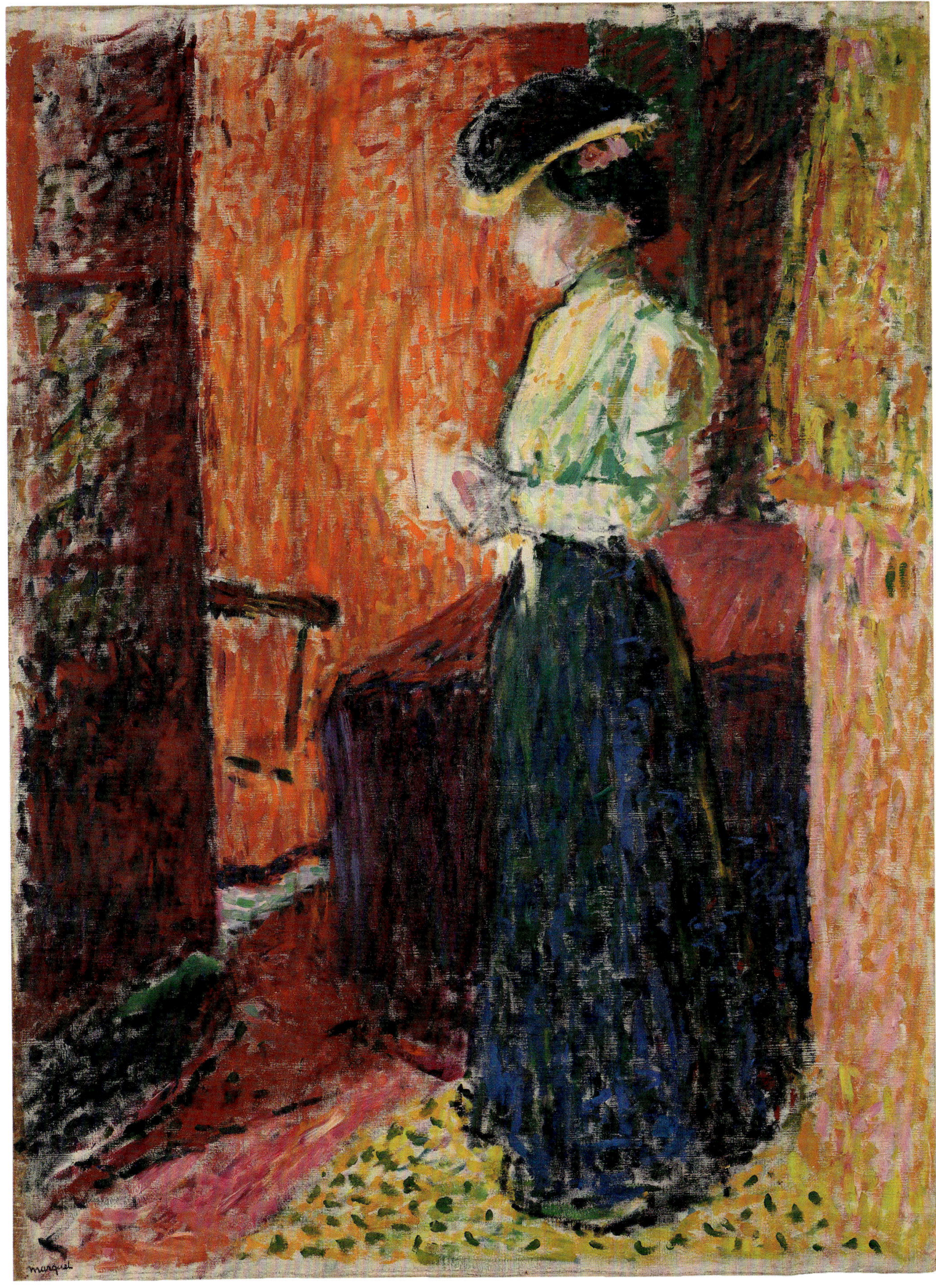

marquet

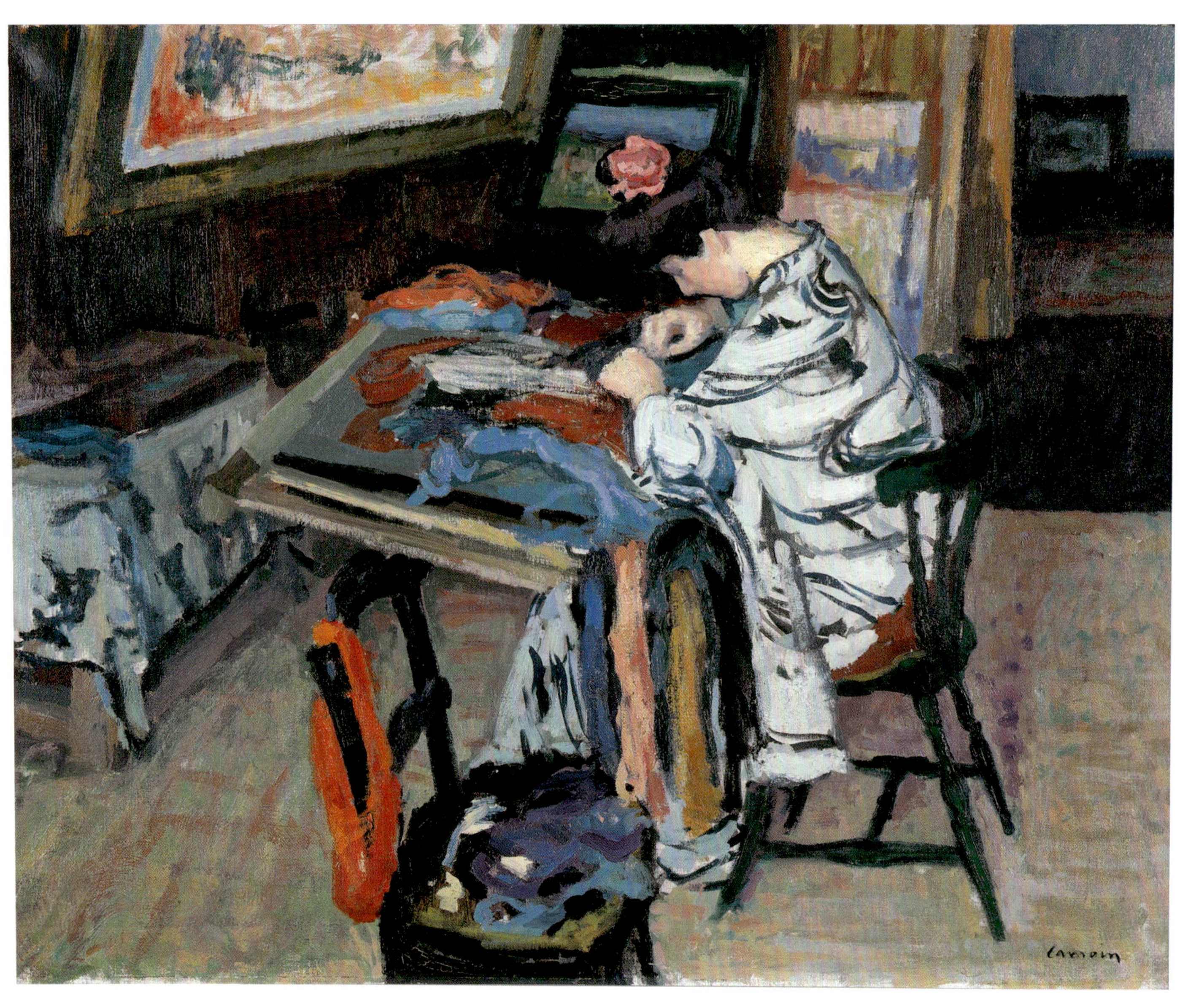

Charles Camoin, *Madame Matisse faisant de la tapisserie* (Madame Matisse Doing Tapestry Work), 1904. Oil on canvas, 25⁹⁄₁₆ × 31⁷⁄₈ in. (65 × 81 cm). Musée d'Art Moderne et Contemporaine, Strasbourg, gift of André Kahn-Wolf, 1966

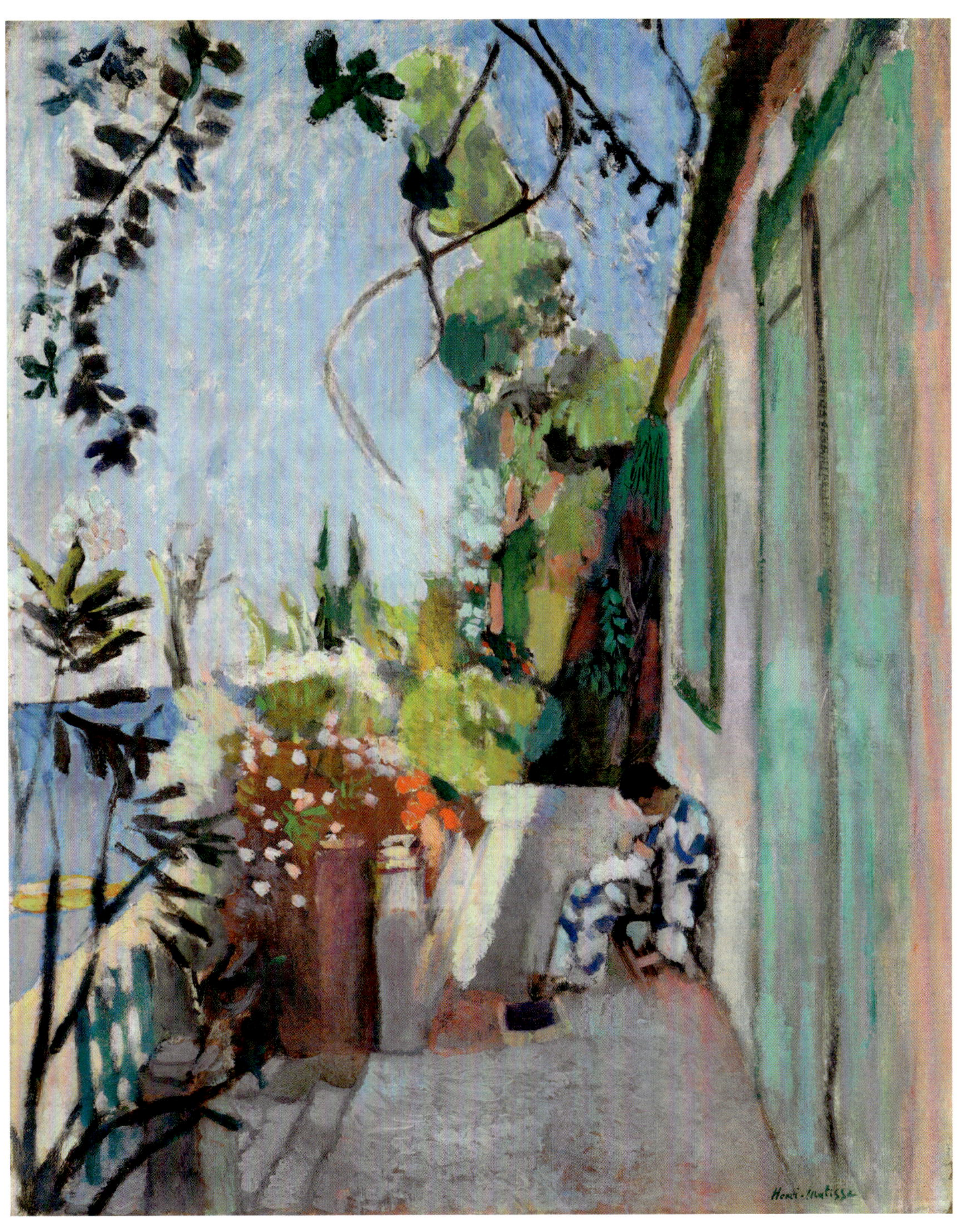

Henri Matisse, *La terrasse (Saint-Tropez)* (The Terrace [Saint-Tropez]), 1904. Oil on
canvas, 28⅜ × 22¹³⁄₁₆ in. (72 × 58 cm). Isabella Stewart Gardner Museum, Boston

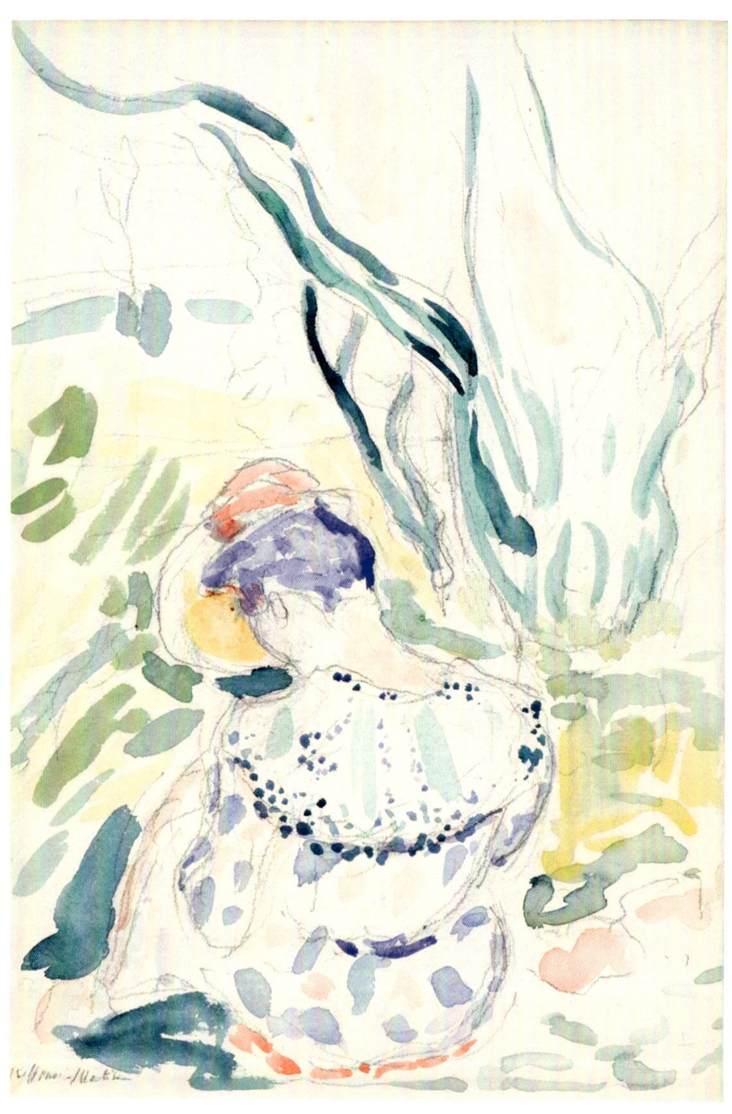

Henri Matisse, *Jeune femme assise de dos—Mme Matisse* (Young Woman Seated
from Behind—Madame Matisse), 1905. Watercolor and graphite on paper, 9$\frac{13}{16}$ × 6$\frac{5}{8}$ in.
(24.9 × 16.9 cm). The Pierre and Tana Matisse Foundation Collection, New York

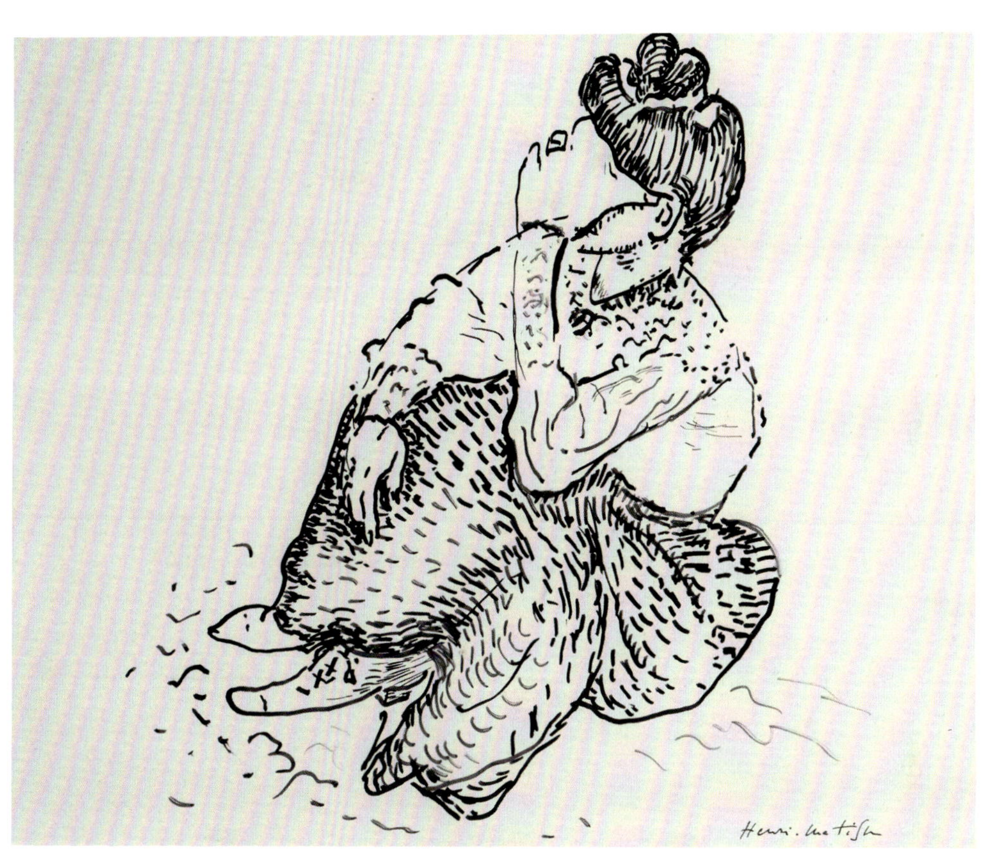

Henri Matisse, *Madame Matisse assise* (Madame Matisse Seated), 1905. Ink on
paper, 7⁹⁄₁₆ × 9⁵⁄₁₆ in. (19.2 × 23.6 cm). Musée National d'Art Moderne/Centre Georges
Pompidou, Paris, purchase, 1984

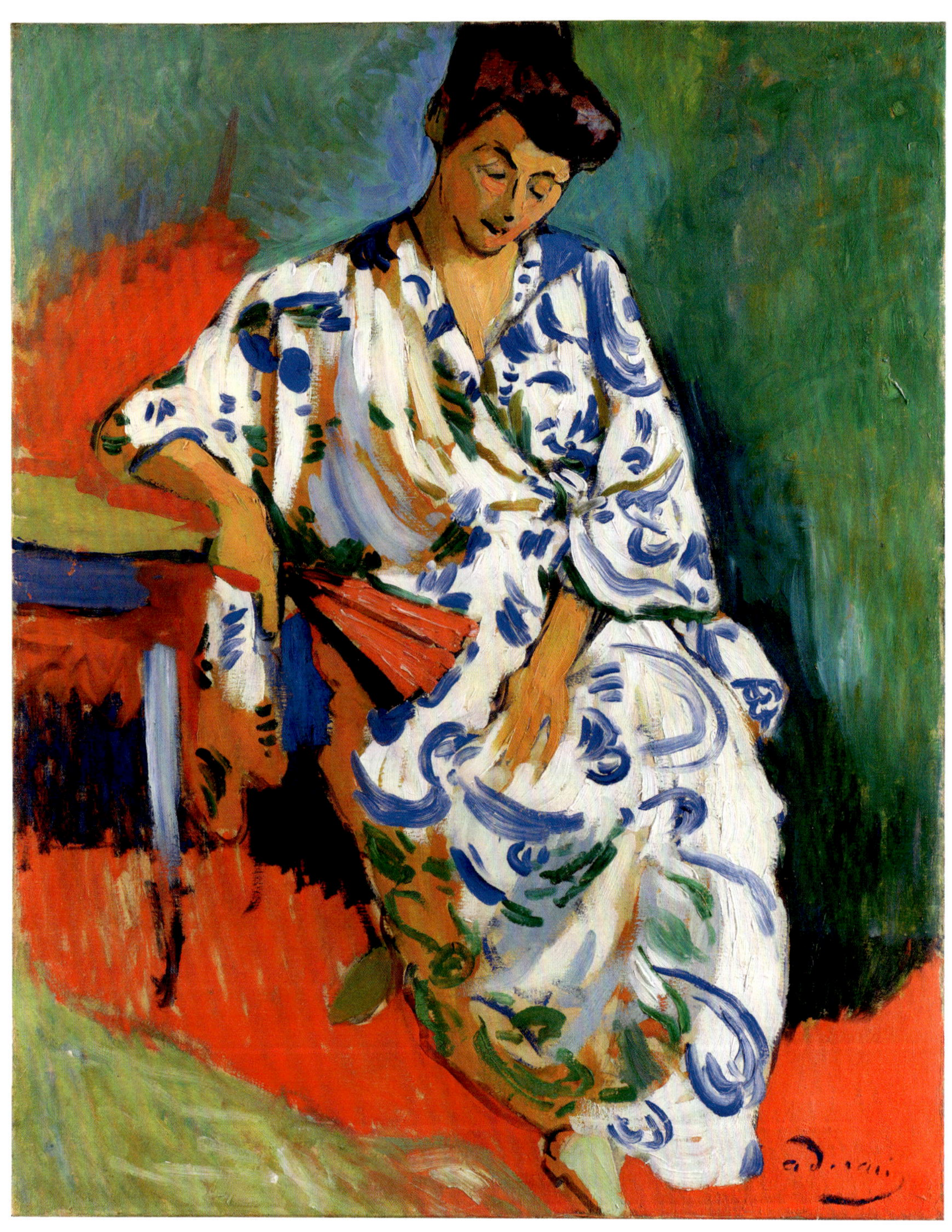

André Derain, *La femme au chale, Madame Matisse en kimono* (Woman with a Shawl,
Madame Matisse in a Kimono), 1905. Oil on canvas, 31¹¹⁄₁₆ × 25⁹⁄₁₆ in. (80.5 × 65 cm).
Private collection, courtesy Nevill Keating Pictures, London

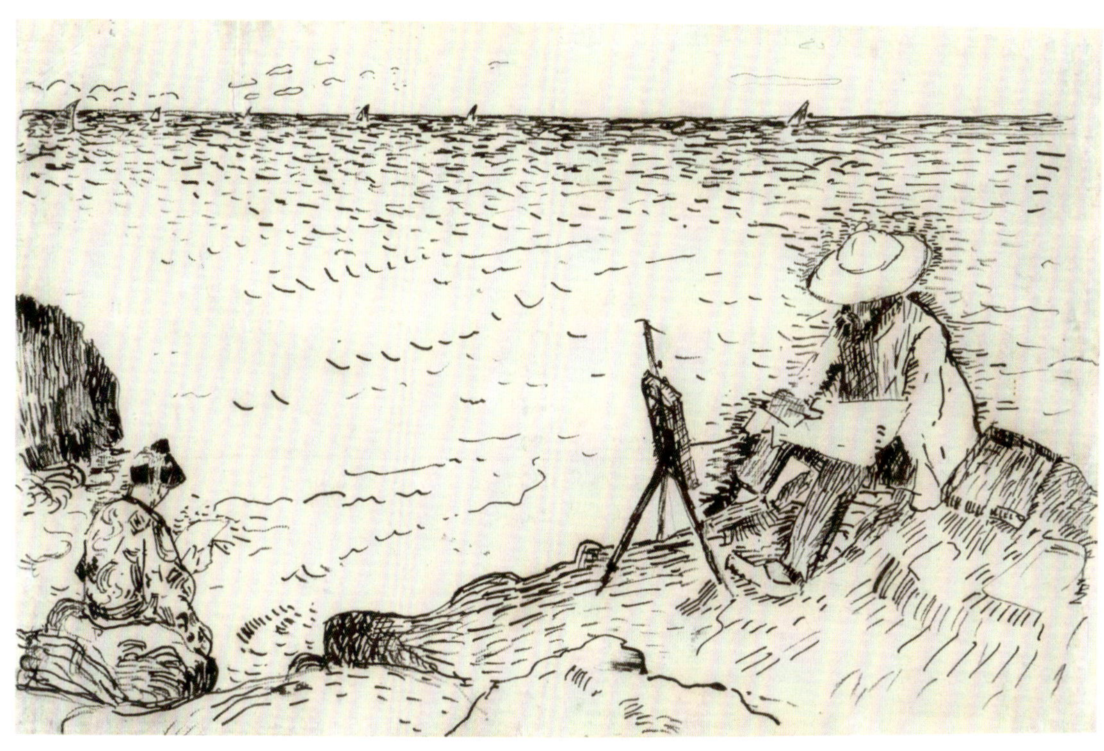

André Derain, *Matisse peignant Madame Matisse en Japonaise au bord de l'eau*
(Matisse Painting Mme Matisse in a Japanese Robe at the Seashore), 1905. Brush and
black ink on paper, 11⅞ × 18⅞ in. (30.2 × 48 cm). The Metropolitan Museum of Art,
New York, Hermina, Movses, Charles, and David Allen Devrishian Fund, 2004

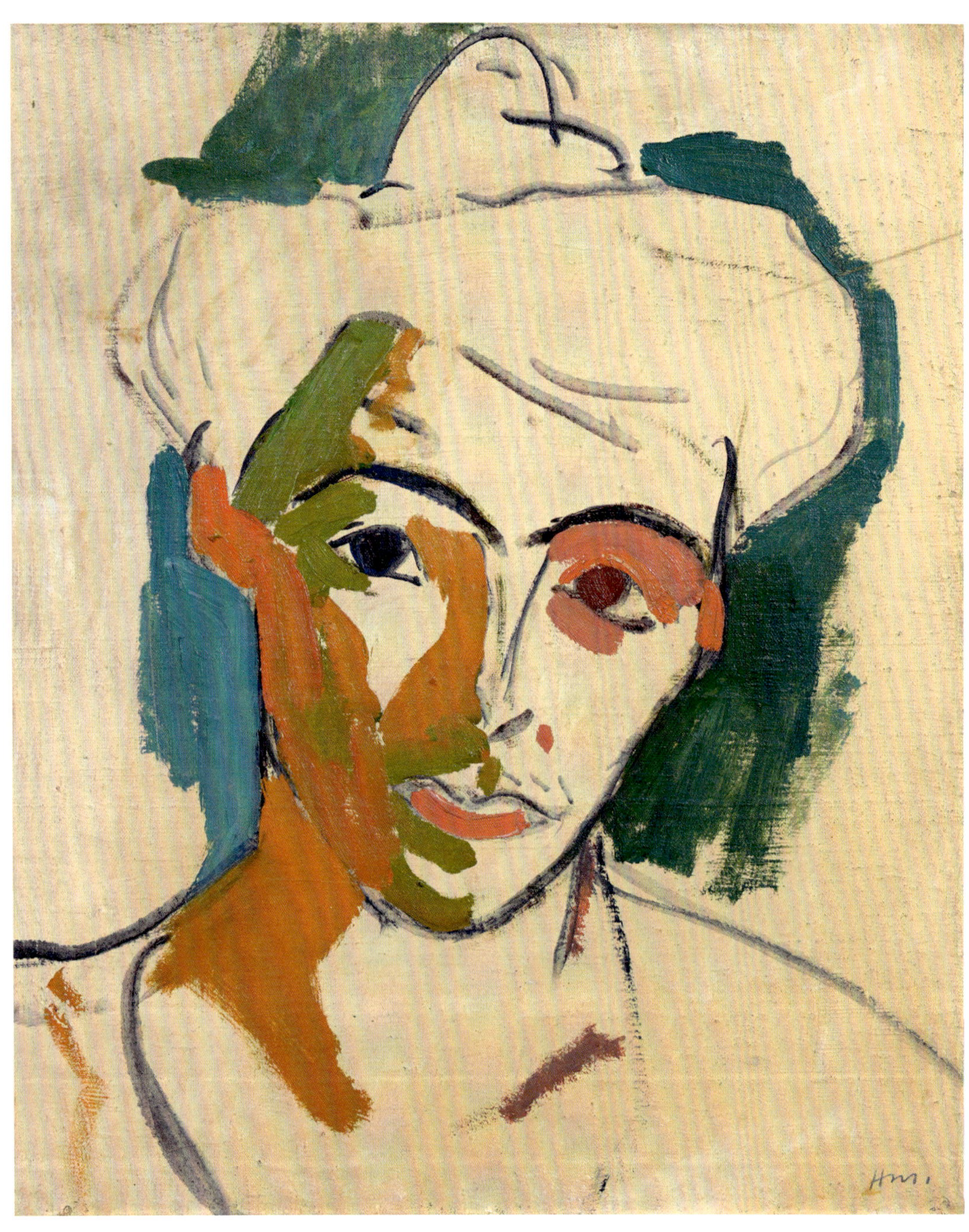

Henri Matisse, *Portrait de Madame Matisse* (Portrait of Madame Matisse), 1905. Oil on canvas, 18⅛ × 15 in. (46 × 38.1 cm). Musée Matisse, Nice, gift of the artist's heirs, 1963

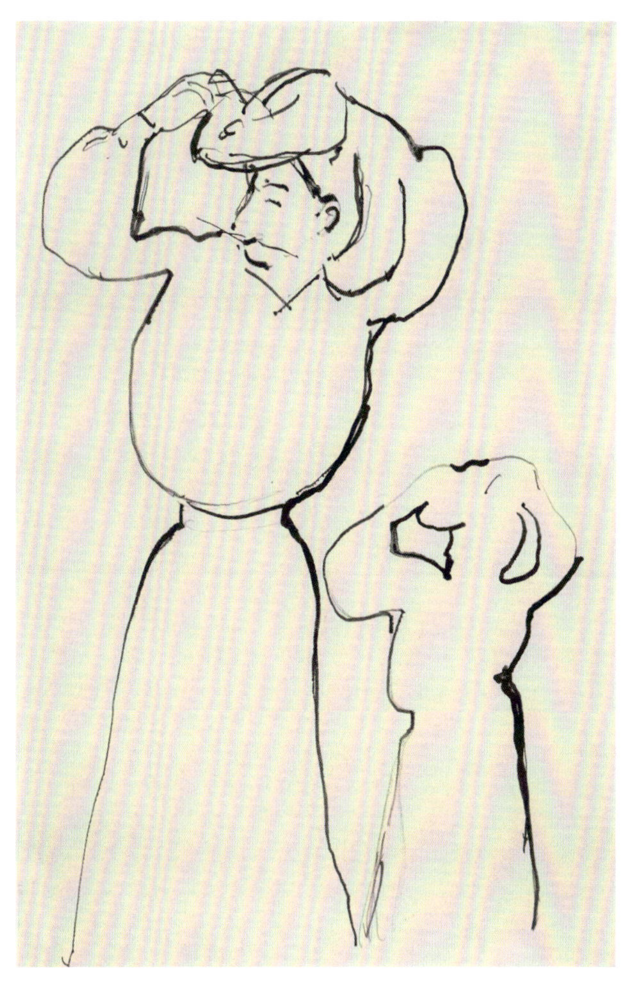

Henri Matisse, *Mme. Matisse Pinning Her Hat to Her Head*, ca. 1906. Ink on paper, 11⅝ × 7⅝ in. (29.5 × 19.4 cm). Gertrude Stein and Alice B. Toklas Papers, Yale Collection of American Literature, Beinecke Rare Book and Manuscript Library, Yale University, New Haven

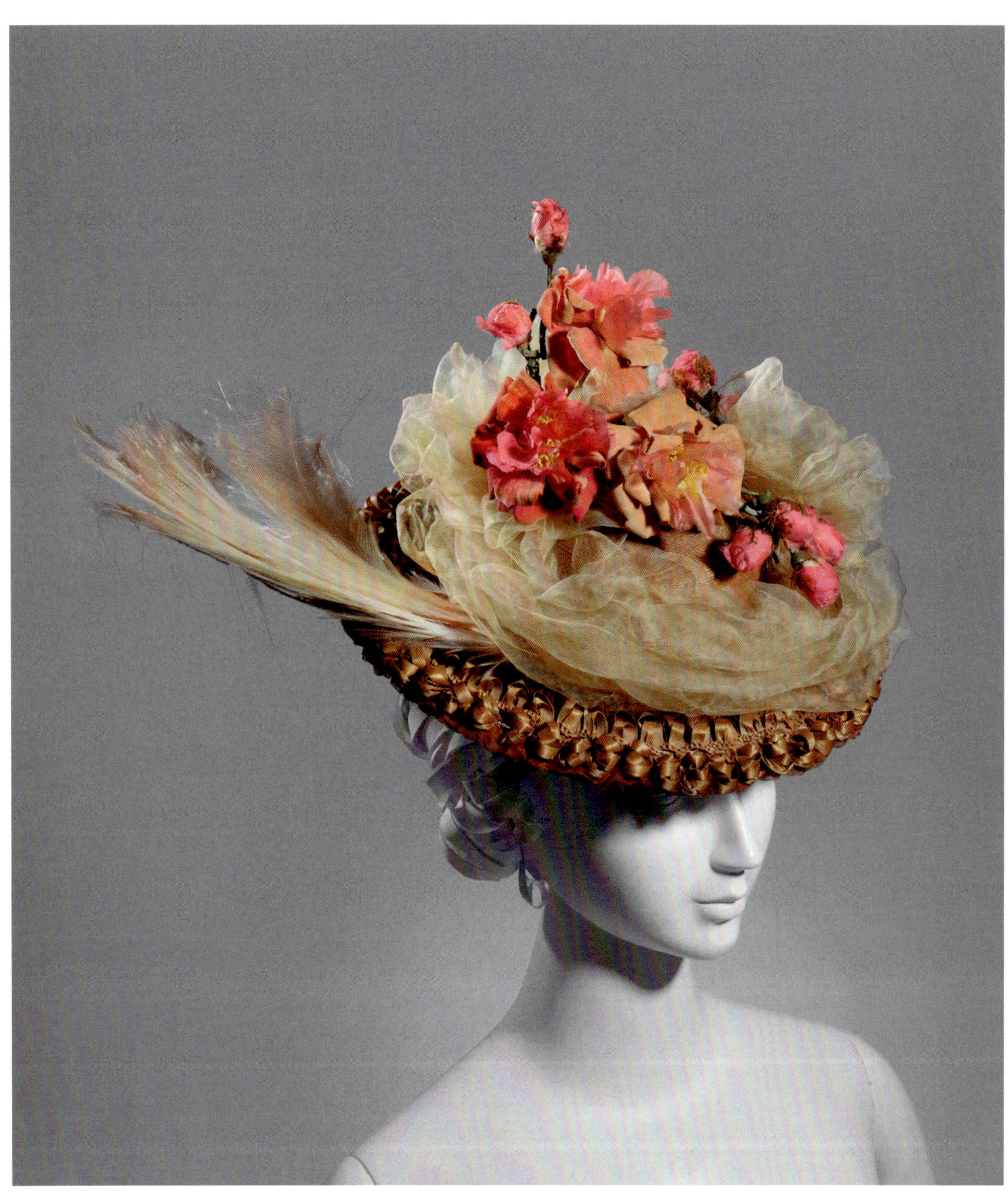

Hat designed by Caroline Reboux, ca. 1900–1905. Straw, shaved wood, silk organza, silk chiffon, bird-of-paradise feathers, and artificial foliage, 12½ in. (31.75 cm) diameter. Arizona State University Fashion Institute of Design and Merchandising (ASU FIDM) Museum, Los Angeles, FIDM Museum Purchase, 2018.5.56

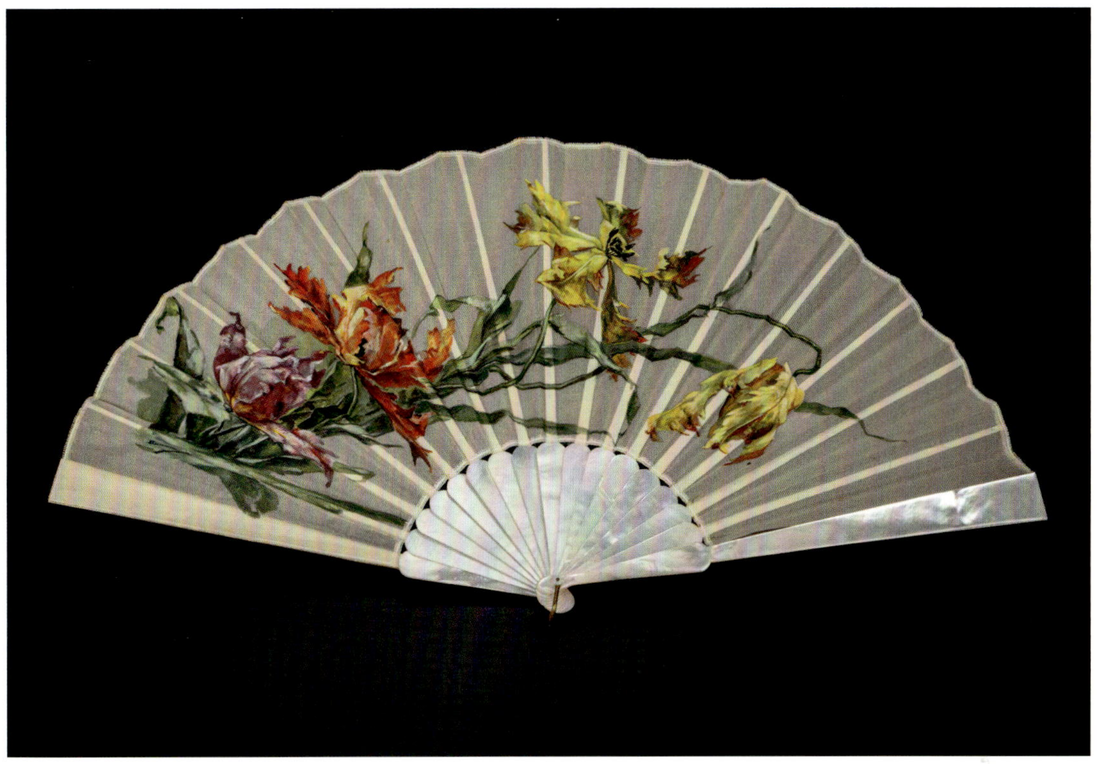

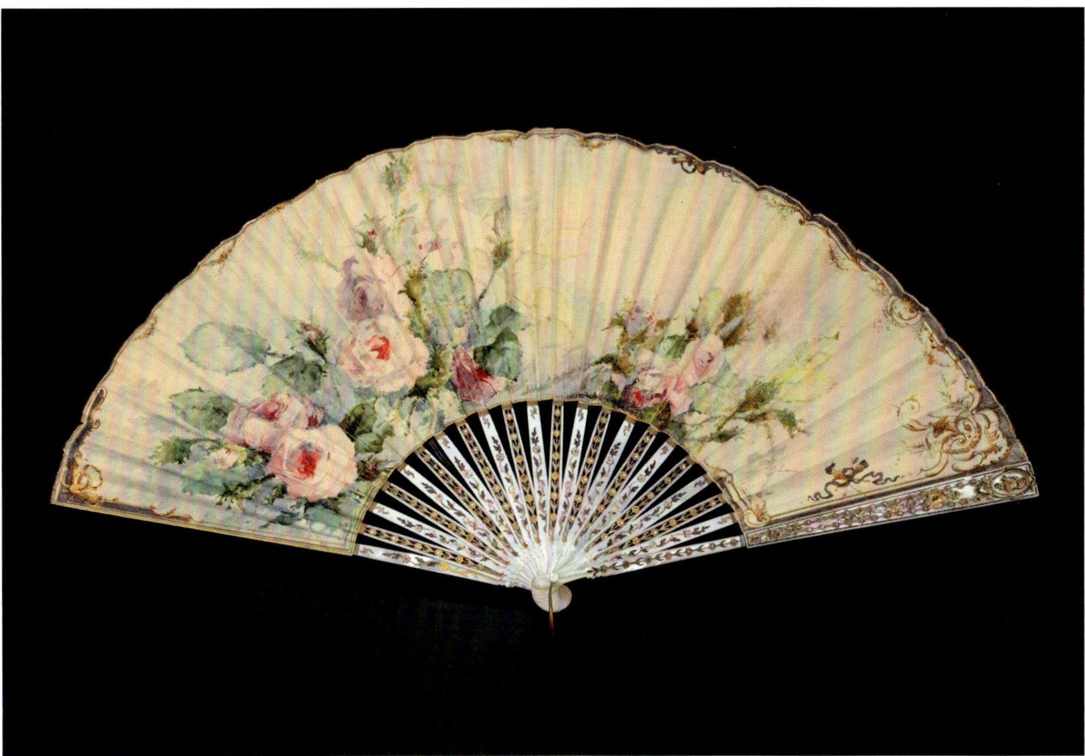

Fan painted by Anna Tacoli, ca. 1900. Hand-painted silk gauze and mother-of-pearl, 13⅜ × 26¾ in. (34 × 68 cm). ASU FIDM Museum, Los Angeles, gift of Mona Lee Nesseth, 2016.975.6

Fan designed by Gustave Beer and painted by G. Lacroix, ca. 1900. Hand-painted paper; pierced, carved, and gilt mother-of-pearl; and crystal rhinestones, 13 × 26 in. (33 × 66 cm). ASU FIDM Museum, Los Angeles, FIDM Museum Purchase: funds donated by Martha Nesseth and Mona Lee Nesseth, 2016.5.139

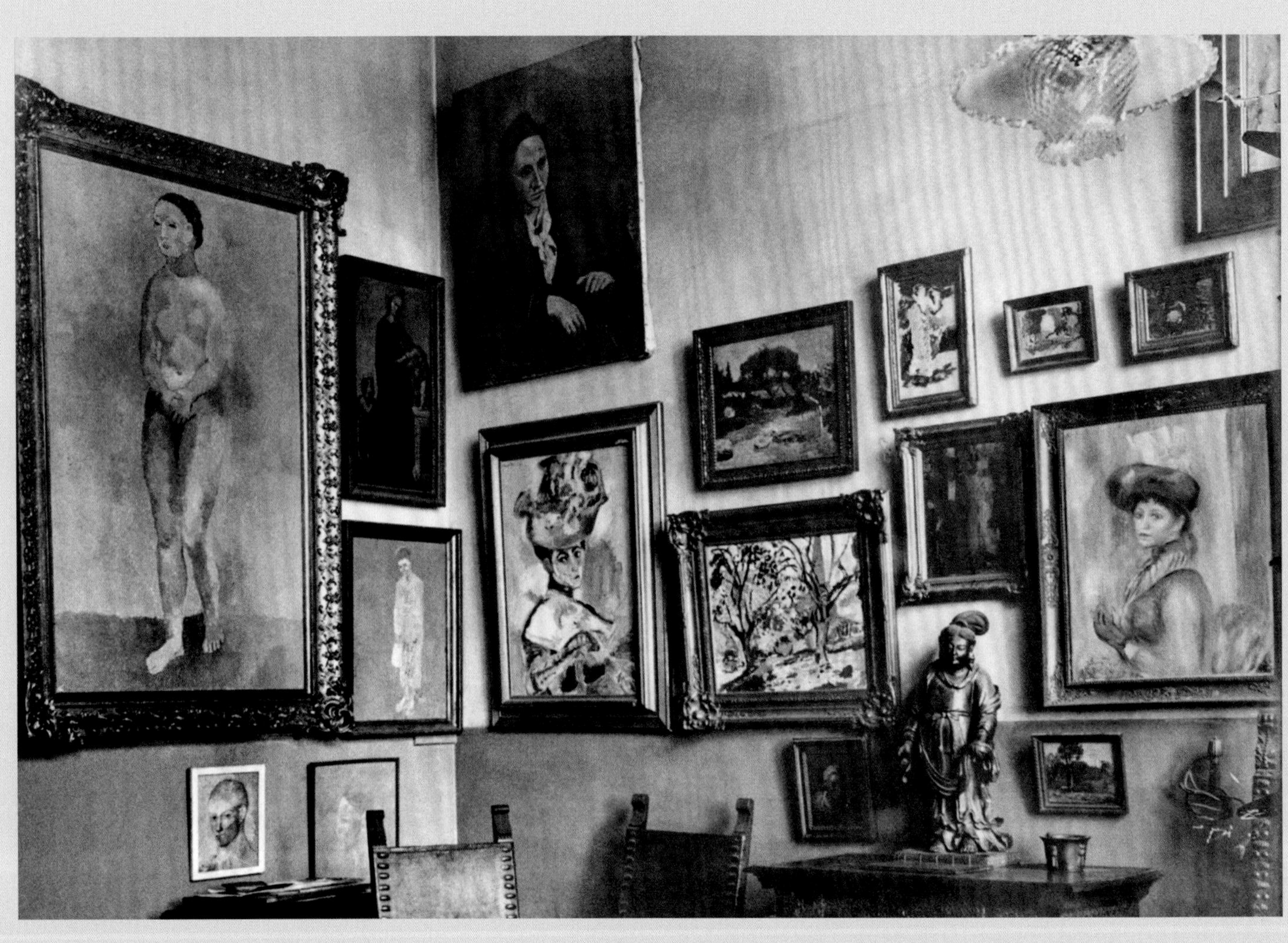

Leo and Gertrude Stein's atelier at 27 rue de Fleurus, Paris, ca. 1908–9, showing *Femme au chapeau* in the company of additional works by Matisse, Picasso, Renoir, and others

Sensual Portraits: Henri Matisse and Gertrude Stein

POPY VENZAL

The American poet Gertrude Stein lived with Matisse's *Femme au chapeau* (Woman with a Hat) in her home in Paris for a decade, from 1905 to 1915 (fig. 1).[1] Over the course of these ten years, and while she was assembling a major painting collection, she produced one of the most radical bodies of early modernist literary works. Stein's acquisition of artworks, her daily engagement with them, and her writing practice were not distinct pursuits but intimately connected ventures.

Acknowledging the significance of painting in her personal journey, Stein suggested that her ability to respond to modernist painting was formed by Italian paintings, notably those by Andrea Mantegna. She also stated that her discovery of Paul Cézanne brought her "a great relief," allowing her to begin her writing.[2] The purchase, in 1904, of *Madame Cézanne à l'éventail* (Madame Cézanne with a Fan, fig. 2) initiated a productive eight years, during which Stein's quest for greater textual autonomy led notably to her practice of syntactic repetition. This device seeks to free traditional narratives from meaning and order, replacing them with a kind of musical and cyclical rhythm in harmony with the rise of contemporary dance, as suggested by Stein's verbal portrait of Isadora Duncan:

> This one is the one being dancing. This one is the
> one thinking in believing in dancing having meaning.
> This one is one believing in thinking. This one is
> one thinking in dancing having meaning. This one
> is one believing in dancing having meaning.[3]

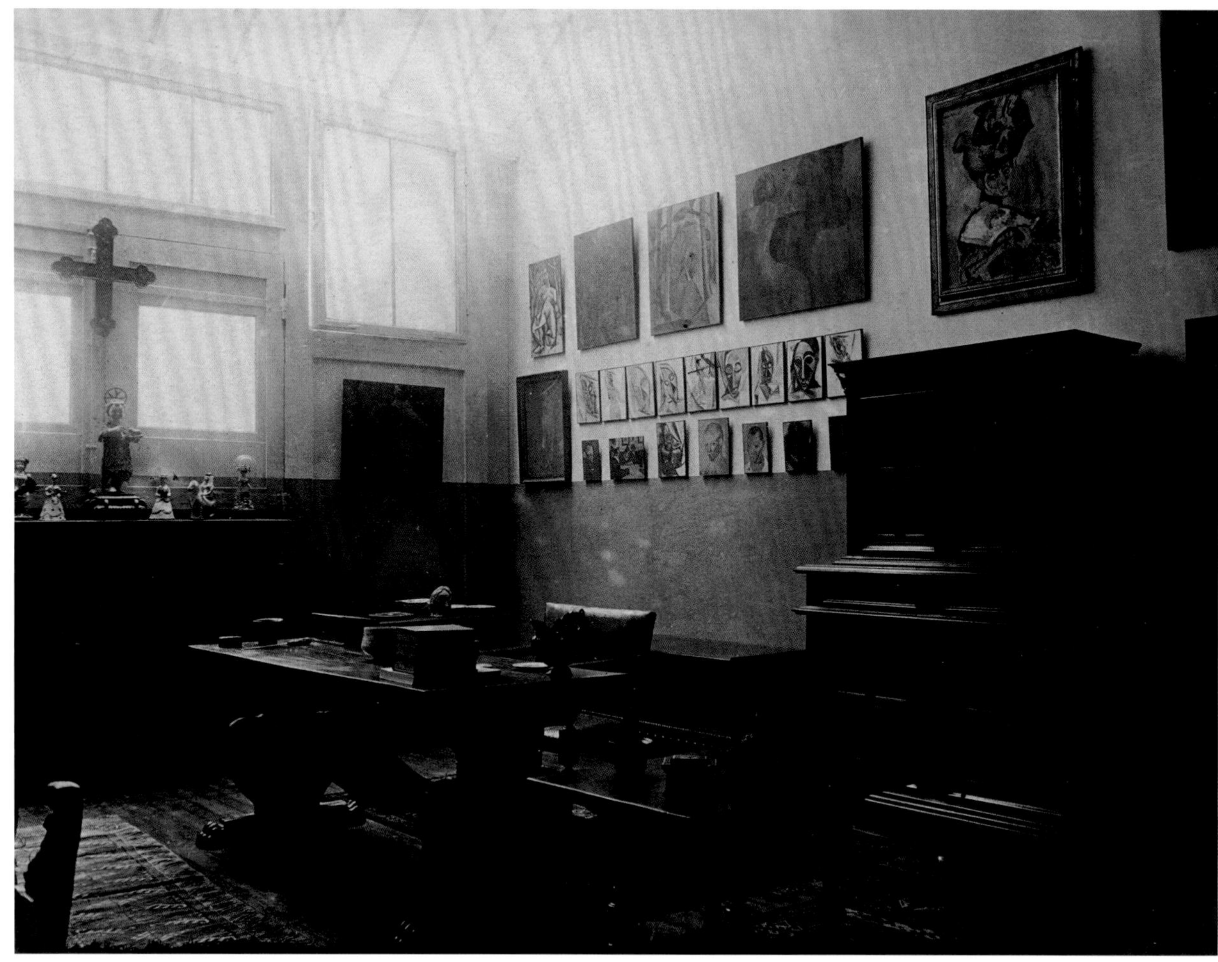

FIG. 1

During these years, Stein and her brother Leo purchased some of Matisse's major works (*Femme au chapeau* in 1905, *Le bonheur de vivre* [The Joy of Life] in 1906, *Blue Nude: Memory of Biskra* in 1907), as well as many works by Pablo Picasso, including the first Cubist paintings of their shared collection. In 1912, Gertrude began to make purchases on her own, no longer together with her brother. That year also marked a significant turn in her writing practice, with the creation of the book *Tender Buttons* (published in 1914), which paved the way for a series of important poems. Stein then abandoned systematic repetition and began to explore unprecedented syntactic deconstruction. In these works, meaning is not abolished but scattered, producing allover effects similar to those of contemporary painting.

While Stein did not shy from drawing parallels between her work and contemporary painting, she remained discreet when it comes to Matisse. It appears that her correspondence features only one short, cryptic statement relating her writings to the painter's work: About her book of stories *Three Lives,* she wrote in 1906, "I am very proud of it, nothing will discourage me. I think it a noble combination of [Jonathan] Swift and Matisse."[4] A few comments in her notebooks around 1909 also refer to the painter but appear to oscillate between like-mindedness and distancing, expressing the ambiguity that characterizes Stein's poem-portrait of the painter, which concludes with these words: "This one was one, some were quite certain, one greatly expressing something being struggling. This one was one, some were quite certain, one not greatly expressing something being struggling."[5]

In spite of Stein's relative silence about Matisse, there are important areas of contact between the writer's work and that of the painter. This is particularly so for *Femme au chapeau* and Stein's post-1912 poems: *Tender Buttons,* considered by the poet as a "portrait of things," and "Sacred Emily" (1913), which can be read as a tribute to Emily Dickinson and as a portrait of Stein's partner, Alice B. Toklas. This is not to suggest that Stein was subject to the influence of Matisse's paintings; rather, both of them appeared to be working through similar questions—whether or not they were aware of this convergence—and both came to offer new compositions, equally beautiful and equally intelligent, within their respective fields.

The subject of portraiture, in particular, is one the painter and the poet address repeatedly both in their works and in related discussions. Stein suggests that each successive generation must wrestle with the question of the portrait, defining it through a mode of composition that in turn generates a specific relationship to portraiture:

> I said nothing changes from generation to generation except the composition in which we live and the composition in which we live makes the art which we see and hear. … The thing that is important is the way that portraits of men and women and children are written, by written I mean made. And by made I mean felt. Portraits of men and women and children are differently felt in every generation and by a generation one means any period of time…. A generation can be from two years to a hundred years.[6]

Both artists sought to articulate the defining feeling of their era through the creation of a mode of portraiture suited to it. They were informed by the example set by Cézanne, notably in the latter's depictions of Madame Cézanne—both saw *Madame Cézanne with a Fan* and *Madame Cézanne au chapeau vert* (Madame Cézanne with Green Hat, fig. 3) at the Salon d'Automne in 1904—which portray simultaneously and in deeply intertwined fashion a beloved woman and the painting practice itself, thereby heralding the advent of modernist portraiture. As they sought to depict their beloveds, both of them engaged in a form of struggle inherent in their respective practices, which in turn became a subject of the work itself. Stein repeatedly underscores the condition of the word sitting on the page, where it oscillates between meaning and materiality:

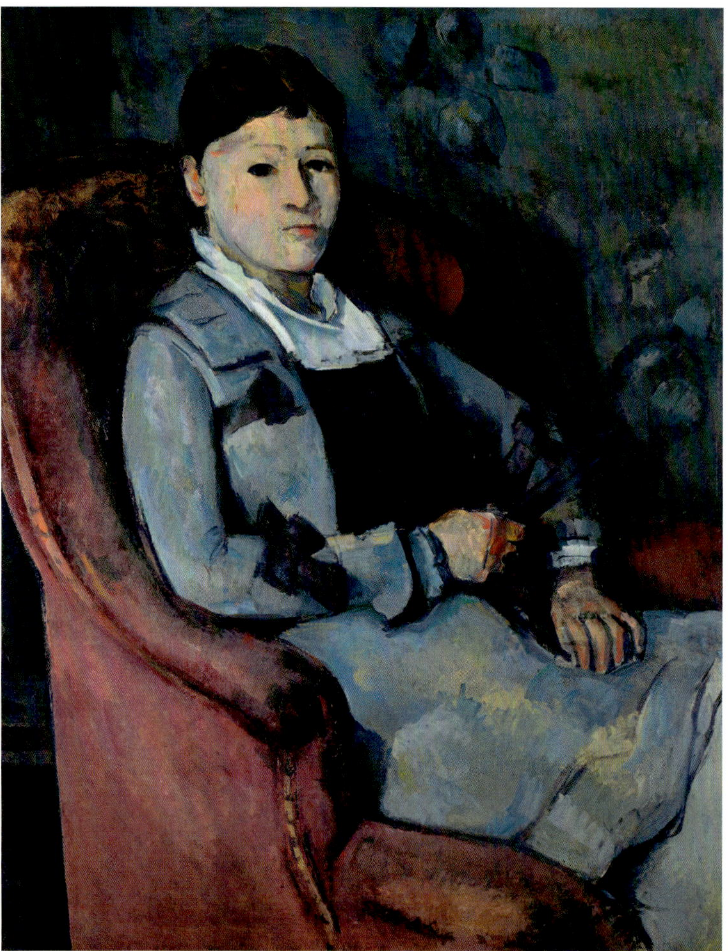

That is a word.
That is a word careless.
Paper peaches.
Paper peaches are tears.[7]

For Matisse, no aspect of the struggle involved in the physical process of creation is to be concealed. Preparatory charcoal lines, material support of the canvas, and successive iterations all remain visible and become the substance of the work itself, which is no longer a finalized and self-enclosed form but instead the product of a mortal hand, embracing a measure of material precariousness. As they openly display their modes of production, Matisse's and Stein's portraits distance themselves from the genre's descriptive and psychological functions and seek new forms of autonomous liveliness. The portrait that eschews verisimilitude is invested less in describing the model than in rendering "the complete rhythm of a personality."[8] In Matisse's work, distancing from strict description involves the pursuit of a surface animated rhythmically by color relations, which he coordinated according to their plastic qualities instead of abiding by notions of "realistic" likeness. Complementary colors are balanced with attention to their respective weights (as with the darker reds and lighter greens). Similarly, beginning with *Tender*

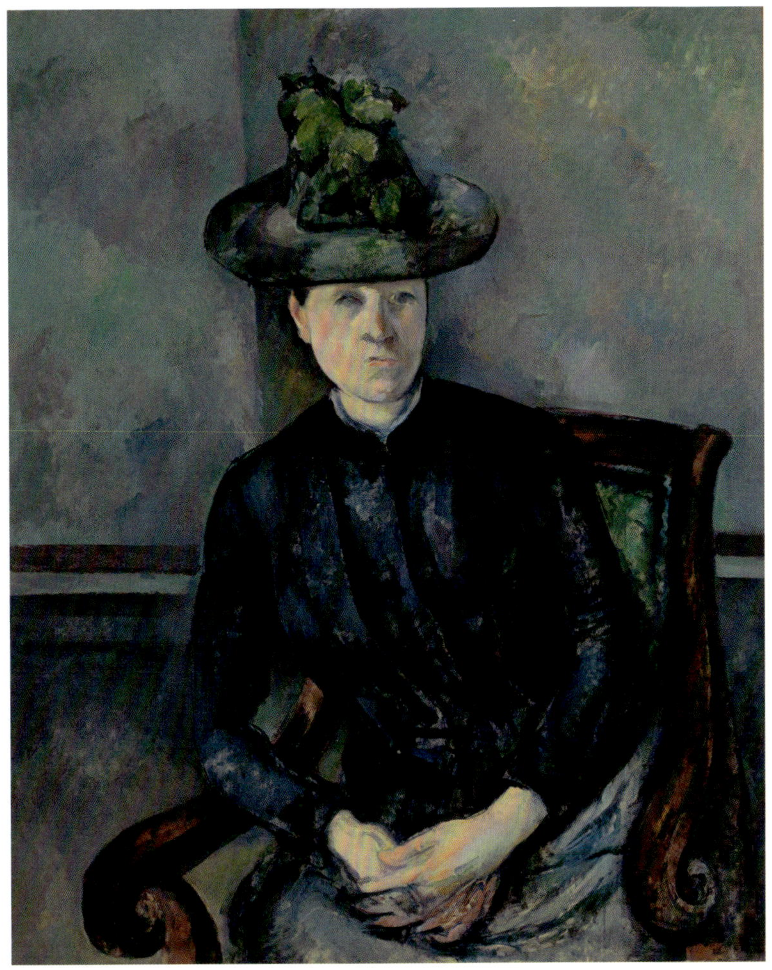
FIG. 3

Buttons and continuing with "Sacred Emily," Stein's words cease to reflect a reality outside the context in which they are placed.[9] They seek not to describe but to generate combinations at once rhythmic and autonomous:

> Rose is a rose is a rose is a rose.
> Loveliness extreme.
> Extra gaiters.
> Loveliness extreme.
> Sweetest ice-cream.
> Page ages page ages page ages.
> Wiped Wiped wire wire.
> Sweeter than peaches and pears and cream.
> Wiped wire wiped wire
> Extra extreme.
> Put measure treasure.[10]

The American poet William Carlos Williams suggests that Stein in her writings "has completely unlinked [the words] from their former relationships in the sentence." In doing so, he says that she imbues words with an abstract quality, so that they become "like a crowd at Coney Island, let us say, seen from an airplane."[11] The novelist and short story writer Sherwood Anderson writes of the shock he felt upon the discovery of this novel mode of writing, which "gives words an oddly new intimate flavor and at the same time makes familiar words seem almost like strangers."[12] This innovative "autonomous" arrangement of the poem's language awakens the reader's sensitivity to the abstract and physical qualities of each word, and to its visual and auditory dimensions. Similarly, in Matisse's work, distancing from imitation signifies the possibility of the purely sensual relationship to color that characterizes a child's experience. Meaning and likeness are not wholly abolished; rather, an equilibrium is struck between the two poles that the poet Paul Valéry identified as "direct sensory stimulation" (sound, color) and "psychic nourishment" (meaning).[13]

In both cases, this recovered sensuality could be seen as a material translation of the artists' physical desire for their respective partners. As the critic Claude Grimald puts it, "For Stein, sex and romantic relationships are directly linked to the writer's work. The bedroom opens onto the kitchen, and the bed leads directly to the worktable."[14] In this way, sexual desire crystallizes into the abstract erotic bonds guiding the works' composition. In a masterful study of Stein's work, Charles Bernstein demonstrates that the composition of *Tender Buttons* is tied to an erotic understanding of the female body.[15] The title itself refers not only to the domestic and decorative realms traditionally associated with the feminine, but also to a woman's erogenous zones, whose distribution across the body is reflected in a work that formally scatters meaning, a "centerless" composition. Similarly, when Matisse insists that he creates portraits only "in the decorative form," he hints at a feminine mode of the portrait, one that seeks to establish equality among the various points on the surface; in the words of the poet Dominique Fourcade, "the center is everywhere."[16]

With this new mode of portraiture, the boundary between identities becomes more porous. In *Femme au chapeau,* color play repeatedly connects the woman to her surroundings, emphasizing the connection between what lies inside and what lies outside (figure and background, human and nonhuman) rather than their division. Green tones, for instance, connect the sitter's face to the space surrounding it. Similarly, complementary colors guide the viewer's gaze in and out of the figure and back again. The boundaries of the body are themselves open spaces, often unpainted, that invite circulation rather than strict definition. It is as if the object of the portrait is not only Madame Matisse but also the quality of her aura in space, the constant interactive flux between a person and her environment. In "Sacred Emily," when the iconic words "Rose is a rose is a rose is a rose" first appear, "Rose" can at first be read as a woman's name that immediately morphs into a common noun, linking uniqueness to commonality, and an individual to the world.[17] ⬢

1   Gertrude and Leo Stein acquired the painting in 1905. She kept it when they divided their collection in 1913–14; in 1915, Michael and Sarah Stein purchased it from her. See Janet Bishop, Cécile Debray, and Rebecca Rabinow, eds., *The Steins Collect: Matisse, Picasso, and the Parisian Avant-Garde,* exh. cat. (San Francisco: San Francisco Museum of Modern Art; New Haven, CT: Yale University Press, 2011), 411.

2   "I liked Mantegna then, because he made me realize that white is a color, and in a way he made me feel something about what oil paintings were that prepared me for much that was to come later." Gertrude Stein, *Lectures in America* (London: Virago, 1988), 71, 77.

3   Gertrude Stein, "Orta or One Dancing" (ca. 1911–12), in *Writings 1903–1932* (New York: Library of America, 1998), 288.

4   Gertrude Stein to Mabel Weeks, undated (late spring 1906), quoted in Bishop et al., *The Steins Collect,* 38.

5   Gertrude Stein, "Matisse" (1909), in *Writings,* 281. See also Jayne L. Walker, *The Making of a Modernist: Gertrude Stein from Three Lives to Tender Buttons* (Amherst: University of Massachusetts Press, 1984), 88–95. Walker compiles all the mentions of Matisse in Stein's notebooks.

6   Gertrude Stein, "Portraits and Repetition," in *Lectures in America,* 165.

7   Gertrude Stein, "Sacred Emily," in *Writings,* 394.

8   Gertrude Stein, "The Gradual Making of the Making of Americans," in *Lectures in America,* 147.

9   See Charles Bernstein, "Gertrude Stein," in *A History of Modern Poetry,* ed. Alex Davis and Lee M. Jenkins (Cambridge, UK: Cambridge University Press, 2015), 255–74.

10 Stein, "Sacred Emily," 395.

11 William Carlos Williams, "The Work of Gertrude Stein," in Davis and Jenkins, *History of Modern Poetry,* 255–74.

12 Sherwood Anderson, "The Work of Gertrude Stein," in *Gertrude Stein, Geography and Plays* (Boston: The Four Seas Company, 1922), 5.

13 Paul Valéry, *Cours de poétique, I: Le corps et l'esprit 1937–1940,* ed. William Marx (Paris: Gallimard, 2023), 75.

14 Claude Grimald, *Gertrude Stein: Le sourire grammatical* (Paris: Bélin, 1996), 99. Desire is far from repressed in Matisse's work, and is explicit in his depictions of Madame Matisse in the nude, as in *Nu dans la forêt* (Nude in a Wood) (1906, Brooklyn Museum 52.150).

15 Bernstein, "Gertrude Stein," 260–64.

16 Henri Matisse, *Écrits et propos sur l'art,* ed. Dominique Fourcade (Paris: Hermann, 1972), 176; Dominique Fourcade, *Rêver a trois aubergines…* (Paris: Éditions du Centre Pompidou, 2012), 39.

17 Marjorie Perloff, "'Une cessation des ressemblances': Stein/Picasso/Duchamp," in *Gertrude Stein et les arts,* ed. Isabelle Alfandary and Vincent Broqua (Dijon: Les Presses du Réel, 2019), 18.

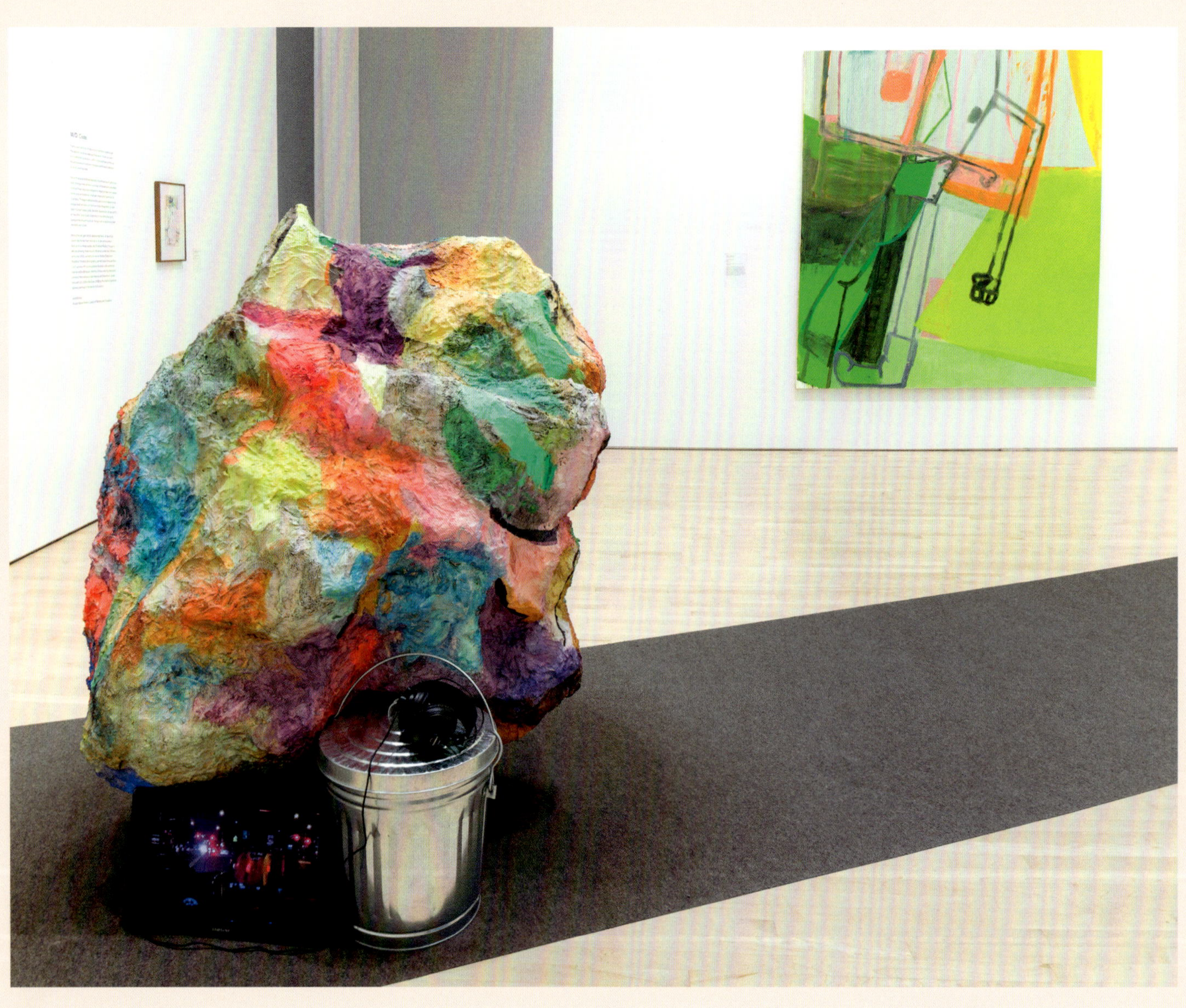

Installation view of *Matisse/Diebenkorn: Coda*, showing Rachel Harrison, *Hoarders* (2012), and Amy Sillman, *U.S. of Alice the Goon* (2008), San Francisco Museum of Modern Art, 2017

Femme au chapeau:
Then and Now

JANET BISHOP

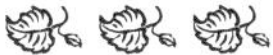

Femme au chapeau has always been a painting that mattered. To Henri Matisse himself, his peers, and to a culturally engaged public in early twentieth-century Paris as well as to subsequent generations of artists, scholars, museum-goers, and stewards of its care, *Femme au chapeau* has been something special, worthy of attention. At the moment it made its public debut at the city's Salon d'Automne, held at the Grand Palais in October and November 1905, *Femme au chapeau* became the talk of the town. As Maria Castro relates in her essay in this volume, the reaction to Matisse's portrait of his wife was passionate and immediate. The picture was so jarring in its formal attributes and attitude, so unbefitting a portrait of a respectable woman, that anyone attuned to painting who experienced it could simply not unsee it.

Completed in haste in Paris after a summer painting in Collioure, in the south of France, *Femme au chapeau* was an eleventh-hour addition to the roster of works Matisse planned for the show. There was, even before the salon opened, a "whiff of scandal in the air," as the curator Ann Dumas has observed.[1] As a highly respected painter and member of the salon's jury him-self—and one whose friends were skeptical, if not outright discouraging about the painting—Matisse had a lot riding on it. The creative breakthrough *Femme au chapeau* represented and the attention it garnered emboldened the artist, paving the way for a career's worth of radical pictures to come. Indeed, *Femme au chapeau* remained a touchstone for Matisse, who, even decades later, con-sidered it one of his "principal works."[2]

Artists who saw the canvas at the salon were absolutely rapt. Some were dismissive: "The young painters were just laughing themselves sick about it," recalled Theresa Ehrman, Sarah and Michael Stein's family nanny.[3]

For others, it was a provocation, inspiring direct dialogue or fresh takes on the long-established trope of the society portrait. Galvanized by the picture and its various attributes—its subject, nonnatural palette, seemingly carefree paint handling, and indeed its audacity and notoriety—they found *Femme au chapeau* a catalyst for their own experimentation, most notably but not exclusively in a proliferation of pictures of women in hats.

Amélie Matisse, a wife, mother, and businesswoman, was hardly a denizen of the Paris underworld. Her portrayal in *Femme au chapeau,* however, with an unnaturally painted face and steely expression, found resonance with artists who were drawn to the city's night culture. Maurice de Vlaminck, for instance, exhibited five landscapes in the salon's Salle VII, or *"la cage au fauves"* (the cage of wild beasts), in the company of *Femme au chapeau.* Also dating from this period is his series depicting hardened, heavily made-up performers and sex workers associated with Le Rat Mort, a popular Montmartre cabaret.[4] Vlaminck's frontal, bust-length *Femme au chapeau* (Woman with a Hat, 1906; p. 112) responds most directly to Matisse's example, whether the self-taught boxer and bicycle racer turned painter would have admitted it. Like Matisse, Vlaminck conjures a bold, indistinct background, and embraces exaggeration as a strategy, emphasizing the woman's massive hat and its abundance of flowery accoutrements. His handling of pigment is not just fast, like Matisse's, but rough. The subject's disquietingly unmatched eyes keep us at a remove from her humanity.

Jacqueline Marval (who would later maintain a studio at 19 quai Saint-Michel, where Matisse painted *Femme au chapeau*) and Kees van Dongen, new in Paris from Rotterdam, were also Salon d'Automne exhibitors.[5] The bright pink

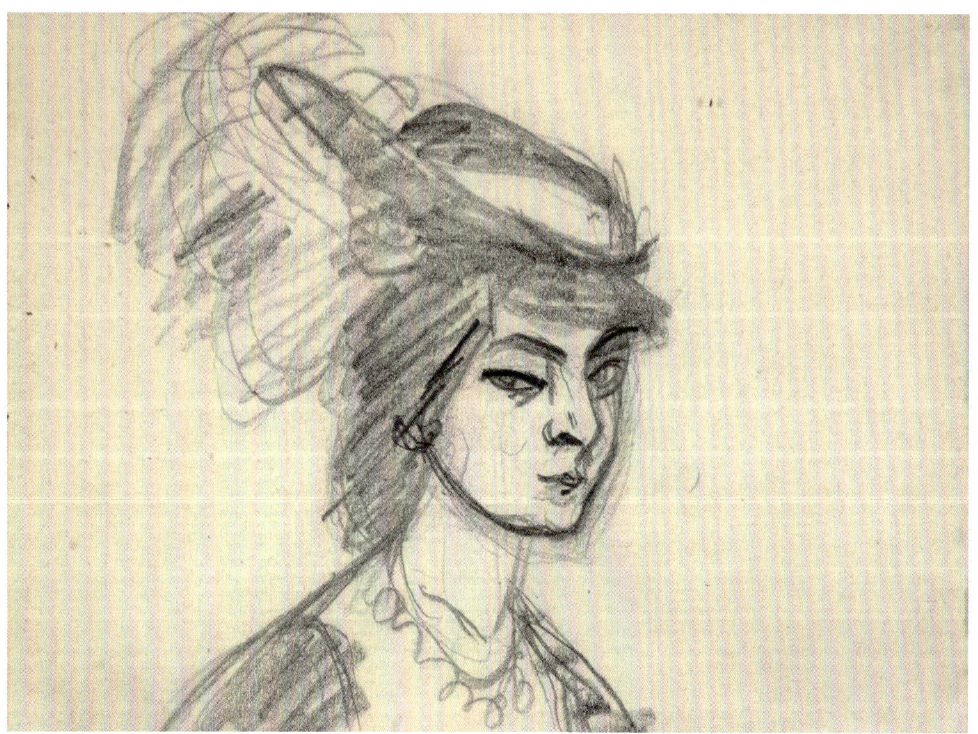

flower adorning the figure's hat in Van Dongen's *Femme au chapeau fleuri* (Woman with a Flowery Hat, 1905; p. 109) is almost as big as her raccoon-eyed face. Elaborate, colorful headwear distinguishes the fair subject of *Portrait* (1905; p. 108) by Marval, whose drawings of herself from the same time connect to Matisse in expression and detail (fig. 1). Conjured through a mosaic of pigment, Jean Metzinger's *Femme au chapeau* (Woman with a Hat, ca. 1906; p. 111), also known as *Lucie au chapeau* (Lucie with a Hat), verges on a riff on Matisse's work in subject, setting, pose, and palette. The artist's pert wife-to-be, Lucie Soubiran, sports a hat with a magnificent bow in a style that would become popular in the years to follow.

◺ • ◿

At the end of the Salon d'Automne's five-week run, Matisse's *Femme au chapeau* found buyers in Leo Stein and his sister Gertrude, with whom he shared a residence and a burgeoning art collection. It was their first Matisse. Leo initially found the painting off-putting. "I would have snatched it at once," he memorably claimed, "if I had not first had to get over the nastiness of the putting on of the paint."[6] Their acquisition of the fall season's most controversial painting established Leo and Gertrude as the most daring collectors in Paris. Matisse's painting took its place within their modest Left Bank apartment at 27 rue de Fleurus amid Chinese art, antique carved wooden furniture, and pictures by Paul Cézanne, Paul Gauguin, Charles Manguin, and Pablo Picasso that Leo had acquired since his 1902 arrival in Paris. With the addition of *Femme au chapeau,* their home became, in effect, "the first museum of modern art," an essential destination for anyone interested in the new, and the only place one could see the painting in the heady years of Fauvism—the city's first art movement of the twentieth century.[7]

The Steins met Matisse soon after their acquisition of *Femme au chapeau*. Early in 1906 they introduced Matisse and Picasso to each other, launching a productive creative rivalry that would span the two artists' lives.[8] As the most talked-about picture at the salon and a new focal point in Leo and Gertrude's apartment, *Femme au chapeau* would have offered a challenge to the ambitious twenty-four-year-old Picasso, who responded not by mimicking aspects of Matisse's picture but by painting the formidable Gertrude in his own proto-Cubist fashion. After eighty or ninety sittings, according to the self-mythologizing subject herself, *Gertrude Stein* (1905–6) was complete and took its place directly above *Femme au chapeau*, even before it was framed (see p. 86).[9]

By spring 1906 interest in Leo and Gertrude's collection was so great that they regularized access to it via weekly evening salons—"Saturdays" or "at-homes" as they called them—that drew throngs of friends, artists and writers, collectors, and lookie-loos from near and far.[10] Sarah and Michael Stein, who began amassing works by Matisse themselves right after the Salon d'Automne, opened their home as well. Marie Laurencin, "no mere *fauvette*," as Matisse purportedly maintained, was a regular on the scene, and one of very few women artists represented in either Stein family collection.[11] Her *Group*

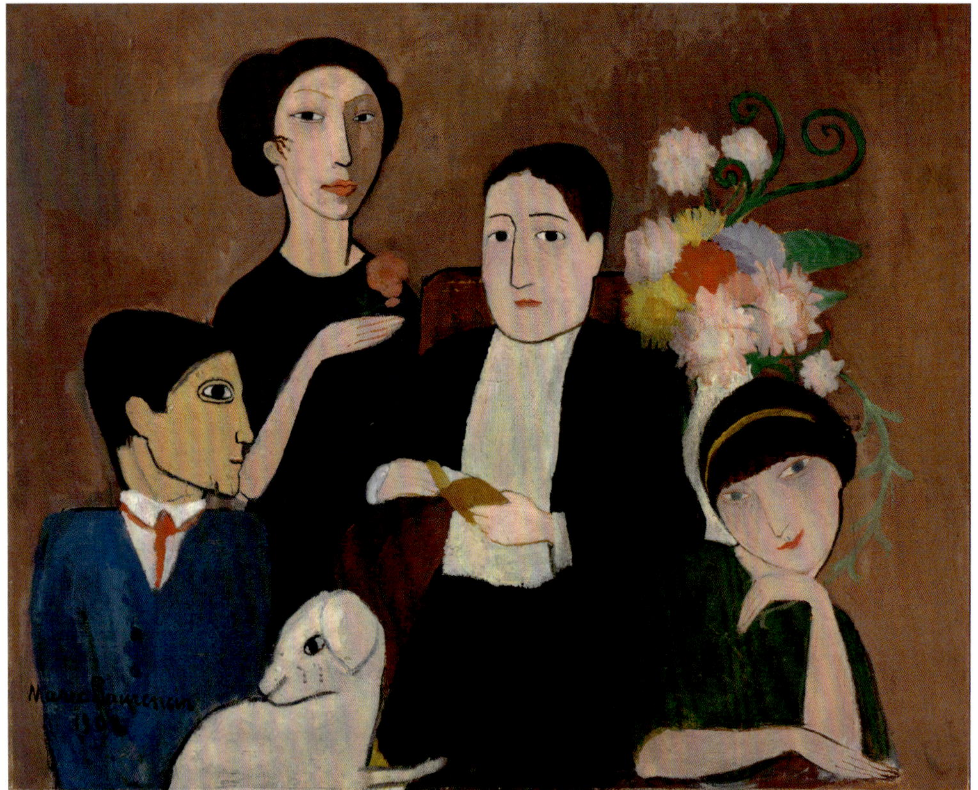

FIG. 2

of Artists features Picasso; his lover and model, Fernande Olivier; Laurencin's lover, the writer Guillaume Apollinaire; and Laurencin herself (fig. 2). Within the enchanting group portrait, the painter cleverly positions a vase of Fauve-bright flowers behind her head that reads like a fanciful sprouting hat.

Germans and Russians were also among Leo and Gertrude's visitors, leading to links between Fauvism and German Expressionism. From late 1906 to spring 1907, the painter Gabriele Münter rented a room above Sarah and Michael's apartment at 58 rue Madame, a three-minute walk from 27 rue de Fleurus, and joined the cadre of individuals interested in new forms of expression who flocked to see the Steins' pictures.[12] Her encounter with *Femme au chapeau* reverberates in her three-quarter-length *Bildnis Marianne von Werefkin* (Portrait of Marianne von Werefkin, 1909; p. 114). Münter adopts elements of Matisse's subject matter, vibrant palette, and paint handling for her own bold portrait of a friend and fellow painter. The catalogue for the 1905 Salon d'Automne lists six paintings by Alexej von Jawlensky, who traveled with Werefkin to Paris in 1906. Several of Jawlensky's works in the years to follow also respond directly to *Femme au chapeau,* such as the fluorescent orange *Mädchen mit Blumenhut* (Girl with a Flowered Hat, 1910; p. 115), its subject pictured with a fan in the same pinks, whites, and greens as Amélie's in *Femme au chapeau.* Jawlensky also made his own version of Matisse's *Le madras rouge* (Red Madras Headdress, 1907; Barnes Collection) in Sarah and Michael's collection, pointing to familiarity with both Stein households.[13]

✑ • ✑

After nearly a decade of what Leo described as their family's "helping to create a new epoch," he and Gertrude parted ways. "There is practically nothing under the heavens that we don't…disagree about," he confided to a friend.[14] Leo left Paris for his villa near Florence, Italy, and the siblings divided their pictures: Leo claimed the most contested object, Cézanne's *Five Apples* (1887–78), and *Femme au chapeau* went to Gertrude, who in turn sold it in 1915 to Sarah and Michael.[15] The purchase was a very welcome addition to their collection. Sarah had championed the purchase of *Femme au chapeau* back in 1905, per Matisse, and long regretted not buying it herself.[16] A decade later, it injected new energy into a collection that, while still impressive, had recently been gutted of many of its important Fauve-era Matisse canvases, such as *Portrait of Madame Matisse (The Green Line)* (1905) and *Pink Onions* (1906–7; both, Statens Museum for Kunst, Denmark). In 1914 Sarah and Michael had lent nineteen paintings at the artist's behest to a gallery exhibition in Berlin. When World War I broke out, the gallery was shuttered, the pictures never to return.[17]

Matisse no doubt painted companion portraits of Sarah and Michael (both 1916, SFMOMA) as consolation for the loss they endured; the Americans had been steadfast supporters, not to mention dear friends. The artist labored over a portrait of Sarah and a related drawing (pp. 116 and 117). Like Amélie, Sarah was fashionable, and how she was dressed would have been a consideration for both Matisse and his sitter as he strove to capture her essence.

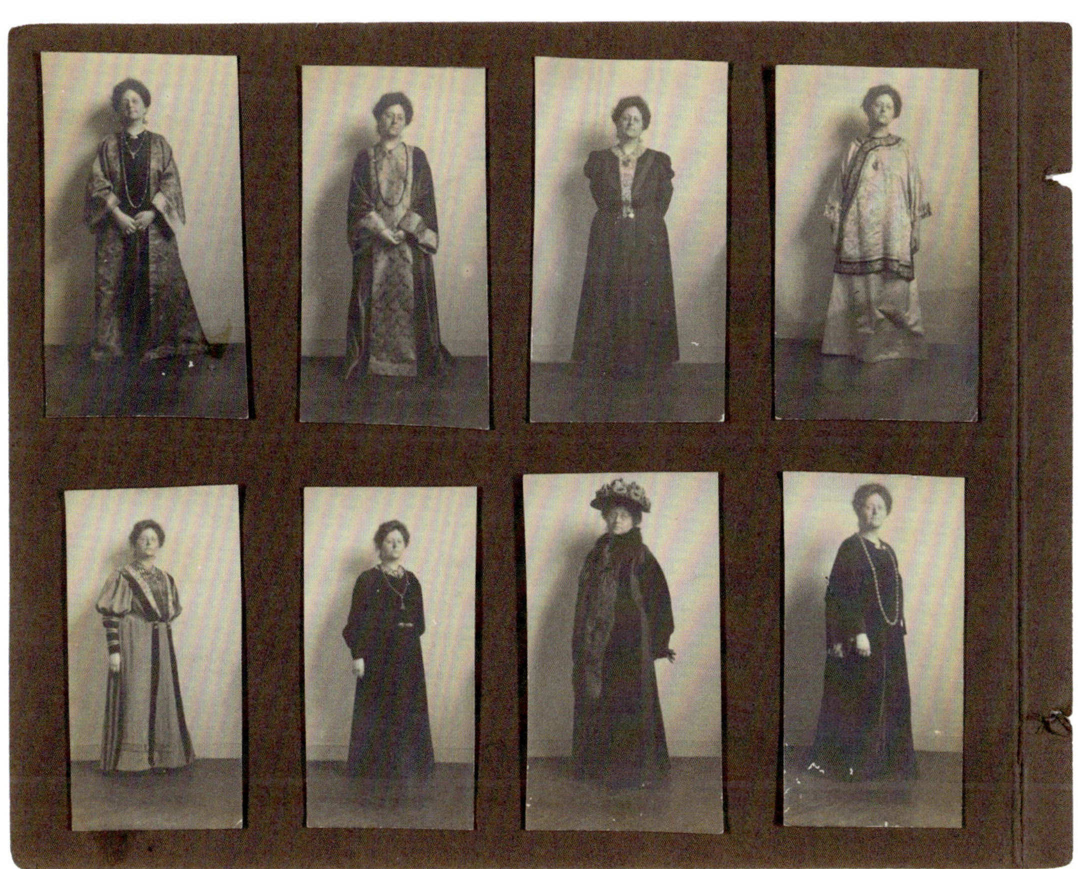

FIG. 3

Ultimately, he forwent the possibilities of jewelry, a fur stole, patterned fabric, or a fancy hat—all of which we see in contemporaneous photographs of Sarah (fig. 3).[18] Instead, he favored a simpler, abstracted approach that emphasizes the character of "Madame Michel Stein"—the woman he considered "the really intelligently sensitive member of the family."[19]

It is not known whether Jeanne Hébuterne, the frequent model for and life partner of Amedeo Modigliani, saw *Femme au chapeau* firsthand. Born in 1898, she would have been a child during the 1905 Salon d'Automne, too young to have attended Gertrude and Leo's Saturdays, and not yet in her teens during Matisse's 1910 gallery show at Bernheim-Jeune. Yet, as an art student in Montparnasse at the time that she painted *Self-Portrait* (ca. 1917; p. 118) and one who was drawn to Fauvism, she would have known of Matisse's famous portrait, by reputation or reproduction.[20] Here Hébuterne assumes something of the subdued palette typical of the war years, as seen in Matisse's portrait of Sarah Stein. Particularly striking are the artist's long red tresses, held in place by a single black headband, and her arresting, confrontational gaze that bears a startling resemblance to Amélie's in *Femme au chapeau.*

Other artists were explicit in their engagement with the piece through reproduction. The New York–based Japanese artist Yasuo Kuniyoshi, who visited Paris in 1928 and exhibited with Matisse in the 1930 Carnegie International, drew from his personal library of art publications for *Untitled* (1934; p. 119).[21] For one of many still lifes by the artist, some of which incorporate printed materials, Kuniyoshi assembled this tabletop scene directly on top of an image of *Femme au chapeau.*[22] Green grapes sprout dramatically from the figure's already elaborate hat. Kuniyoshi painted partly in color and partly in the grisaille of the reproduction, which he almost certainly sourced from the 1931 edition of *Cahiers d'Art* dedicated to Matisse.

In 1935 *Femme au chapeau* crossed the Atlantic for the first time.[23] After thirty-one years in France, Sarah and Michael Stein returned to California, ushering in a new chapter in which Matisse's Fauve masterwork served as a source of inspiration, particularly for artists in the Bay Area. By year's end the painting was installed at the Steins' new residence, at 433 Kingsley Avenue in Palo Alto. As Sarah reported to Matisse, "Our paintings have been hung for two weeks now and we were finally feeling at home . . . when, voilà today a large part of them (eleven canvases) are leaving for an exhibition of your work in San Francisco."[24]

Grace L. McCann Morley, founding director of the San Francisco Museum of Art (SFMA), had sought an introduction to the Steins upon their arrival. She soon launched plans for an exhibition of works by Matisse from Bay Area collections, anchored by *Femme au chapeau,* which made its San Francisco debut in January 1936, just a year after the museum opened its doors. An eager contingent of artists would have seen the show. Matisse met faculty and students at the California School of Fine Arts during his one and only visit to San Francisco, en route to Tahiti in 1930. The sculptor Ralph Stackpole, who was at work on figures for the new San Francisco Stock Exchange building, hosted Matisse in his Montgomery Street studio, where the teenage apprentices David Park and Gordon Newell were lucky flies on the wall.

Morley was proud that the SFMA was the first museum in the country to display Sarah and Michael's collection, and that one of its "first major enterprises early in its present phase as a museum of modern art and its sources" was dedicated to Matisse.[25] At the close of the show, she wrote the Steins to thank them for the loans and report on its success, singling out *Femme au chapeau,* which graced the cover of the accompanying brochure: "We were very sorry indeed to see the paintings go, especially your *Lady in the Blue Hat,* and the little landscapes."[26] In retrospect, however, Morley acknowledged that, as special as the 1936 exhibition had been, the "San Francisco public in general had then not as yet had enough experience of modern art to understand fully the importance of Matisse."[27] The picture's real impact in California began at mid-century, after it entered the collection of the San Francisco philanthropist Elise S. Haas in 1948. In declining health and compelled to raise funds to address her grandson Danny Stein's horse-racing debts, Sarah Stein had sold several works including *Femme au chapeau* to Haas and her husband, Walter. "How to thank Elise Haas for the beautiful colored copy of Matisse's 'femme au chapeau'?" wrote Sarah of a reproduction Haas offered her upon the sale. "I am not well . . . but very grateful, as I should be."[28]

In the care of Haas, who owned the piece until her death in 1990, *Femme au chapeau* enjoyed a far more public life than before. It was part of at least seventeen museum presentations from the 1950s to the 1970s, ten of them in San Francisco. Most significant for local painters was Matisse's traveling US retrospective, organized by Alfred H. Barr Jr. for The Museum of Modern Art in New York, which the SFMA hosted in 1952. In a recap of the museum's presentation, Morley described the 1952 show, much larger and more highly attended than the one in 1936, as "a satisfying sequel," with a "large proportion of artists and students" in attendance.[29]

The regular opportunities that local painters had to see *Femme au chapeau* at the SFMA throughout the 1950s coincided with the emergence of the region's first distinctive artistic style: Bay Area Figurative art. David Park, for instance, having worked through various modes of expression, made a decisive switch from gestural abstraction toward a new figuration in 1949, with others soon following suit. A favorite model was his wife, Lydia Newell, who, like Amélie, appears in paintings with needle in hand, as in *Portrait of Lydia Sewing* (1955). *Femme au chapeau* reverberates in some of the more strident examples of Park's portraiture, such as *Woman with Red Mouth* (1954–55; Smithsonian American Art Museum), with her smeared lipstick, triple strand of pearls, and cigarette, or *Mother-in-Law* (1954–55; p. 120), in which a hat casts an olive green shadow on a convincing likeness of Lydia's mother, Harriet See Newell.[30]

Richard Diebenkorn first encountered *Femme au chapeau* as a Stanford undergraduate in 1943, when his professor Daniel Mendelowitz brought the promising young painter to Sarah Stein's home to see her collection.

The experience marked the beginning of Diebenkorn's career-long fascination with Matisse, with subsequent encounters in museums and close study of reproductions fueling the direction of his work.[31] Within his significant personal library of Matisse books, Diebenkorn especially cherished Barr's 1951 *Matisse: His Art and His Public,* which features *Femme au chapeau,* reproduced in color in an art book for the first time, as its frontispiece (fig. 4). Like Matisse and Park, Diebenkorn found a ready model and muse in his wife. He made many of his own *femmes aux chapeaux:* notably, a smartly accessorized Phyllis Diebenkorn in *Woman in Hat and Gloves* (1963; p. 121), and *Seated Figure with Hat* (1967; p. 122), the latter of which brings to mind the side view and shallow space of James Abbott McNeill Whistler's *Arrangement in Grey and Black No. 1* (1871, popularly known as *Whistler's Mother*), as well as the exuberant palette and brushwork of Matisse.

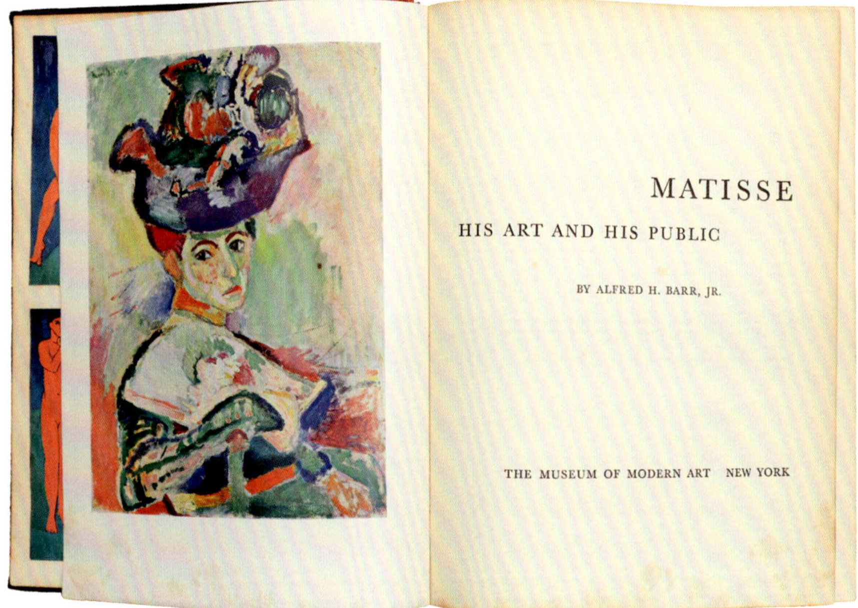

FIG. 4

Femme au chapeau's proliferation through print reproduction allowed it to be used as a teaching tool, as in the art classes at Yale that Hermine Ford attended in 1960–61.[32] In a color course designed by Josef Albers and taught that year by Si Sillman, students made torn-paper collages of famous paintings.[33] Ford's *Femme au chapeau* (fig. 5) is one of two such collages inspired by the "masters" that were published in Albers's seminal two-volume *Interaction of Color* (1963).[34] In it, Albers described the collages (without crediting their female makers) as "consciously condensed records of…a painting's color instrumentation, or, in usual terms, of its palette and color relatedness."[35] Asked whether she was assigned *Femme au chapeau* or chose it, Ford replied, "I certainly chose that Matisse painting because I loved it and felt it would be great to spend that much concentrated time with it, and that it would make the assignment fun for me."[36]

The artists Joan Brown and Wayne Thiebaud, devoted educators as well as lifelong students of painting, both counted Matisse among their heroes. Brown's highly expressive, thickly painted canvases of the 1960s take on classical subjects like nudes and bathers. Ambiguous headwear notwithstanding, her *Girl Sitting* engages with *Femme au chapeau* in its approach to facture, color, pose, and a certain fanlike blue shape at her chest (fig. 6). Her interest in Matisse persisted as her style flattened out. Brown loved painting her face, and painting her face in paintings. She also loved switching out her headwear. *Self-Portrait in Fur Hat* (1972; p. 123) is one of several self-portraits from that year

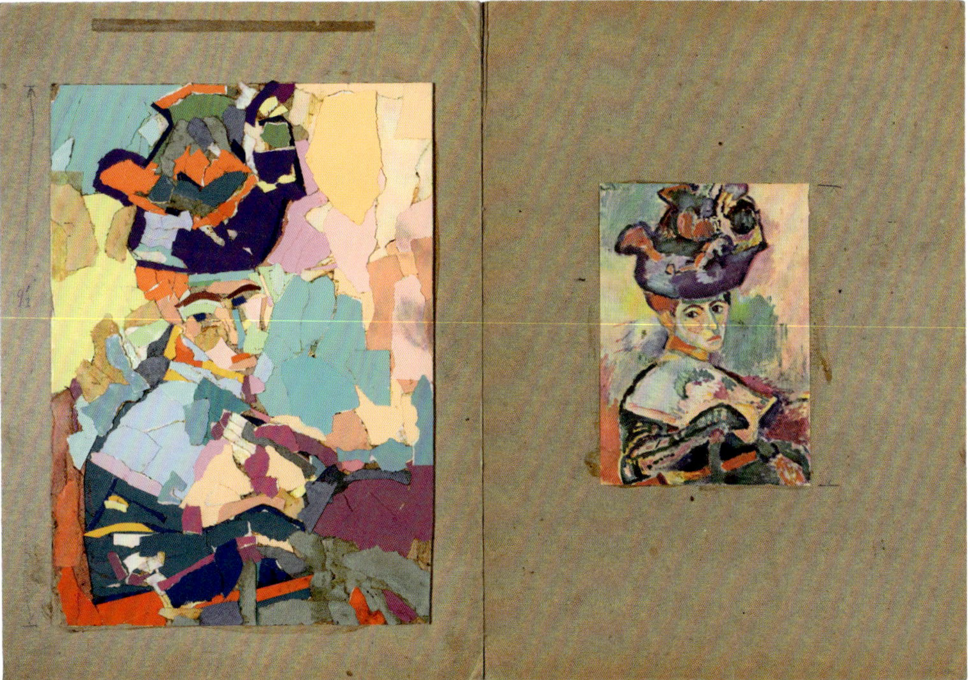

FIG. 5

whose frontal format calls to mind Matisse's *La fille aux yeux verts* (Girl with Green Eyes, 1908; p. 113). In addition to fur, we see Brown decked out in various headscarves, a knitted cap, and a turban with an Inuit dog pin, to name a few.[37] Thiebaud's *Girl with Pink Hat* (1973; p. 124) taps into the unexpected within *Femme au chapeau*. The prominence of the hat—typically the last thing one puts on or first thing one takes off—underscores his subject's toplessness.

While Matisse, Park, and Diebenkorn painted their wives, and Brown painted herself again and again, David Hockney found a regular muse in his friend Celia Birtwell, the British textile designer. *Celia in a Green Hat* (1984; p. 125) shows his effervescent, singularly talented subject commanding the sheet with her open face, bright red hair, and bright green eyes. Hockney was increasingly inspired by early twentieth-century European artists at the time, favoring effect over naturalism, with a specific affinity for Matisse's color, line, sensibility, and sustained relationships with models.[38]

Mickalene Thomas's monumental *Qusuquzah, une très belle négresse 1* (2011; p. 127), like *Femme au chapeau*, commands the room. As the museum director and curator Thelma Golden noted the year it was painted, "She simultaneously reinvents and pays tribute to centuries of artistic depictions of women as she draws on an astonishing and inspired range of esthetic, historical, and social references."[39] Thomas's subtitle honors the subject of Édouard Manet's modest canvas known until recently as *La négresse* and now as *Portrait of Laure* (1862–63; fig. 7), whose subject is the Black woman pictured in shadow in the artist's famous *Olympia* (1863, Musée d'Orsay), offering flowers to a recumbent white prostitute. Here Thomas, a longtime Matisse fan, taps

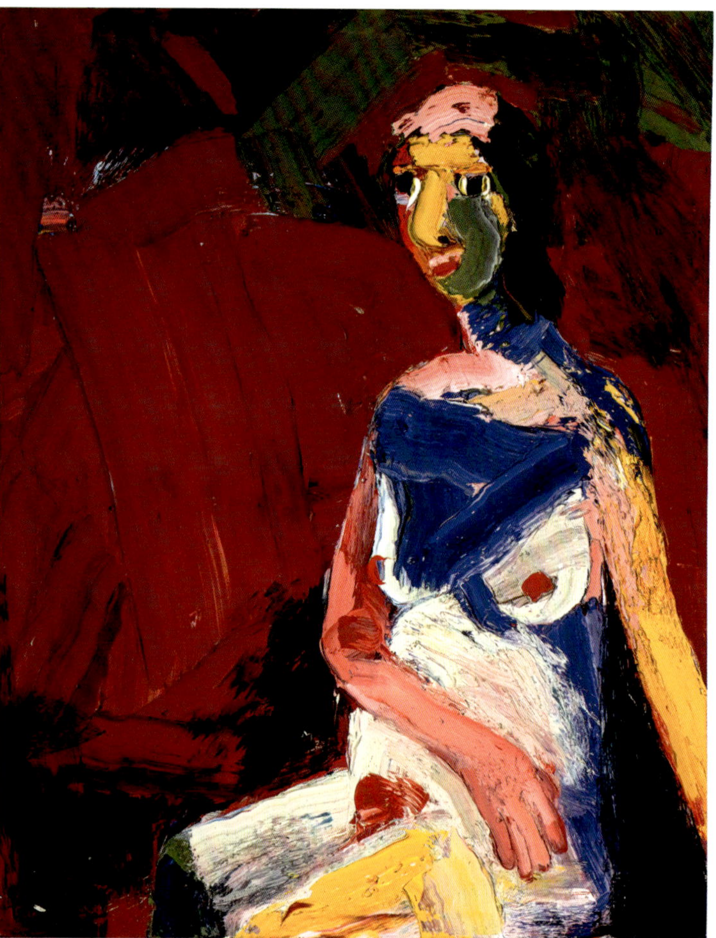

FIG. 6
Joan Brown, *Girl Sitting*, 1962. Oil on canvas, 60 × 47¾ in. (152.4 × 121.3 cm). Oakland Museum of California, gift of Dr. Samuel West

FIG. 7
Édouard Manet, *Portrait of Laure* (formerly *La négresse*), 1862–63. Oil on canvas, 24 × 20 in. (61 × 50 cm). Pinacoteca Giovanni e Marella Agnelli, Turin

into elements of both *Femme au chapeau* and *Girl with Green Eyes*, the former offering precedent in strength, sass, and subject matter, and the latter for a straight-on bust-length view of a sitter set in a shallow decorative space. In bedazzling Qusuquzah's veiled blue hat, hair, and other details with rhinestones, Thomas takes the already vibrant picture over the top, creating a twenty-first-century *Femme au chapeau*.

In 2011–12, the San Francisco Museum of Modern Art, Réunion des Musées Nationaux–Grand Palais, and The Metropolitan Museum of Art collaborated on an exhibition that united the collections of Gertrude, Leo, Michael, and Sarah Stein, whose legendary status as the most important champions of modern art in early twentieth-century Paris began with Leo and Gertrude's 1905 acquisition of Matisse's *Femme au chapeau*. The exhibition *The Steins Collect: Matisse, Picasso, and the Parisian Avant-Garde,* as it was known at its American venues, marked the first time the picture had left San Francisco in thirty years. Hundreds of thousands of people saw the show, introducing a new generation to *Femme au chapeau* and its various attributes. The cover of the English-language edition of the accompanying catalogue, which featured the framed *Femme au chapeau*, made its way into a twenty-first-century still life by Elizabeth Peyton: *The Stein's Collect and Flowers* (2011; p. 128).

Rachel Harrison was preparing for a solo exhibition at Greene Naftali gallery when she saw *The Steins Collect* at The Metropolitan Museum of Art in the spring of 2012.[40] She knew Matisse's famous Fauve portrait from books, and had likely seen it at SFMOMA.[41] But after encountering it at the Met, surrounded by quieter pictures—including Pierre Bonnard's *Siesta* (1900; National Gallery of Victoria, Melbourne) and Pablo Picasso's *Lady with a Fan*

(1905; p. 139)—Harrison changed course. The main, blob-like element of her sculpture titled *Hoarders* (2012; pp. 94 and 129), which would include a metal pail and video monitor in its final form, was underway in her Brooklyn studio. Working from a postcard of the Matisse, she adapted the sculpture's painted surface, covering it with patches of high-keyed colors mimicking the background of *Femme au chapeau,* and once it was complete, dramatically situating it on a purple runway carpet.

Femme au chapeau makes several cameos in Hilary Harkness's *Life with Alice and Gertrude,* a series of meticulous, intimately scaled paintings that reimagine sex, gender, and power dynamics within the famous couple's circle. The tiny *Woman with the Hat* (2011; p. 131)—the piece she considers her *Femme au chapeau*—presents a glamorous Alice B. Toklas grasping the severed head of Ernest Hemingway, with highly specific anatomical details.[42] Her gesture mirrors the image of Amélie Matisse's hand holding her fan, which can be seen in the provocatively cropped detail of *Femme au chapeau* on the wall in the upper left. A nude, tanned Alice returns with the same trophy in *Girl with a Basket of Flowers* (2011; p. 130), where Matisse's famous portrait finds company among additional canvases from the Steins' storied collection. Things continue to go awry in *Answered Prayers* (2024; p. 8), where Harkness's Alice, pictured as a Hollywood starlet, enjoys a cocktail while acknowledging neither the head sitting on a table shelf nor the corpse behind her. Meanwhile, Amélie, whose eyes follow you, observes from the wall. As we share the story of *Femme au chapeau* in this volume and on the walls of SFMOMA, now and into the future, we look forward to seeing how artists might continue to respond, through their own lenses and in their own time. ❁

1   Ann Dumas, "The Salon d'Automne of 1905: A Baptism of Fire," in *Vertigo of Color: Matisse, Derain, and the Origins of Fauvism,* by Dita Amory and Ann Dumas (New York: Metropolitan Museum of Art, 2023), 52.

2   Regarding a presentation of the artist's work as part of the 1937 exhibition *The Masters of Independent Art, 1895–1937,* at the Petit Palais, Paris, Matisse wrote to Sarah Stein: "[The city] is placing at my disposition a large gallery to fill with my works, and gave me the authority to choose what I would like to see there. I thought of my principal works and naturally of *la femme au chapeau.*" Henri Matisse to Sarah Stein, March 31, 1937, Estate of Daniel M. Stein, courtesy William J. Ashton.

3   Theresa [Ehrman] Jelenko, "My Life with the Steins," transcript of dictation to Elise S. Haas, ca. 1965, Theresa Ehrman papers and photographs, Magnes Collection of Jewish Art and Life, Bancroft Library, University of California, Berkeley. Transfer: Judah L. Magnes Museum, MSS 92/810c, ctn. 6.

4   Daniel Zamani, "Anarchy of Color: Vlaminck's Fauvist Painting," in *Maurice de Vlaminck: Modern Art Rebel,* by Anna Storm and Daniel Zamani (Munich: Prestel, 2024), 31–33.

5   Marval displayed a single painting titled *Le printemps* (Spring), whereas Van Dongen showed two: *La chemise* (The Shirt) and *Torse* (Torso).

6   Leo Stein, *Appreciation: Painting, Poetry, and Prose* (Lincoln: University of Nebraska Press, 1996), 158.

7   "In the early decades of the century, hundreds of visitors flocked to the display of vanguard art: many came to scoff, but several went away converted. It was a brilliant scene—and a historic one. For all intents and purposes, Leo and Gertrude Stein had inaugurated, at 27 Rue de Fleurus, the first museum of modern art." James R. Mellow, "The Stein Salon Was the First Museum of Modern Art," *New York Times,* Dec. 1, 1968.

8   "You have got to be able to picture side by side everything Matisse and I were doing at that time. No one has ever looked at Matisse's painting more carefully than I; and no one has looked at mine more carefully than he," stated Picasso toward the end of his life. Quoted in John Golding, "Introduction," in *Matisse Picasso,* ed.

Elizabeth Cowling, Anne Baldassari, John Elderfield, John Golding, Isabelle Monod-Fontaine, and Kirk Varnedoe (New York: Museum of Modern Art, 2002), 13.

9   Gertrude Stein, *The Autobiography of Alice B. Toklas* (New York: Vintage, 1990), 45.

10   For a detailed accounting of the Stein family salons, see Emily Braun, "Saturday Evenings at the Steins," in *The Steins Collect: Matisse, Picasso, and the Parisian Avant-Garde,* ed. Janet Bishop, Cécile Debray, and Rebecca Rabinow, exh. cat. (San Francisco: San Francisco Museum of Modern Art; New Haven, CT: Yale University Press, 2011), 49–67.

11   Of the 442 Stein-owned works documented in *The Steins Collect,* five are by women: two by Marie Laurencin, two by Dora Maar, and one by Mathilde Vollmoeller-Purrmann.

12   Hélène Leroy, "Premiers pas sur la scène Parisienne," in *Gabriele Münter: Peindre sans détours* (Paris: Musée d'Art Moderne de Paris, 2025), 52–53.

13   See, for instance, plates 2, 5, and 6 in Frank Schmidt, "Mit Matisse unterhielt ich mich längere Zeit sehr interessant über Kunst," in *Horizont Jawlensky: Alexej Jawlensky im Spiegel seiner künstlerischen Begegnungen 1900–1914,* exh. cat., ed. Roman Zieglgänsberger (Munich: Hirmer, 2014), 233–35.

14   Leo Stein to Sarah Stein, September 9, 1938, Estate of Daniel M. Stein, courtesy William J. Ashton; Leo Stein to Mabel Weeks, February 7, 1913, in *Leo Stein, Journey into the Self: Being the Letters, Papers, and Journals of Leo Stein,* ed. Edmund Fuller (New York: Crown, 1950), 52.

15   Rebecca Rabinow, "Discovering Modern Art: The Steins' Early Years in Paris, 1903–1907," in Bishop et al., *The Steins Collect,* 32.

16   Henri Matisse, in Georges Braque, Eugene Jolas, Maria Jolas, Henri Matisse, André Salmon, and Tristan Tzara, *Testimony against Gertrude Stein* (The Hague: Servire Press, February 1935), 3; Rabinow, "Discovering Modern Art," 32.

17   For full accounting of the Steins' loss, see Claudine Grammont, "Matisse as Religion: The 'Mike Steins' and Matisse, 1908–1918," in Bishop et al., *The Steins Collect,* 160–63.

18   Details of the paper and the crease of the

now-loose page suggest that it came from the same album as a photograph of Michael Stein posing for Matisse in fall 1916.

19   Matisse, in Braque et al., *Testimony against Gertrude Stein,* 3.

20   See, for instance, *L'Illustration,* Nov. 4, 1905 (see p. 21).

21   According to Kuniyoshi expert Tom Wolf and Woodstock Artists Association and Museum archivist Emily Jones, Kuniyoshi's art library included several Matisse publications that predate *Untitled* (1934), including the 1931 edition of *Cahiers d'Art,* which features a full-page, black-and-white reproduction of *Femme au chapeau* with a white border. Tom Wolf, email to Robert McD. Parker, Maria Castro, and the author, June 16, 2025.

22   Works incorporating print materials include *Accordion* (1938) and *Broken Objects* (1944; both, Metropolitan Museum of Art, New York).

23   Sarah Stein wrote that she and Michael made the crossing on the *Statendam* with their grandson Danny [Daniel M. Stein] in July; their "paintings, bronzes and some of the furniture from Vaucresson" arrived in September. Sarah Stein to Henri Matisse, July 6, 1935, and September 1935, Archives Matisse Paris.

24   Sarah Stein to Henri Matisse, Jan. 7, 1936, Archives Matisse Paris.

25   Grace L. McCann Morley in *San Francisco Museum of Art Quarterly Bulletin,* series II, vol. I, no. 1–2, 1952, p. 6.

26   Grace L. McCann Morley to Mr. and Mrs. Michael Stein, March 4, 1936, Estate of Daniel M. Stein, courtesy William J. Ashton. The landscapes she refers to were *Bonheur de vivre* and *Paysage: Les genêts,* which were bequeathed by Elise S. Haas to SFMOMA along with *Femme au chapeau.*

27   *San Francisco Museum of Art Quarterly Bulletin,* 1952, p. 7.

28   Sarah Stein, handwritten note to unknown recipient on Mrs. Michael Stein stationery, ca. 1948, Estate of Daniel M. Stein, courtesy William J. Ashton.

29   *San Francisco Museum of Art Quarterly Bulletin,* 1952, p. 8.

30   Confirmation of the identity of the subject from email exchange with Park's daughter, Helen Park Bigelow, Nov. 24, 2025.

31 For a thorough examination of
Diebenkorn's connection to Matisse,
see Janet Bishop and Katy Rothkopf,
Matisse/Diebenkorn (Baltimore
Museum of Art and San Francisco
Museum of Modern Art; Munich:
DelMonico Books-Prestel, 2016).

32 Hermine Ford, interview by Judith Olch
Richards, Feb. 18–19, 2010, Archives of
American Art, Smithsonian Institution.

33 Jeannette Redensek, email to the
author, June 2, 2023.

34 Josef Albers, *Interaction of Color: New
Complete Edition* (New Haven, CT: Yale
University Press and the Josef and
Anni Albers Foundation, 2009), vol. 2,
pp. IXI-1 and XIX-2.

35 Albers, *Interaction of Color*, vol. 1, p. 108.
The second pairing features a reproduction of a painting by Georges Rouault
and a collage of the same by the student
Karen Allen. Jeannette Redensek,
email to the author, Nov. 20, 2025.

36 Hermine Ford, email to the author,
Nov. 24, 2025.

37 For color plates, see Janet Bishop and
Nancy Lim, *Joan Brown* (San Francisco:
San Francisco Museum of Modern
Art; Oakland: University of California
Press, 2022), 87–89.

38 See, for instance, Claudine Grammont,
Hockney–Matisse: Un paradis retrouvé
(Nice: Musée Museum Nice, 2022).

39 Quoted in Barbara Pollack,
"Rhinestone Odalisques," *ArtNews,*
Jan. 2011, www.artnews.com/art-news/
retrospective/archives-mickalene-
thomas-work-goes-beyond-black-
esthetic-2011-10971/.

40 Rachel Harrison, telephone conversation with the author, Nov. 10, 2025.
The first two venues for the exhibition
were SFMOMA and the Réunion des
Musées Nationaux–Grand Palais, Paris.

41 Harrison was the subject of a solo
exhibition at SFMOMA (*New Work:
Rachel Harrison,* Nov. 12, 2004–
March 13, 2005), during which *Femme au
chapeau* was on view in the museum's
second-floor collection galleries.

42 Ivy Haldeman, "A Conversation with
Hilary Harkness," in *Hilary Harkness:
Everything for You,* exh. cat. (London:
Black Dog Press, 2024), 212.

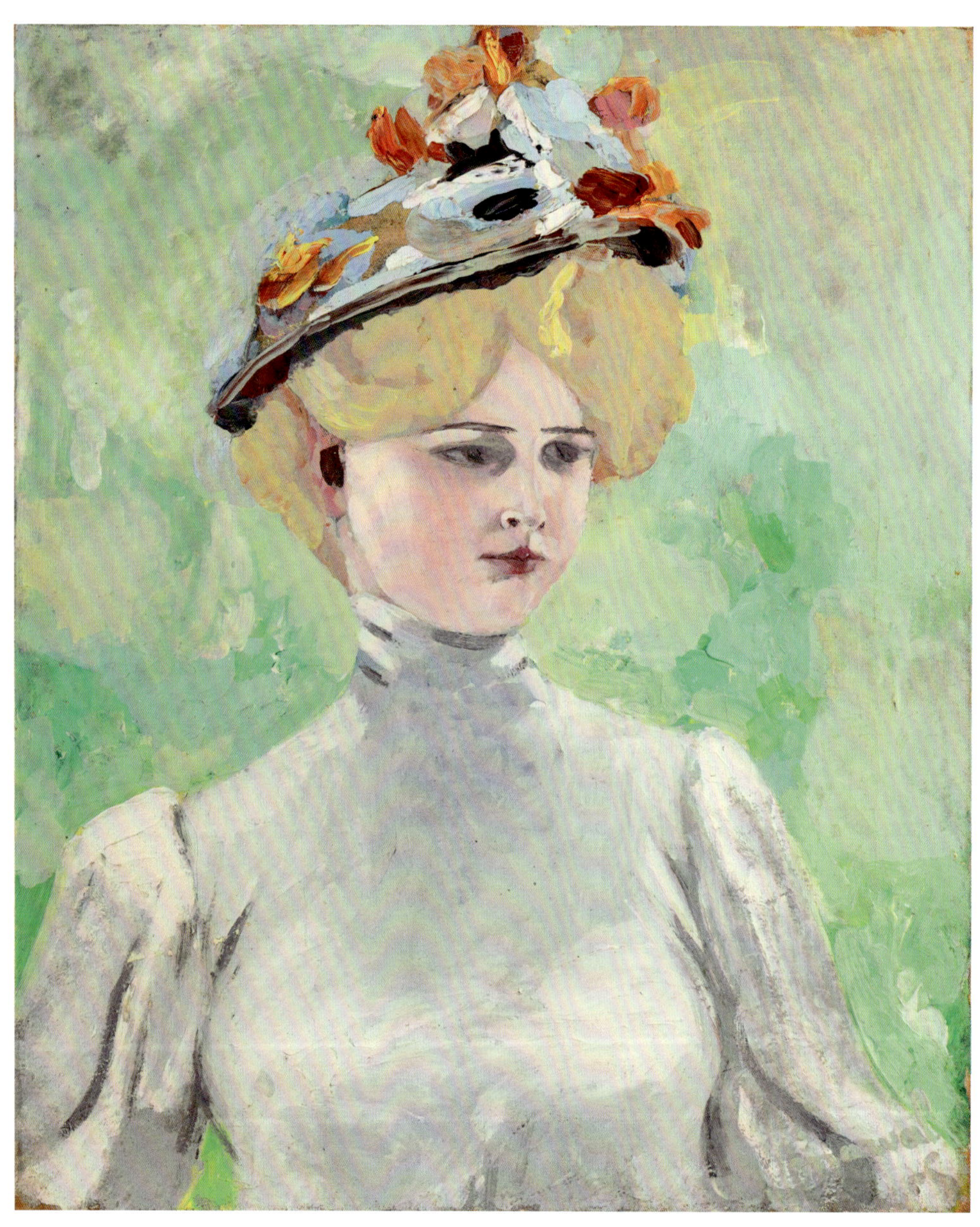

Jacqueline Marval, *Portrait*, 1905. Oil on canvas, 25⅝ × 21¼ in. (65 × 54 cm).
Private collection, courtesy Comité Jacqueline Marval, Paris

108

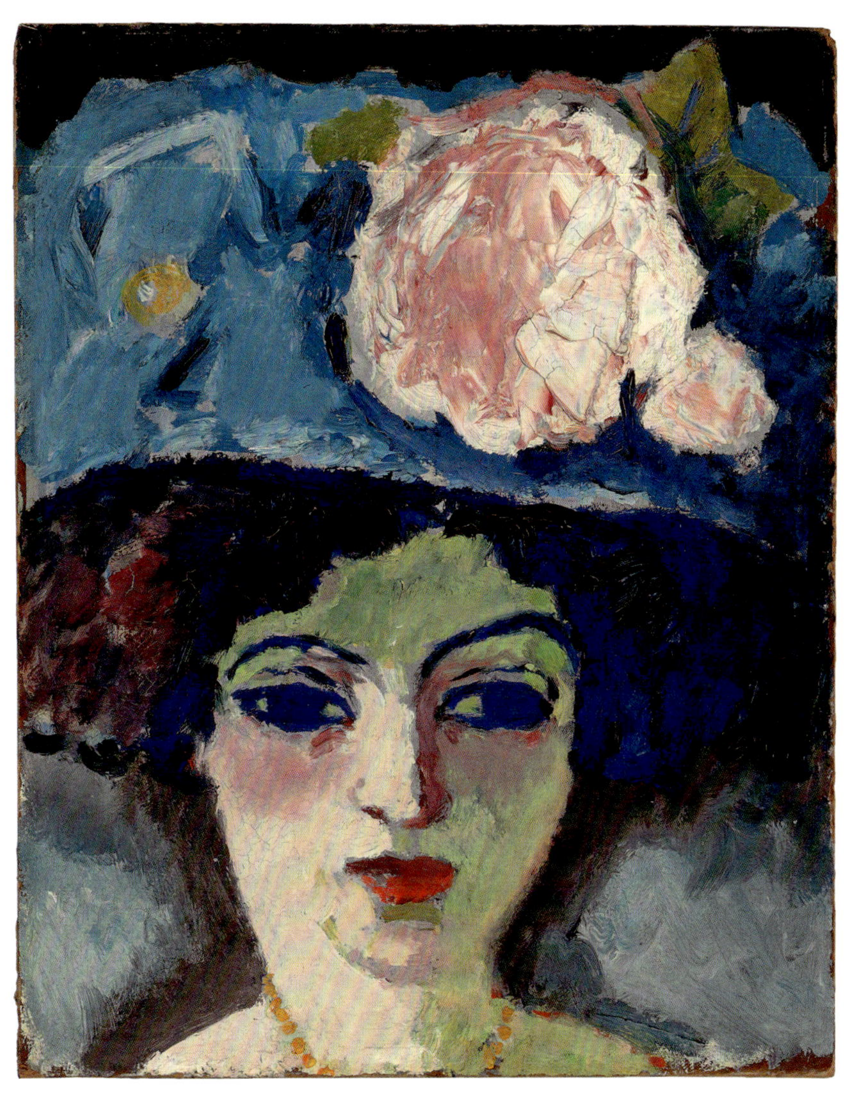

Kees van Dongen, *Femme au chapeau fleuri* (Woman with a Flowered Hat), 1905.
Oil on board, 18⅓ × 14¾ in. (47.5 × 37.5 cm). AAA Fondation

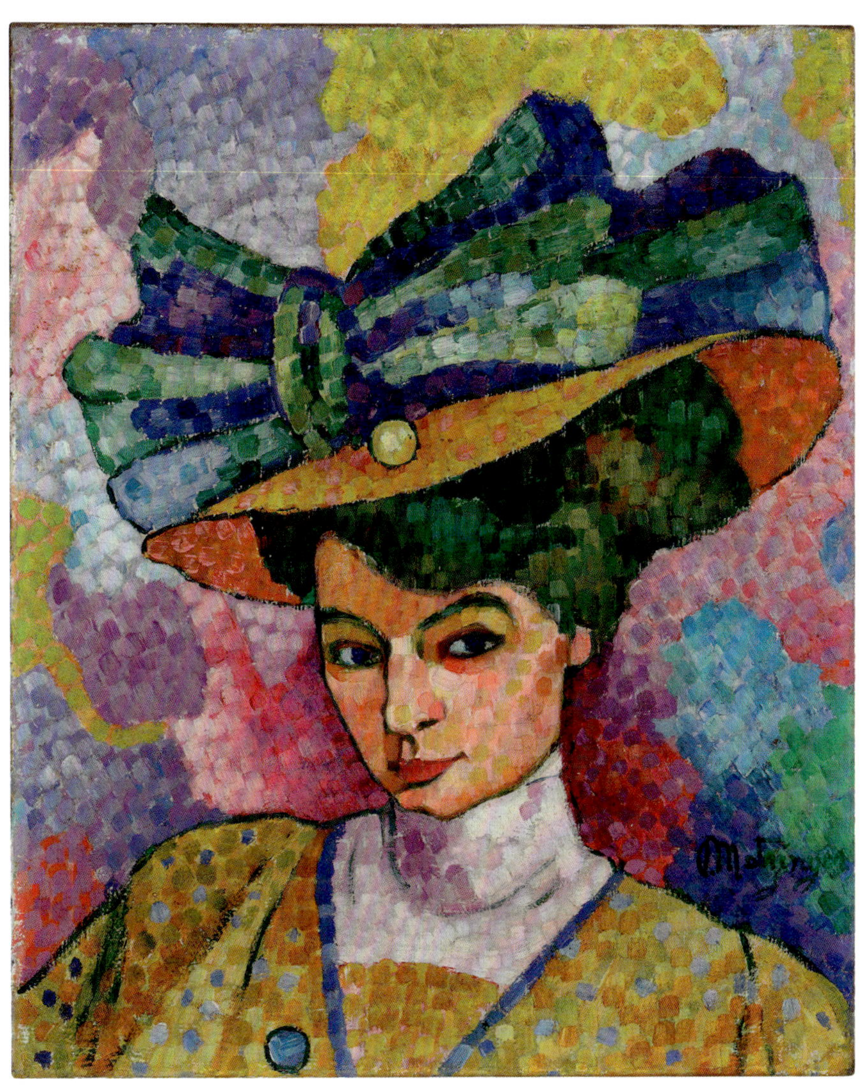

Jean Metzinger, *Femme au chapeau* (Woman with a Hat), ca. 1906. Oil on canvas,
17⅝ × 14½ in. (44.7 × 36.8 cm). AAA Fondation

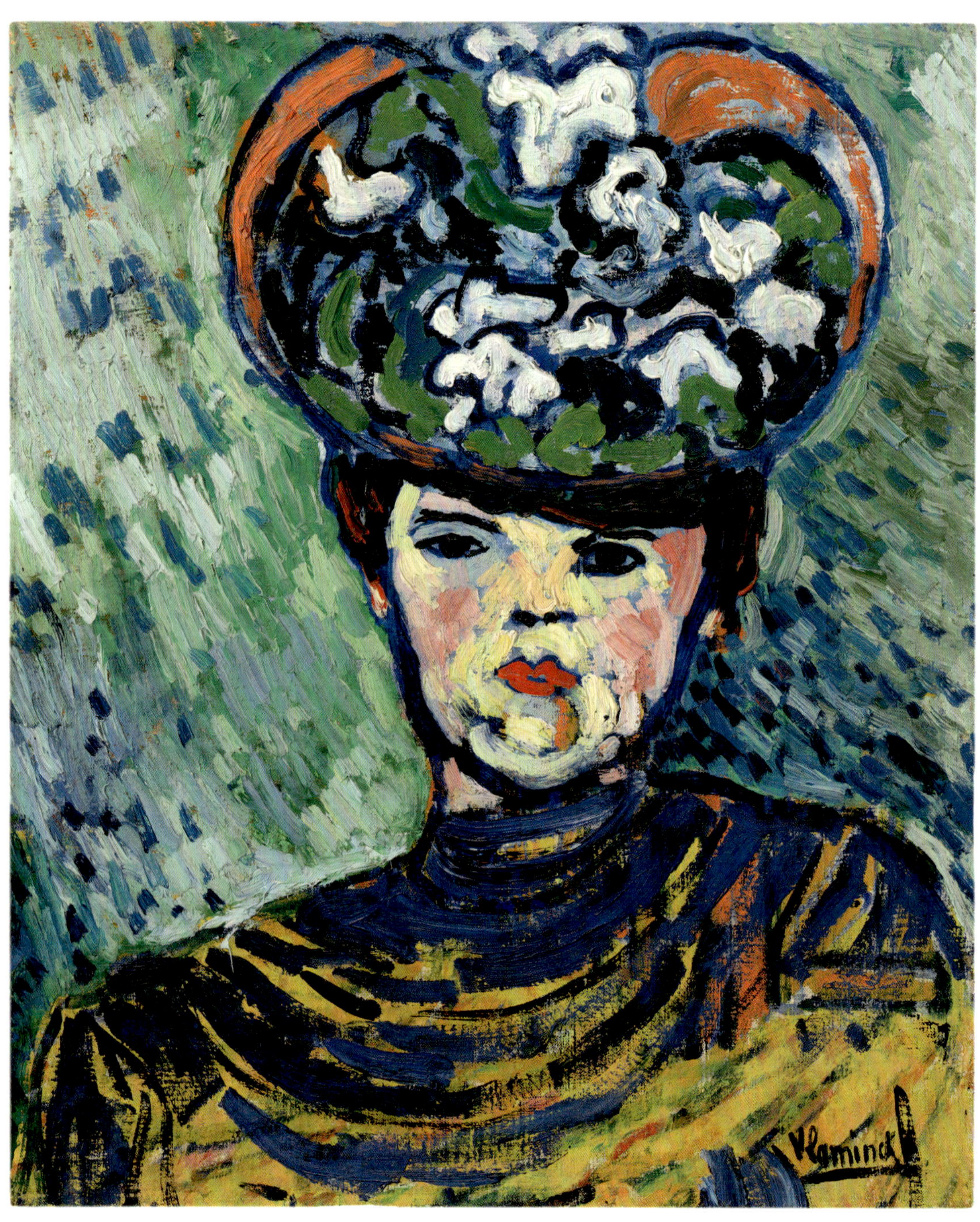

Maurice de Vlaminck, *Femme au chapeau* (Woman with a Hat), 1906. Oil on canvas, 22¼ × 18¾ (56.5 × 47.6 cm). National Gallery of Art, Washington, DC, donated by Lolo Sarnoff in memory of her parents, Mr. and Mrs. Robert von Hirsch, 1981.84.1

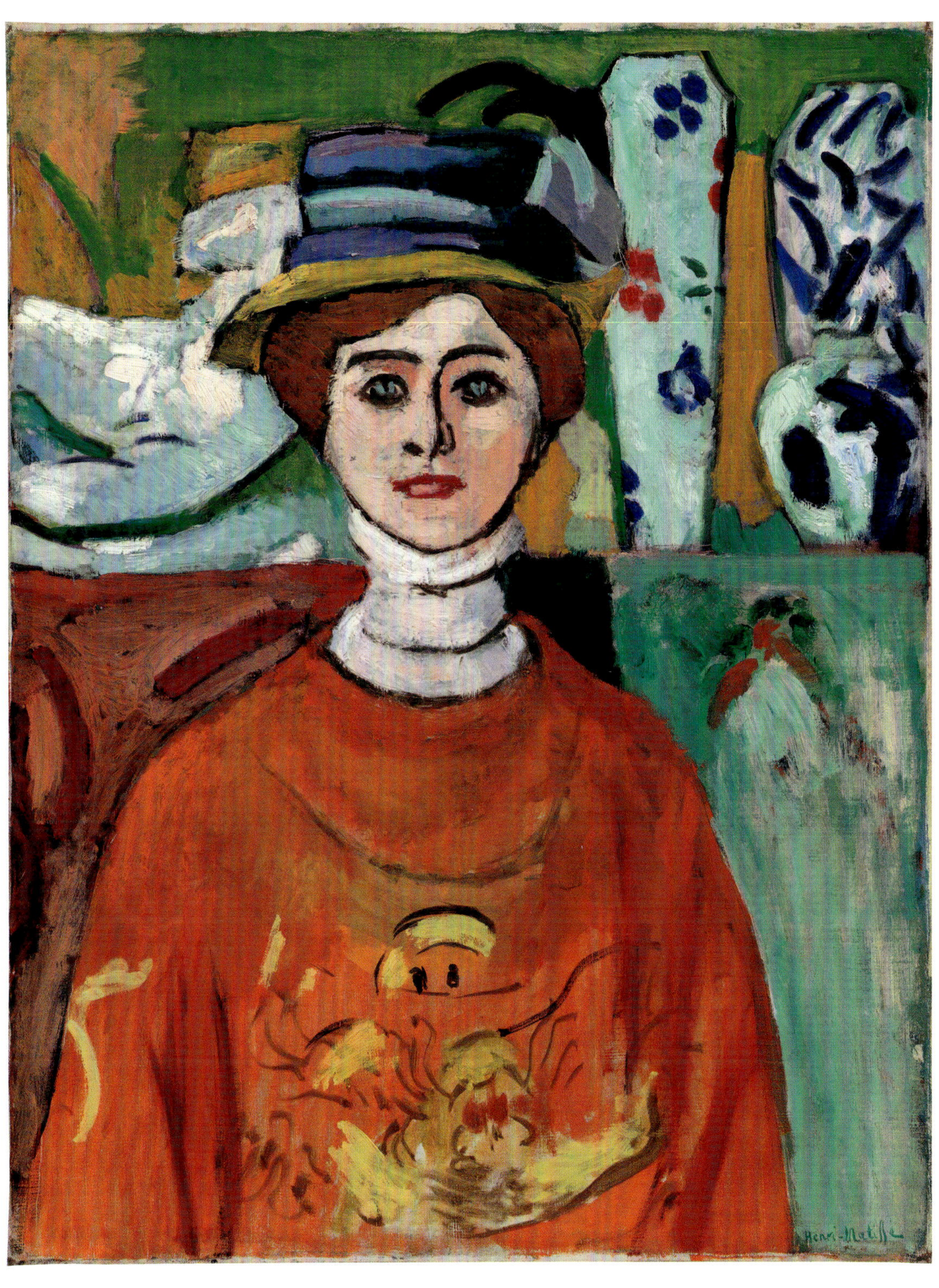

Henri Matisse, *La fille aux yeux verts* (The Girl with Green Eyes), 1908.
Oil on canvas, 26 × 20 in. (66 × 50.8 cm). San Francisco Museum of Modern Art,
bequest of Harriet Lane Levy, 1950

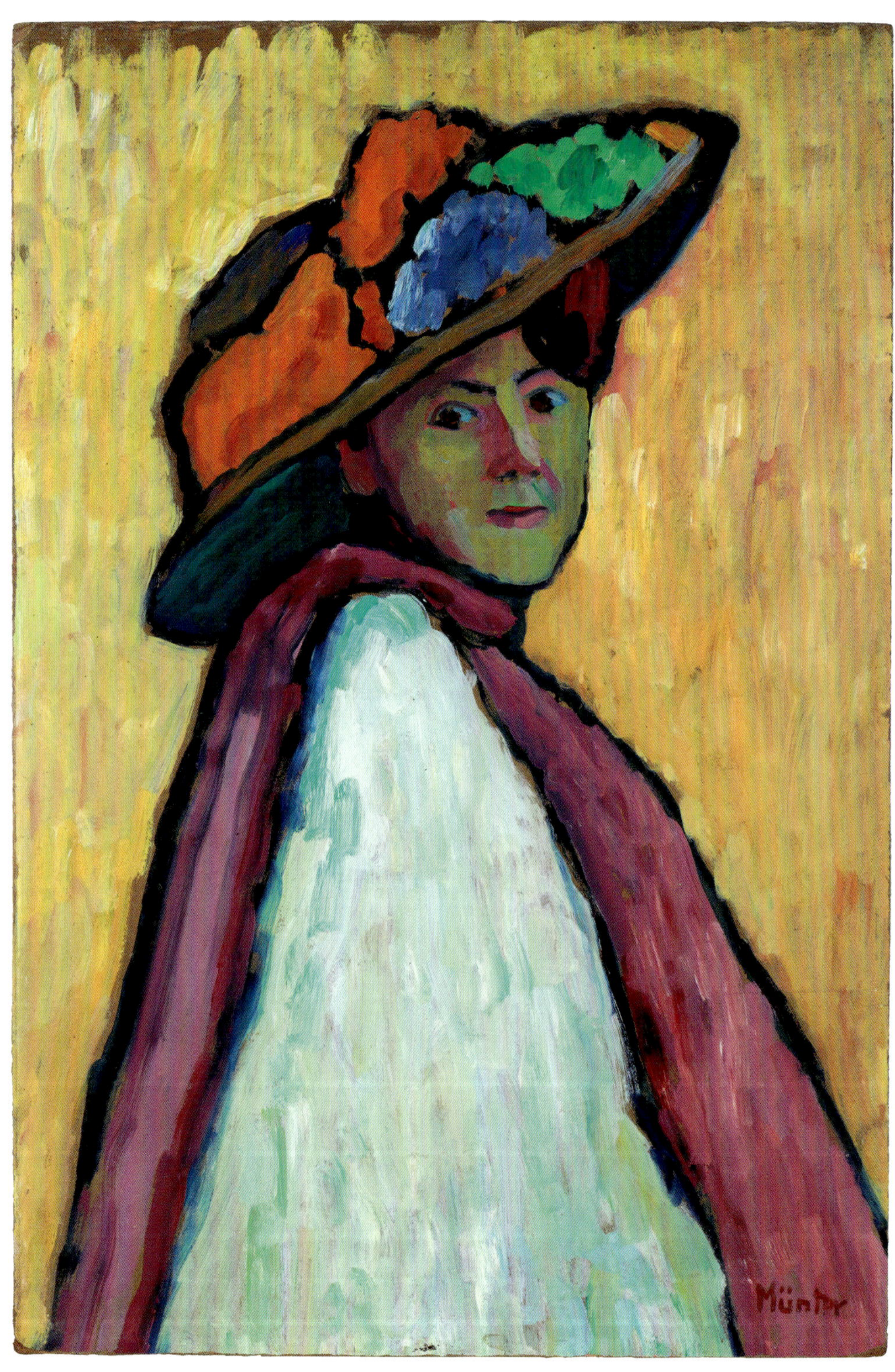

Gabriele Münter, *Bildnis Marianne von Werefkin* (Portrait of Marianne von
Werefkin), 1909. Oil on cardboard, 31⅞ × 21⅝ in. (81 × 55 cm). Städtische Galerie im
Lenbachhaus und Kunstbau, Munich, Gabriele Münter Collection, 1957

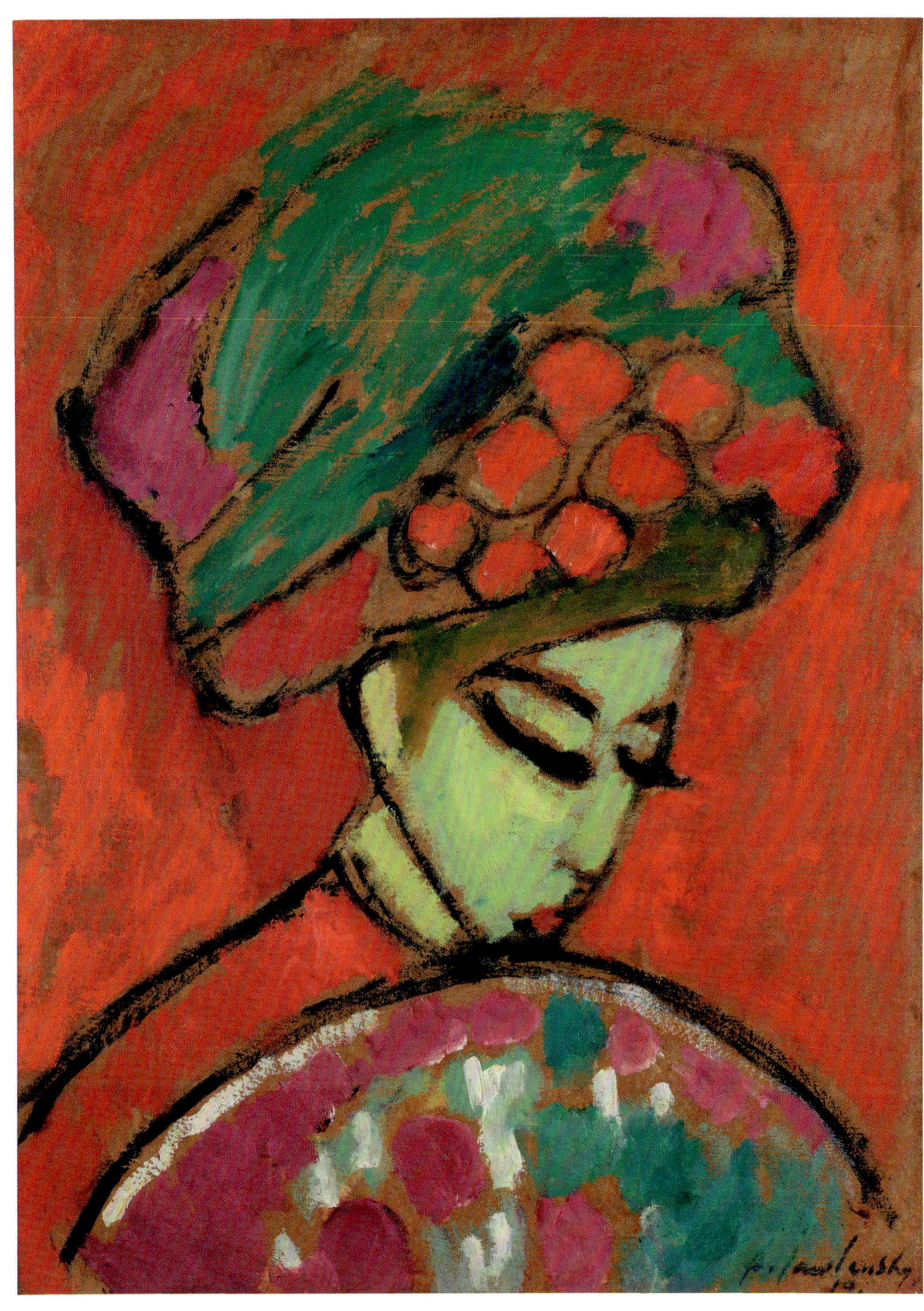

Alexej von Jawlensky, *Mädchen mit Blumenhut* (Girl with a Flowered Hat), 1910.
Oil on cardboard, 26⅜ × 19¼ in. (67.5 × 49 cm). Albertina Museum, Batliner Collection

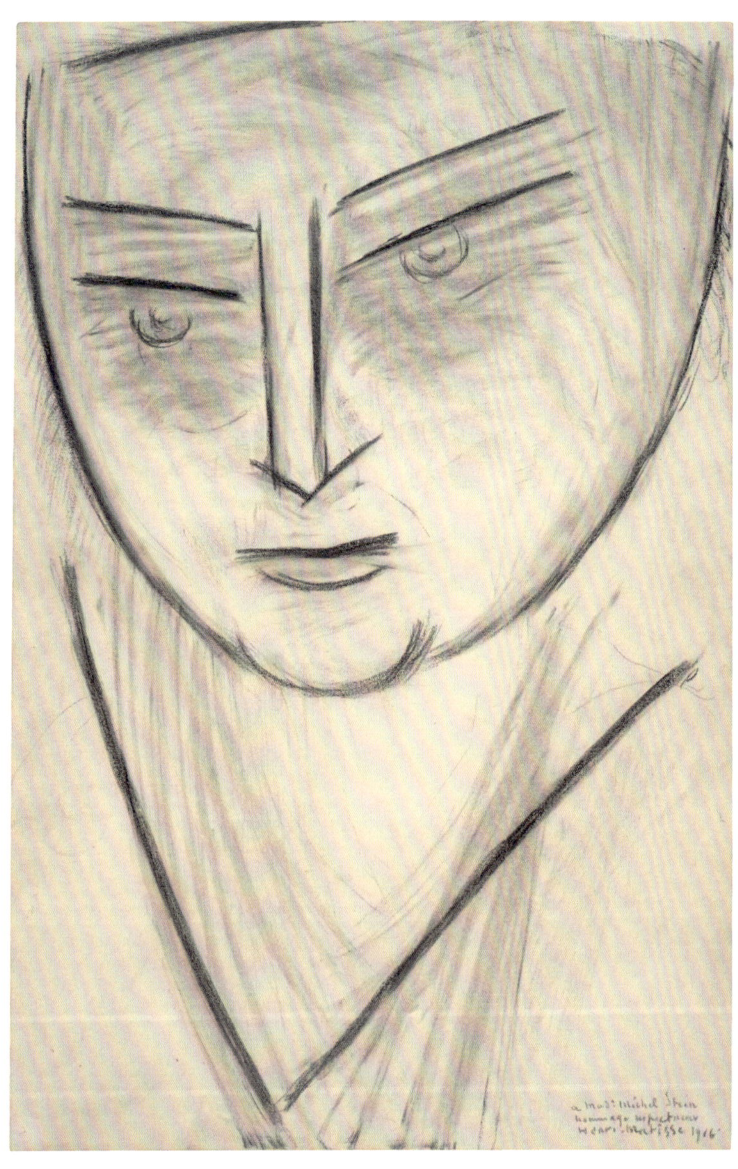

Henri Matisse, *Study of Sarah Stein,* 1916. Graphite on paper, 19⅛ × 12⅝ in. (48.5 × 32 cm). San Francisco Museum of Modern Art, gift of Mr. and Mrs. Walter A. Haas, 1962

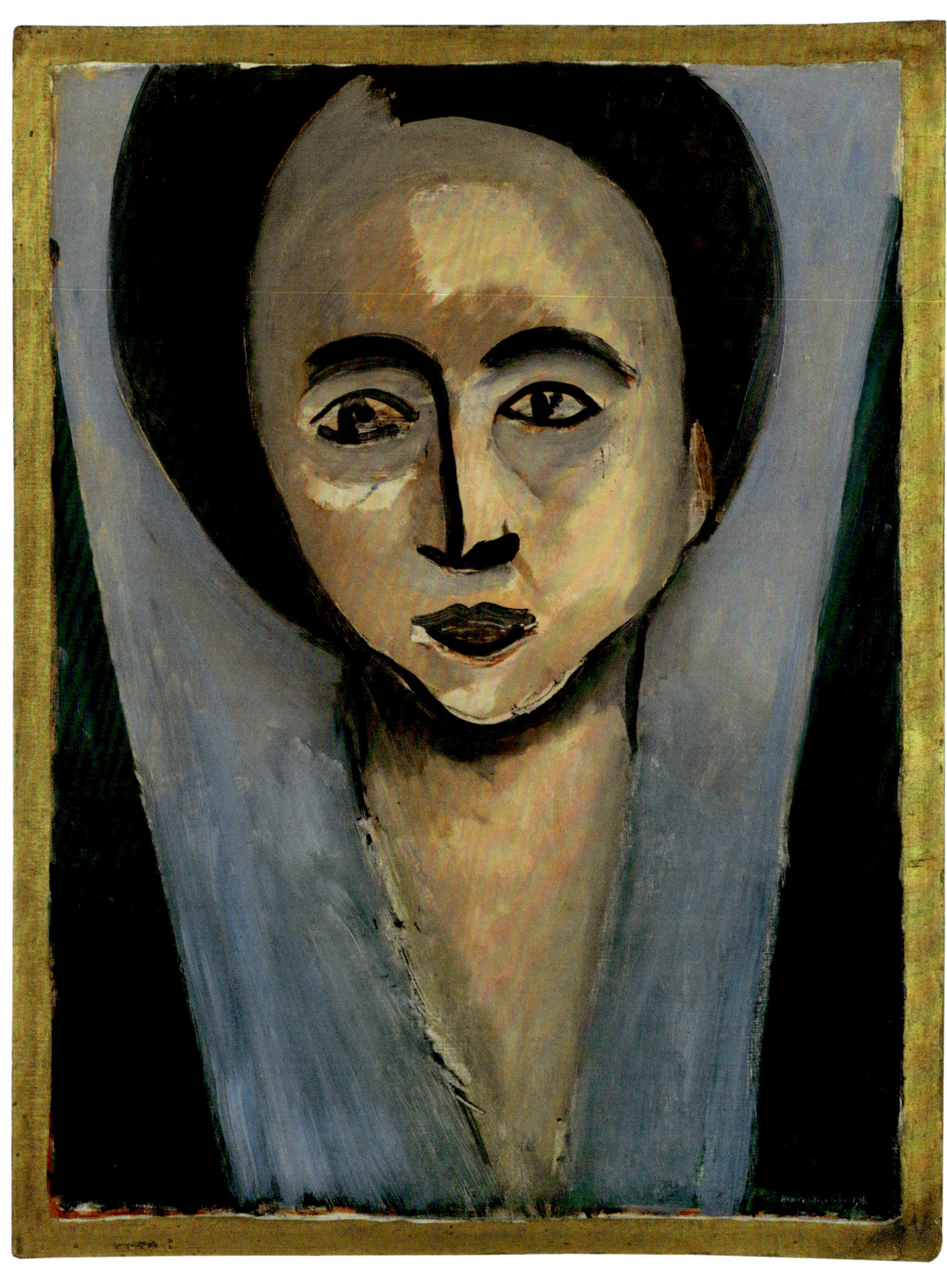

Henri Matisse, *Sarah Stein,* 1916. Oil on canvas, 28½ × 22¼ in. (72.4 × 56.5 cm).
San Francisco Museum of Modern Art, Sarah and Michael Stein Memorial Collection,
gift of Elise S. Haas, 1954

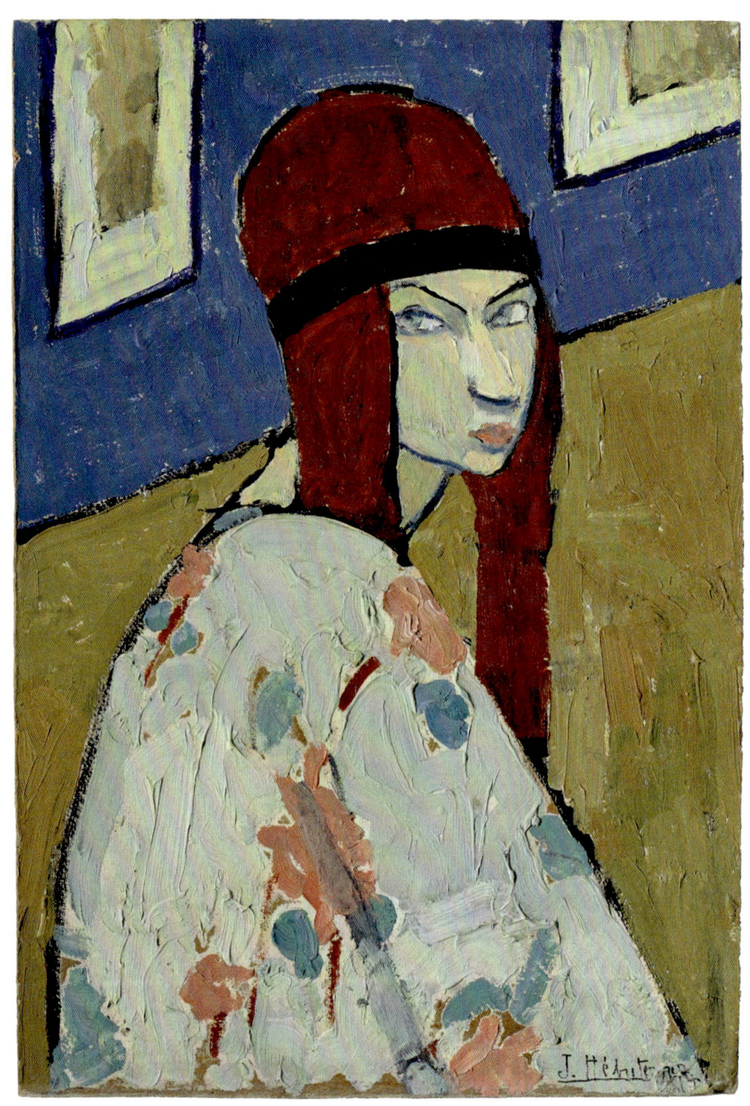

Jeanne Hébuterne, *Self-Portrait*, ca. 1917. Oil on board, 17½ × 12 in. (44.5 × 30.5 cm).
Collection of Dr. Harald Link

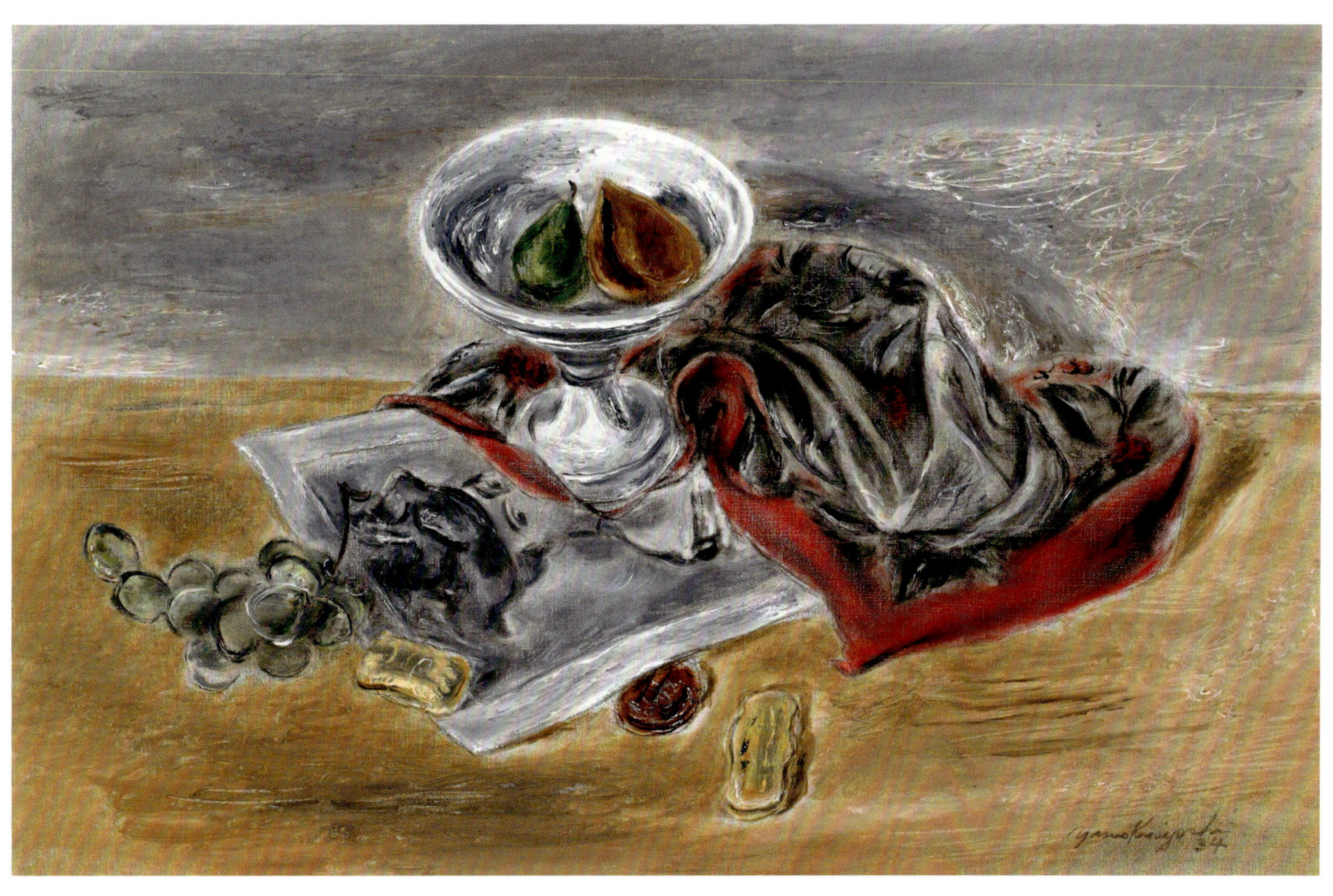

Yasuo Kuniyoshi, *Untitled*, 1934. Oil on canvas, 17½ × 27⅝ in. (44.45 × 70.2 cm). Harn Museum of Art, University of Florida, gift of Eloise Ricks Chandler

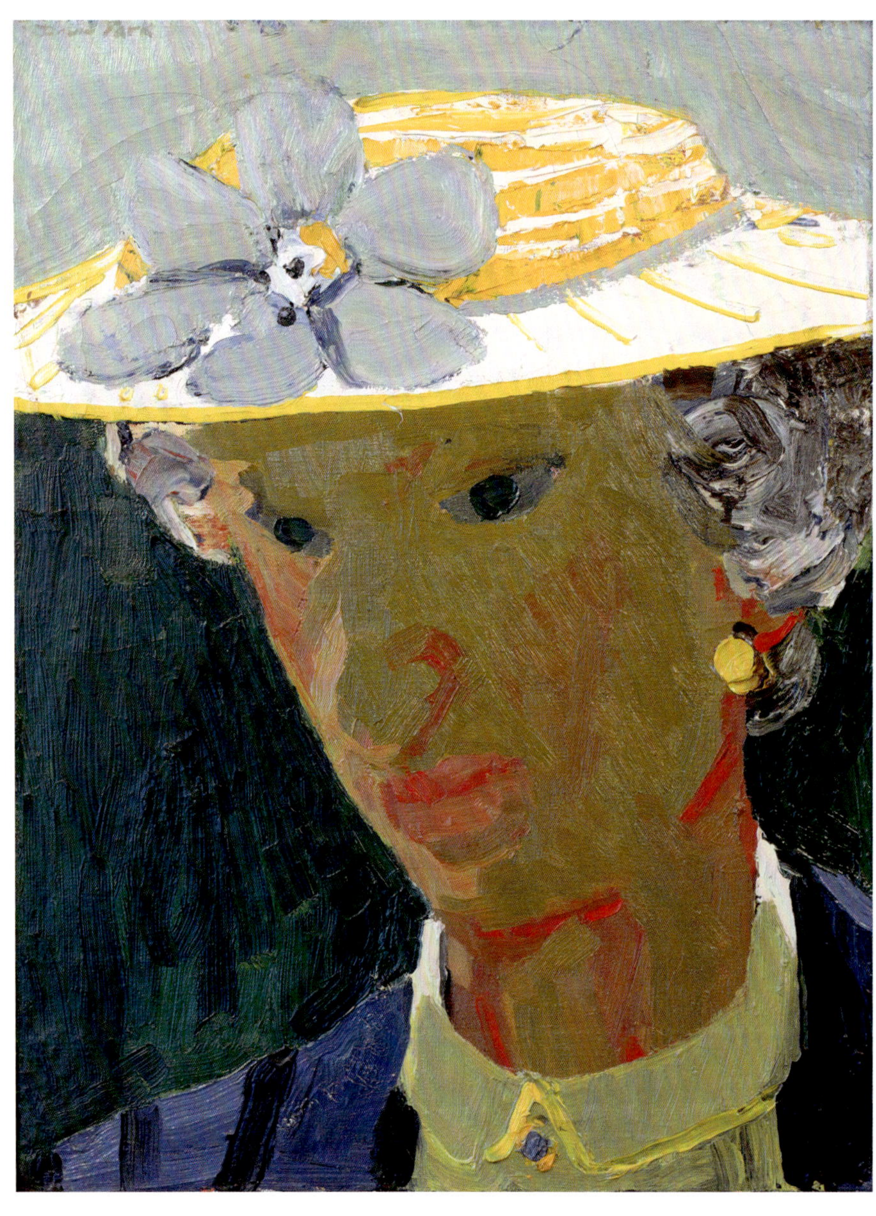

David Park, *Mother-in-Law,* 1954–55. Oil on canvas, 26 × 19½ in. (66 × 49.5 cm).
Collection of Vicki and Kent Logan, fractional and promised gift to the San Francisco
Museum of Modern Art

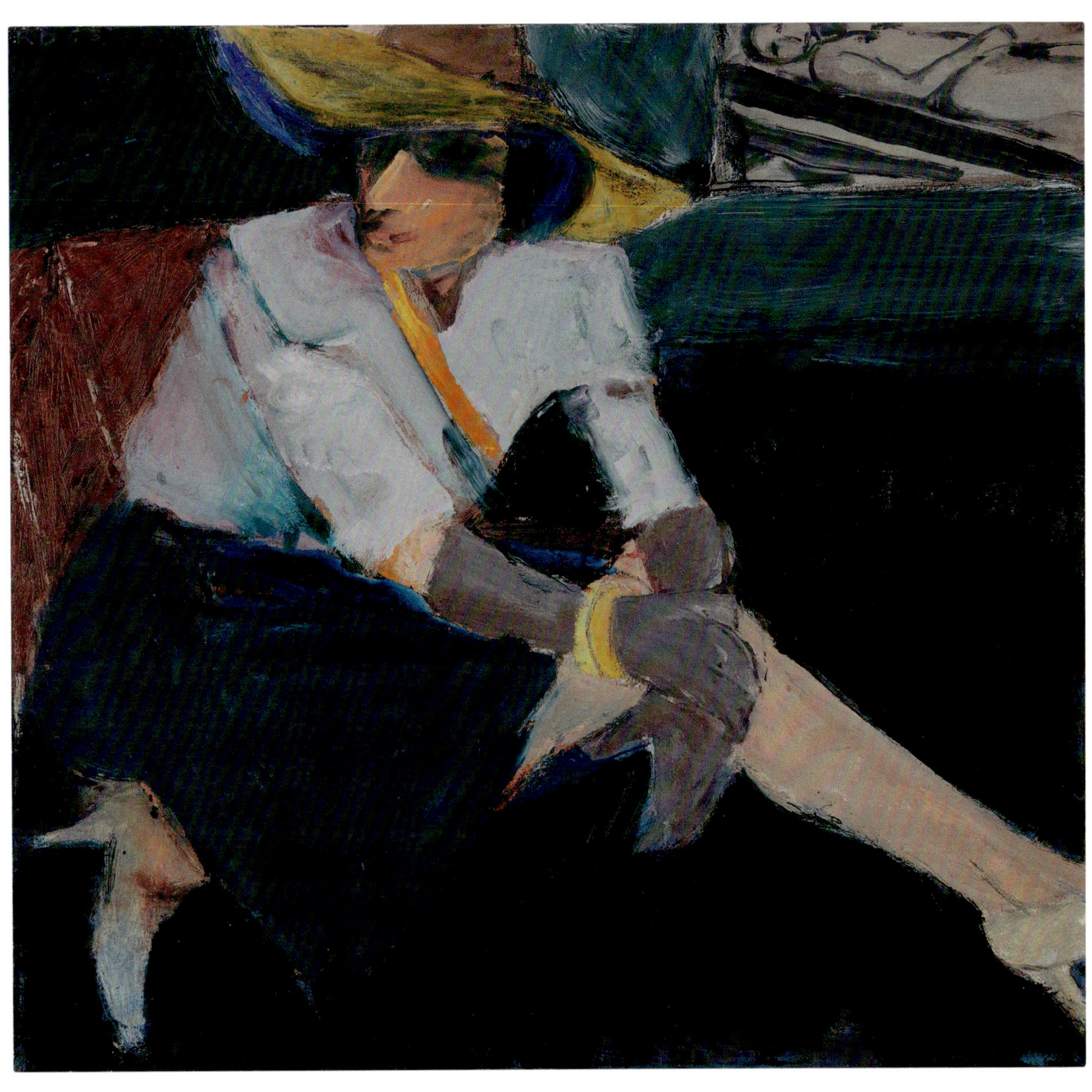

Richard Diebenkorn, *Woman in Hat and Gloves*, 1963. Oil on canvas, 33¾ × 36 in.
(85.7 × 91.4 cm). Private collection

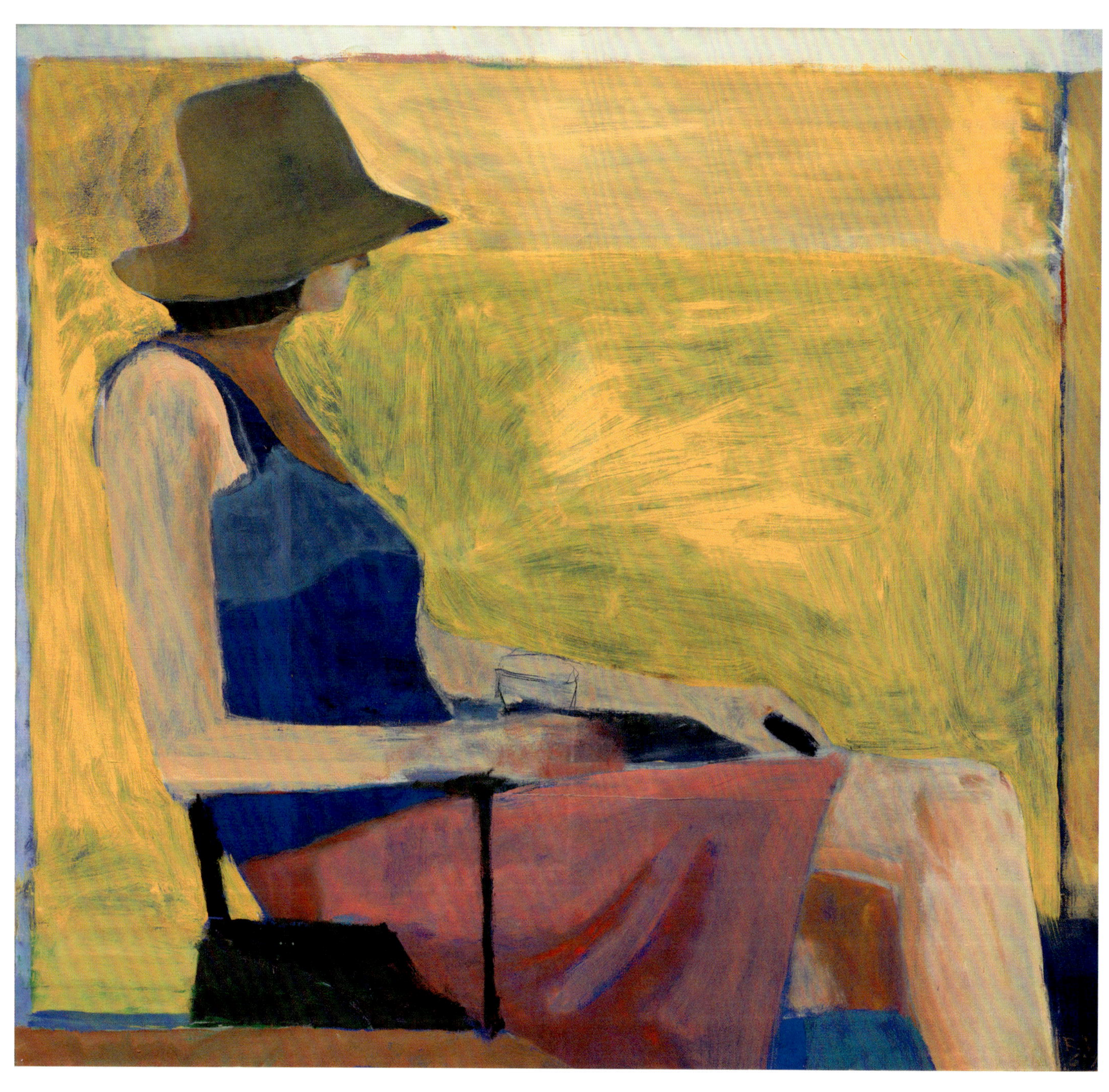

Richard Diebenkorn, *Seated Figure with Hat,* 1967. Oil on canvas, 57¾ × 61¾ in. (146.7 × 156.9 cm). National Gallery of Art, Washington, DC, gift of the Collectors Committee and Mr. and Mrs. Lawrence Rubin

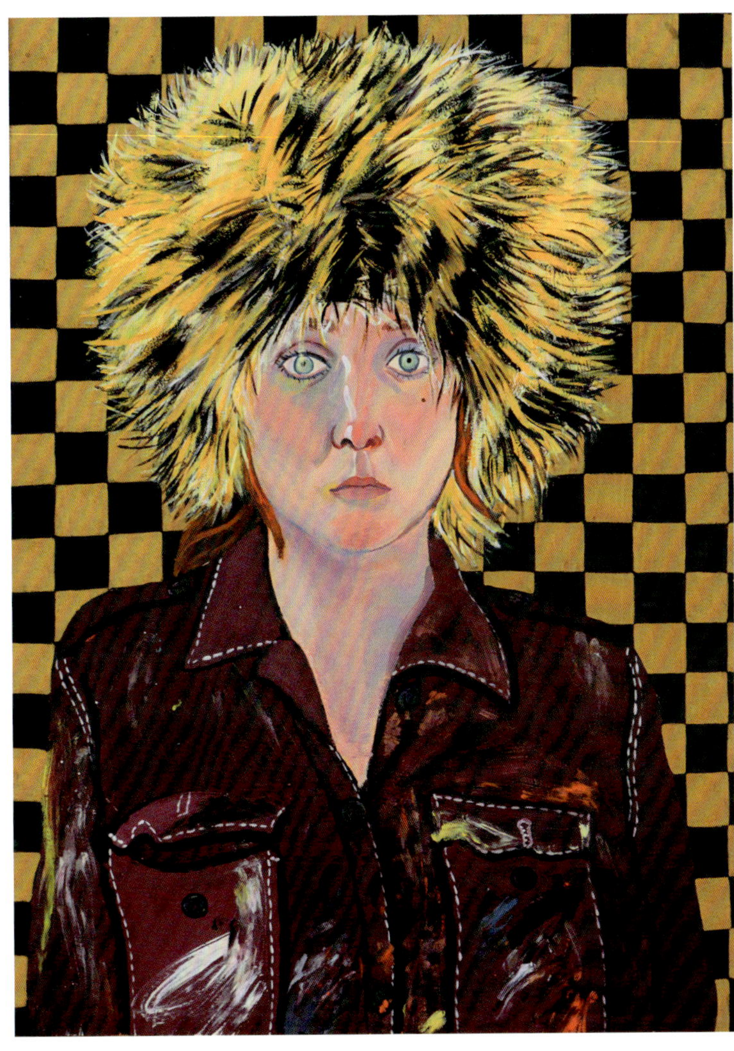

Joan Brown, *Self-Portrait in Fur Hat,* 1972. Enamel on panel, 40¾ × 29¾ in. (103.2 × 75.6 cm). di Rosa Center for Contemporary Art, Napa

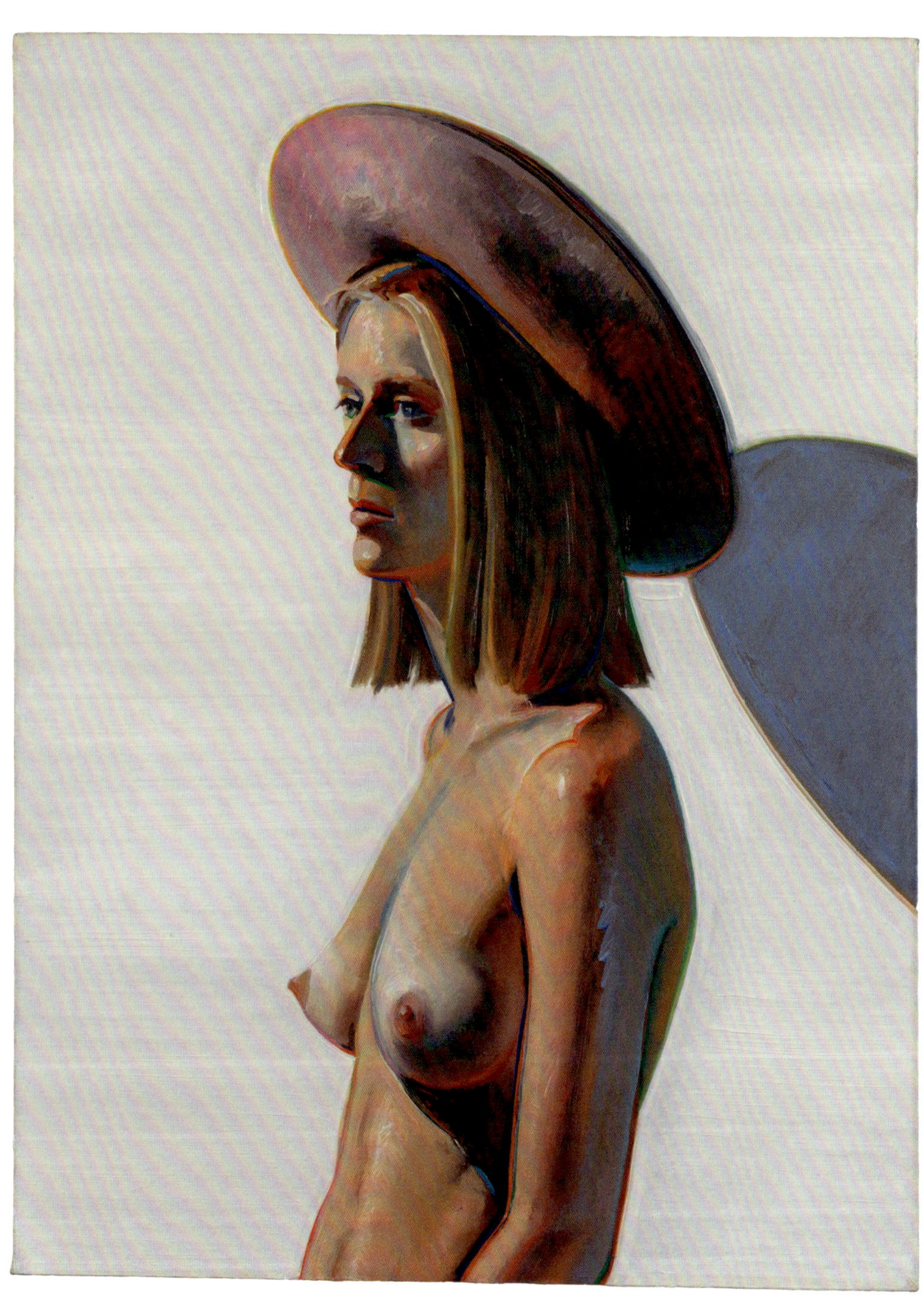

Wayne Thiebaud, *Girl with Pink Hat,* 1973. Oil on canvas, 29½ × 22⅜ × 2 in. (74.9 × 56.9 × 5.1 cm). San Francisco Museum of Modern Art, gift of Jeannette Powell, 2010

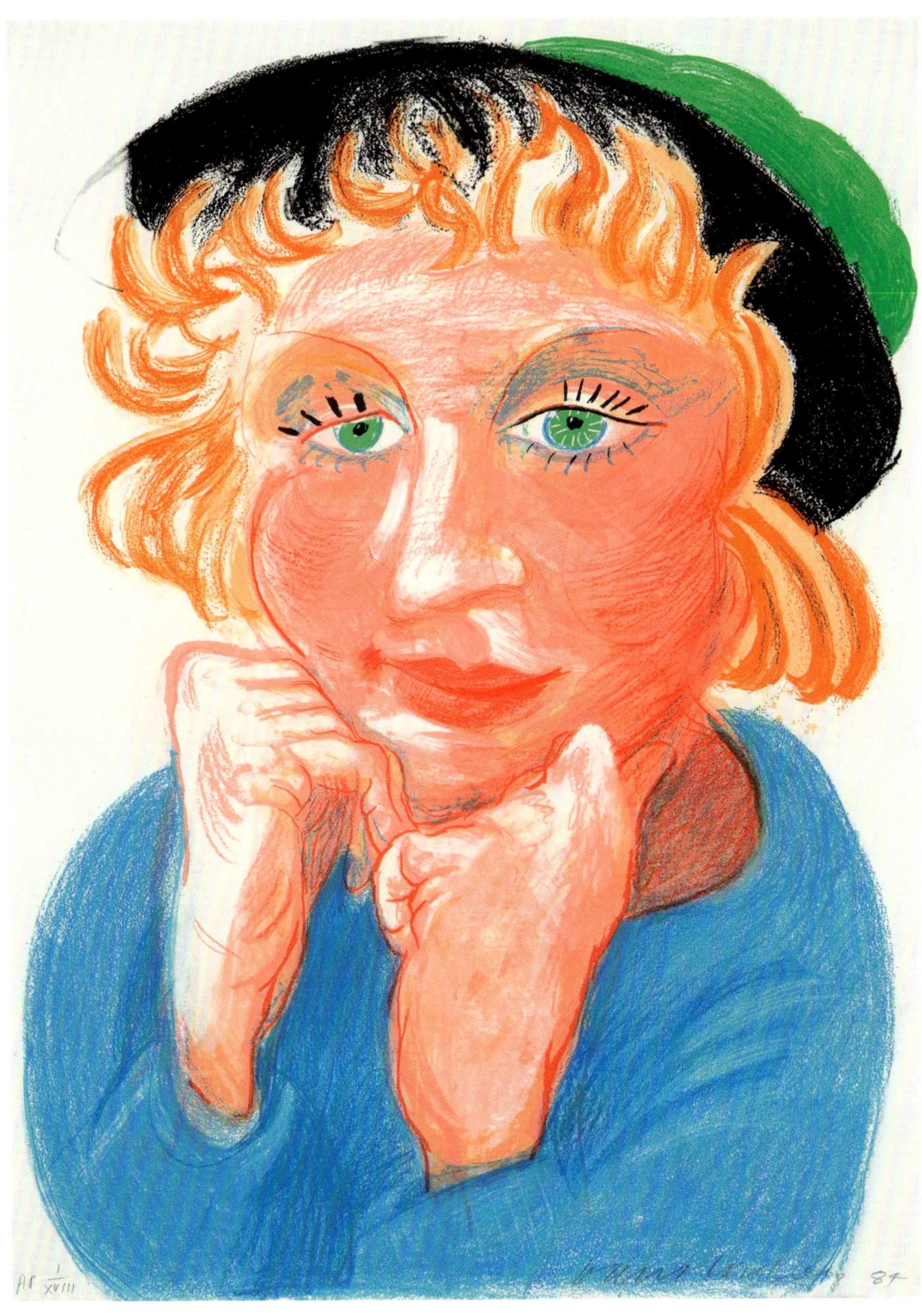

David Hockney, *Celia in a Green Hat,* 1984. Color lithograph, 30 × 22 in. (76.2 × 55.9 cm).
Collection of the David Hockney Foundation

Mickalene Thomas, *Qusuquzah, une très belle négresse 1* (Qusuquzah, a Very Beautiful Black Woman 1), 2011. Rhinestones, acrylic paint, oil, and enamel on wood panel, 96 × 80 × 2 in. (243.8 × 203.2 × 5.1 cm). San Francisco Museum of Modern Art, purchase, by exchange, through a gift of Peggy Guggenheim, 2019

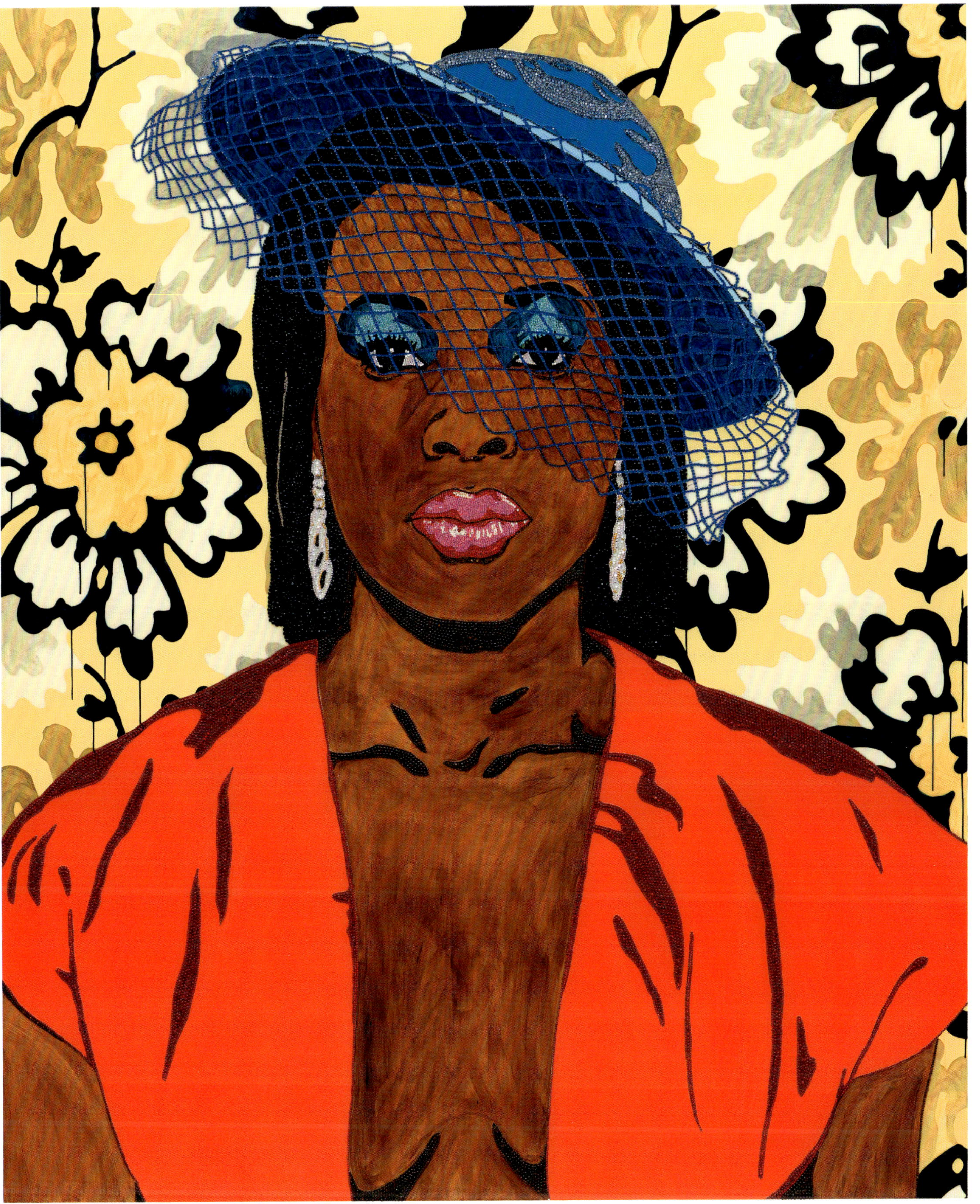

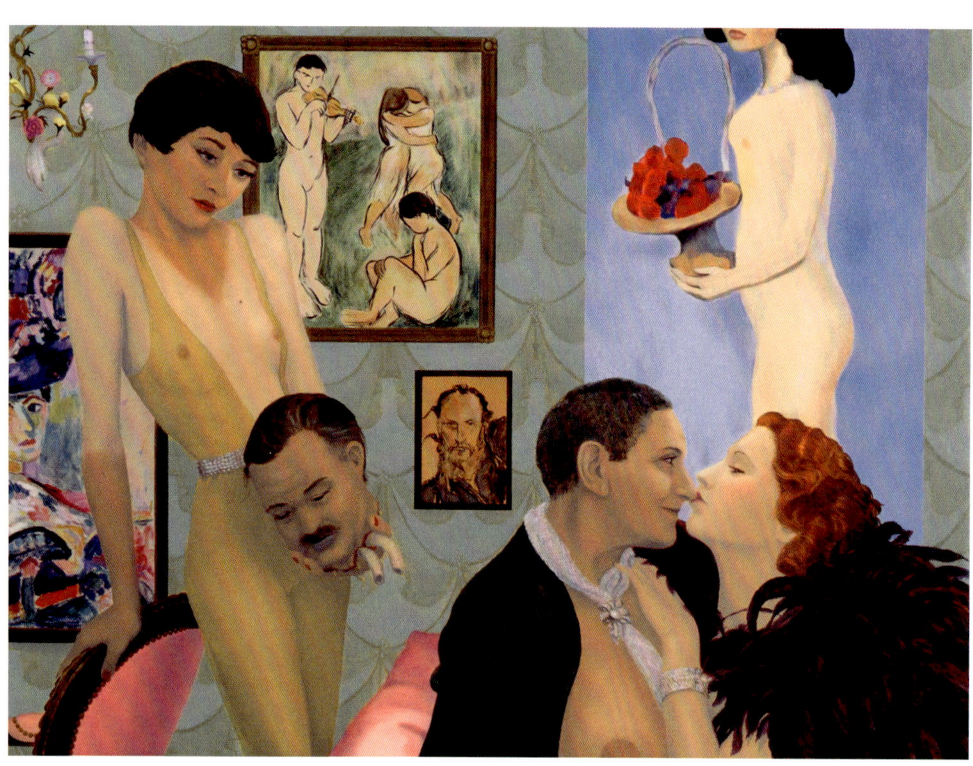

Hilary Harkness, *Girl with a Basket of Flowers,* 2011. Oil on linen mounted on panel, 8½ × 11 in. (21.6 × 27.9 cm). Collection of Glenn and Amanda Fuhrman, New York, courtesy the FLAG Art Foundation

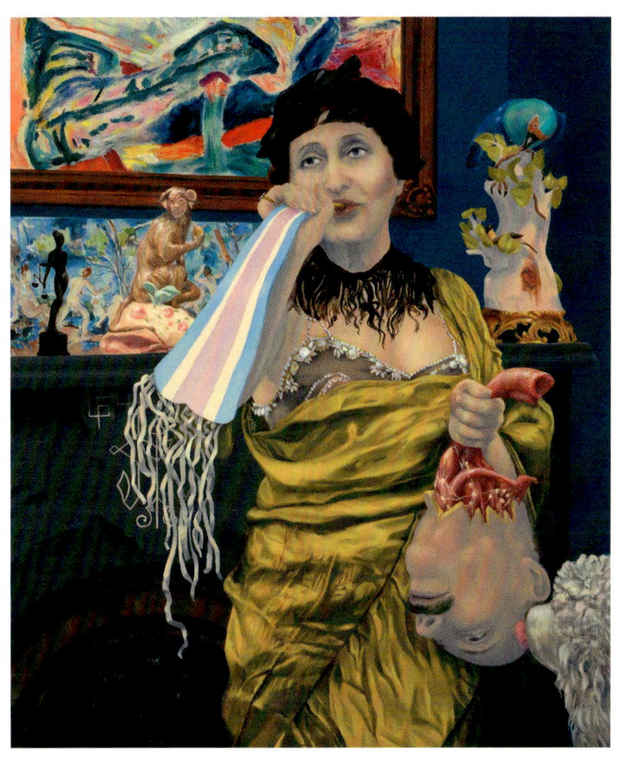

Hilary Harkness, *Woman with the Hat,* 2011. Oil on paper mounted on panel,
8½ × 7 in. (21.6 × 17.8 cm). Collection of Stuart Smith

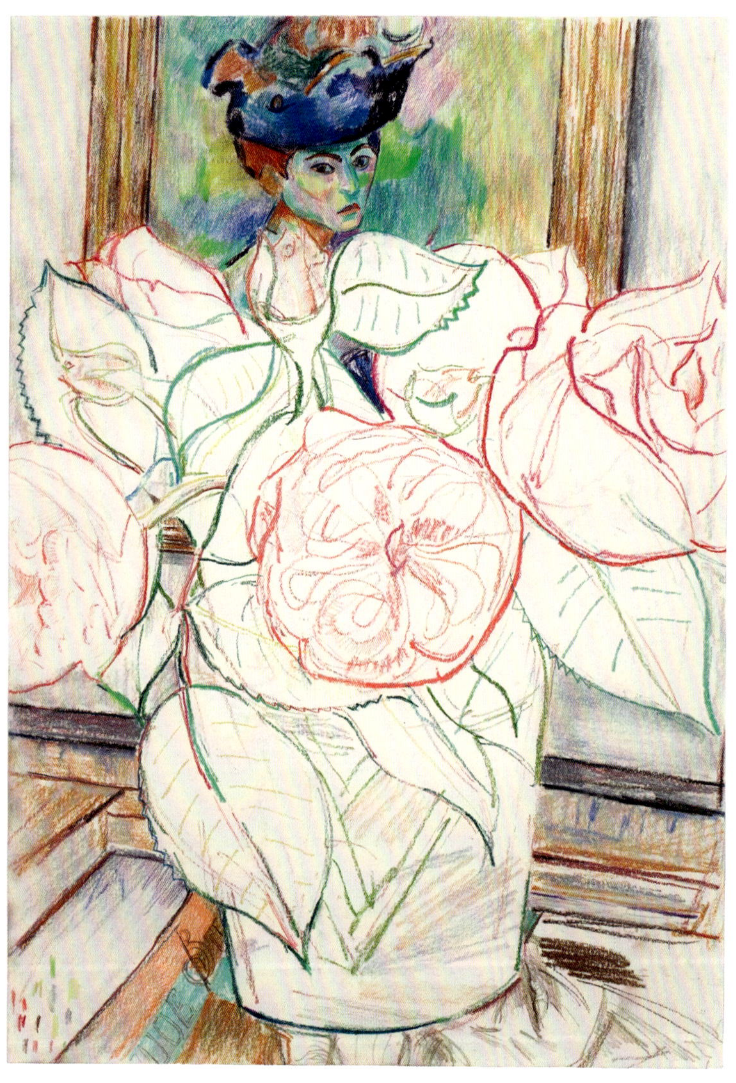

Elizabeth Peyton, *The Stein's Collect and Flowers,* 2011. Pastel and colored pencil on paper, 11⅝ × 8¼ in. (29.5 × 21.1 cm). Private collection

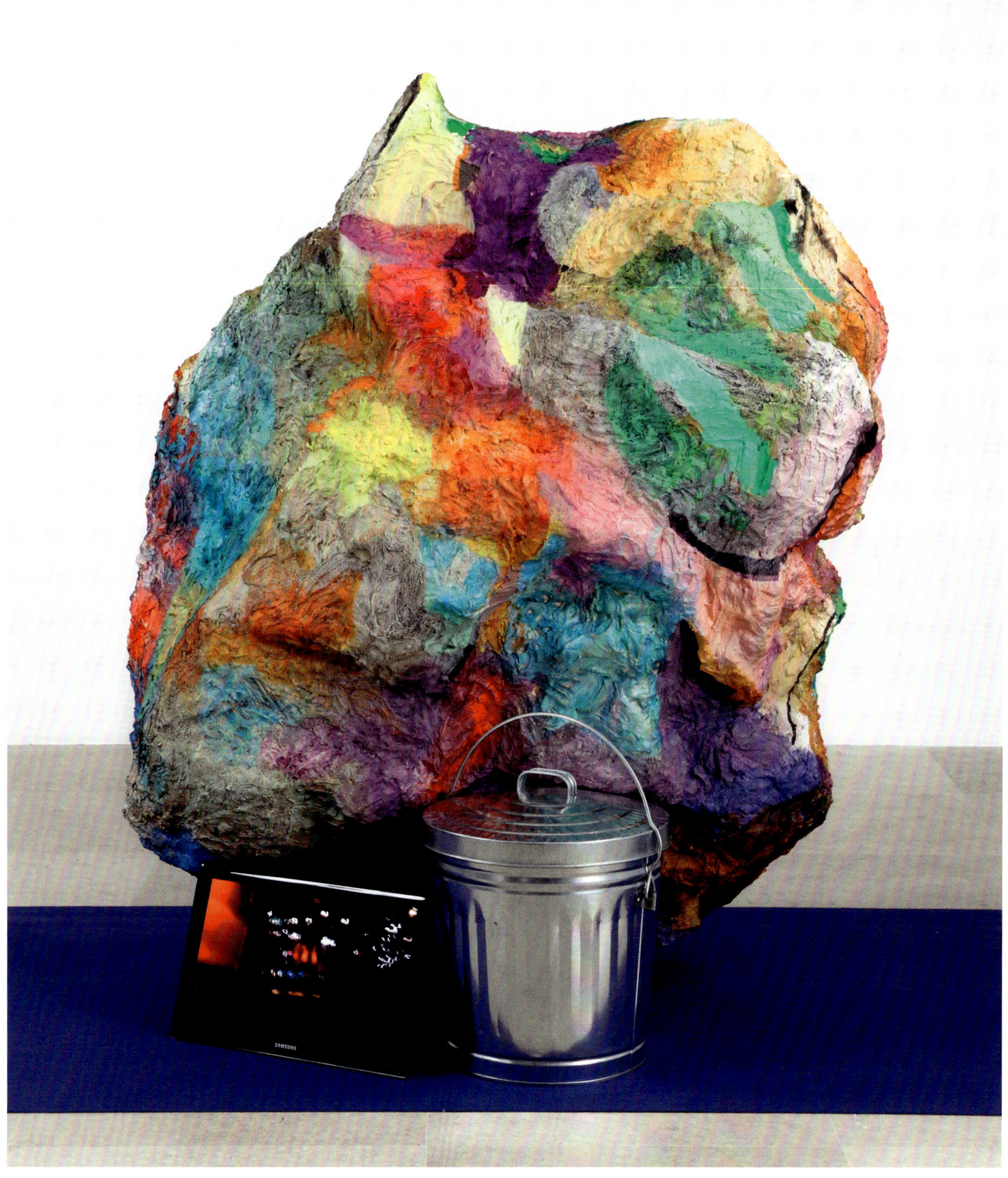

Rachel Harrison, *Hoarders,* 2012. Wood, polystyrene, chicken wire, cement, cardboard, acrylic paint, metal pail, flat-screen monitor, wireless headphones, runway carpet, and digital video (color, with sound; 10:39 min.), overall dimensions variable. Courtesy the artist and Greene Naftali, New York

Femme au chapeau:
An Illustrated History

ALISON GUH

South and west walls of Leo and Gertrude Stein's atelier at 27 rue de Fleurus, Paris, ca. 1906, featuring *Femme au chapeau* near Paul Cézanne's *Madame Cézanne with a Fan,* 1878/1888, and Pierre-Auguste Renoir's *Two Nudes,* ca. 1897, among other works

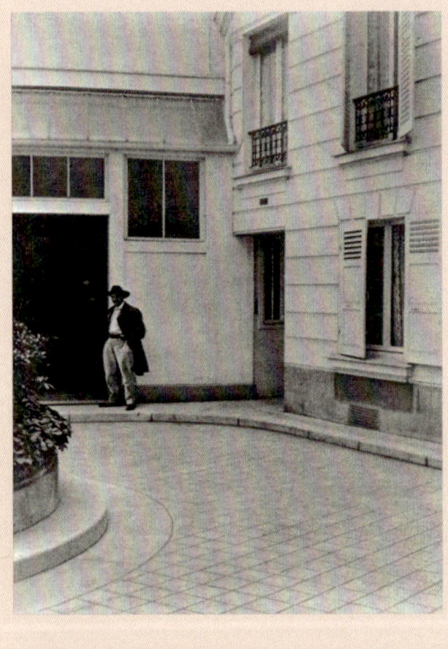

Leo Stein in the courtyard at 27 rue de Fleurus, Paris, ca. 1905

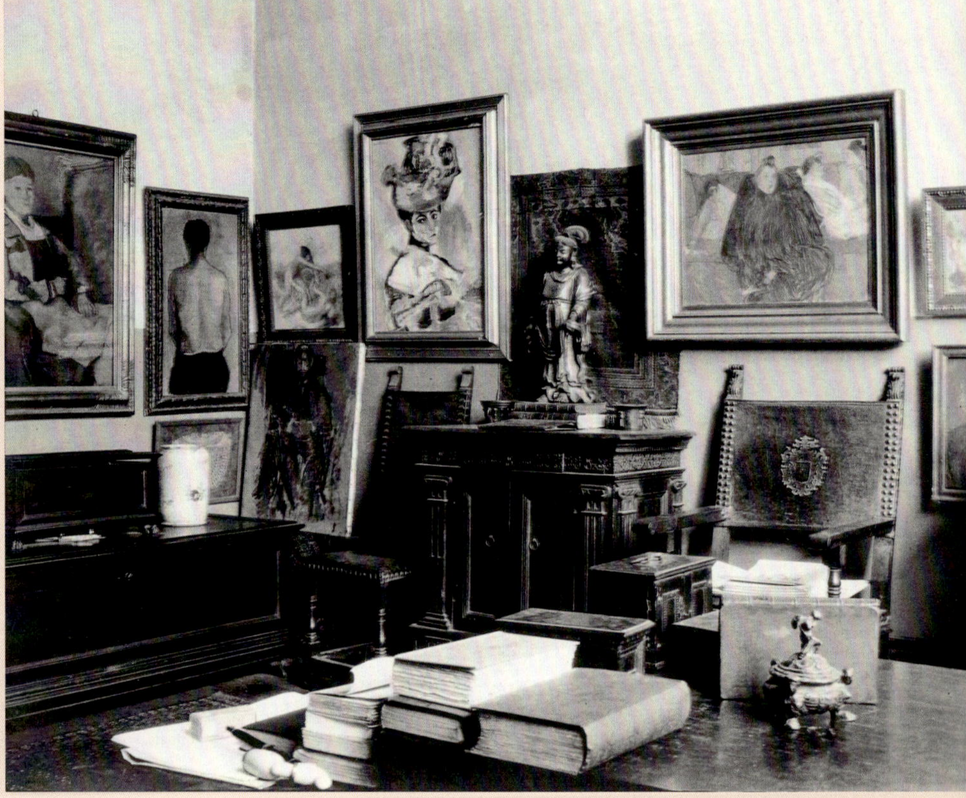

OCTOBER 18–NOVEMBER 25, 1905

🖾 *Femme au chapeau* (Woman with a Hat) makes its public debut in Gallery VII at the third Salon d'Automne at the Grand Palais, Paris (cat. no. 717).

AUTUMN 1905

🖾 Purchased by the collector and art critic Leo Stein at the 1905 Salon d'Automne.[1] He shares ownership of the work until 1913 or 1914 with his sister—the novelist, poet, and collector Gertrude Stein.[2] The painting is displayed in the American expatriates' shared Paris residence at 27 rue de Fleurus and seen by a wide array of guests at the siblings' regular Saturday evening salons.[3]

FEBRUARY 14–MARCH 5, 1910

🖾 Exhibited in *Exposition Henri Matisse* at the Galerie Bernheim-Jeune, Paris (cat. no. 32), which features 91 paintings and drawings. The exhibition is extended past its original closing date of February 22.

1913/14–15

🖾 After a falling-out between Leo and Gertrude Stein, the two divide their collection and Gertrude takes sole ownership of *Femme au chapeau.*

FEBRUARY 12, 1915

🖾 The businessman and collector Michael Stein purchases *Femme au chapeau* from his younger sister Gertrude for $4,000, confirming the sale in a letter to her.[4] Michael owns the painting jointly with his wife, Sarah Stein—like him, a notable patron of the arts.

1915–22

Sarah and Michael move with their art collection within Paris from 58 rue Madame to 14 rue de l'Assomption (1917), then to 248 boulevard Raspail (1918), and finally to 59 rue de la Tour (1922).[5]

Femme au chapeau displayed in one of the salons in Sarah and Michael Stein's apartment at 59 rue de la Tour, Paris, ca. 1922–28

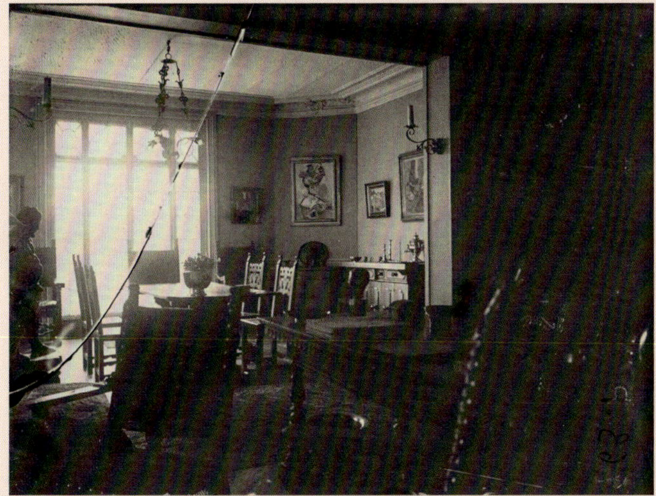

Sarah and Michael Stein's home at 433 Kingsley Avenue, Palo Alto, California, ca. 1935–38

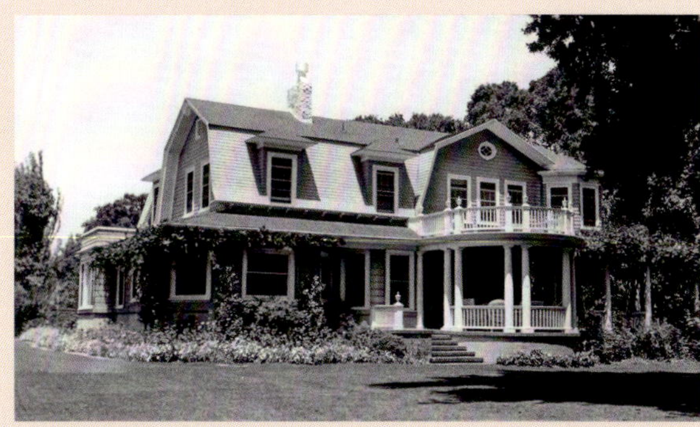

← *Femme au chapeau* displayed in the living room at the Villa Stein–de Monzie, also known as "Les Terrasses," Vaucresson, France, ca. 1928

↓ Exterior of "Les Terrasses," ca. 1928

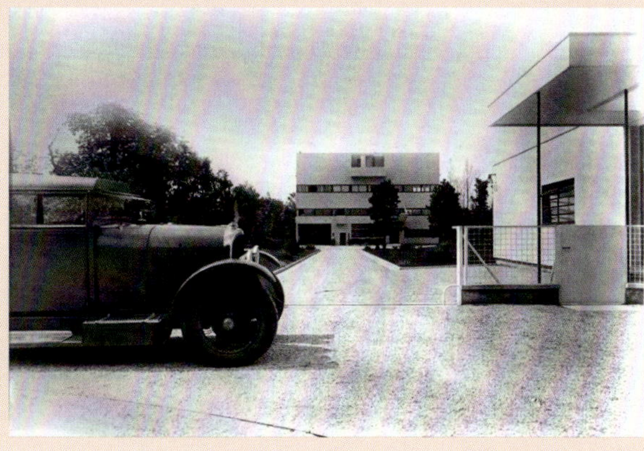

AUGUST 1922–SPRING 1928

⟐ While living at 59 rue de la Tour, Sarah and Michael Stein hang *Femme au chapeau* prominently in one of the salons of the apartment they share with their friend Gabrielle Colaço-Osorio and her daughter, Jacqueline.[6]

1928–35

⟐ Drawn to the prospect of life in the countryside, in May 1926 Sarah and Michael commission architects Le Corbusier and Pierre Jeanneret to design a modern home in Vaucresson, outside Paris, for themselves and Colaço-Osorio (the estranged wife of Count Anatole de Monzie).[7] While living at the Villa Stein–de Monzie from spring 1928 until July 1935, the Steins display *Femme au chapeau* in their living room.

JUNE 16–JULY 25, 1931

⟐ *Femme au chapeau* is exhibited in *Henri-Matisse: Exposition organisée au profit de l'Orphelinat des Arts* at Galeries Georges Petit, Paris (cat. no. 9). The exhibition features 142 paintings, pastels, and bronzes.

1935–48

⟐ After 31 years abroad, Sarah and Michael Stein leave France for the San Francisco Bay Area in 1935. They bring their modern art collection with them and take up residence at 433 Kingsley Avenue, Palo Alto.

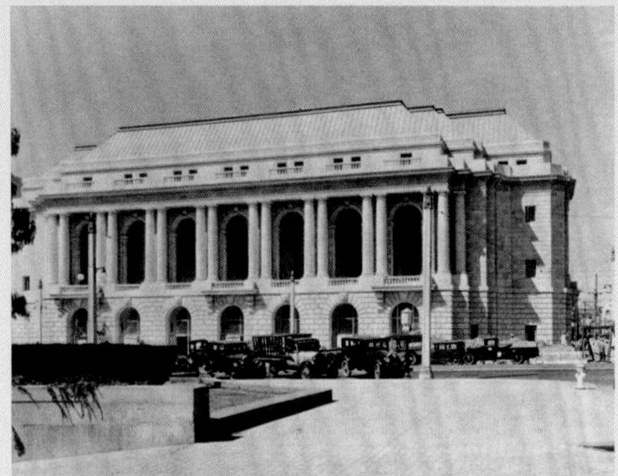

Exterior of the War Memorial Veterans Building at 401 Van Ness Avenue, home to the San Francisco Museum of Art (SFMA) from 1935–1995, ca. 1930s

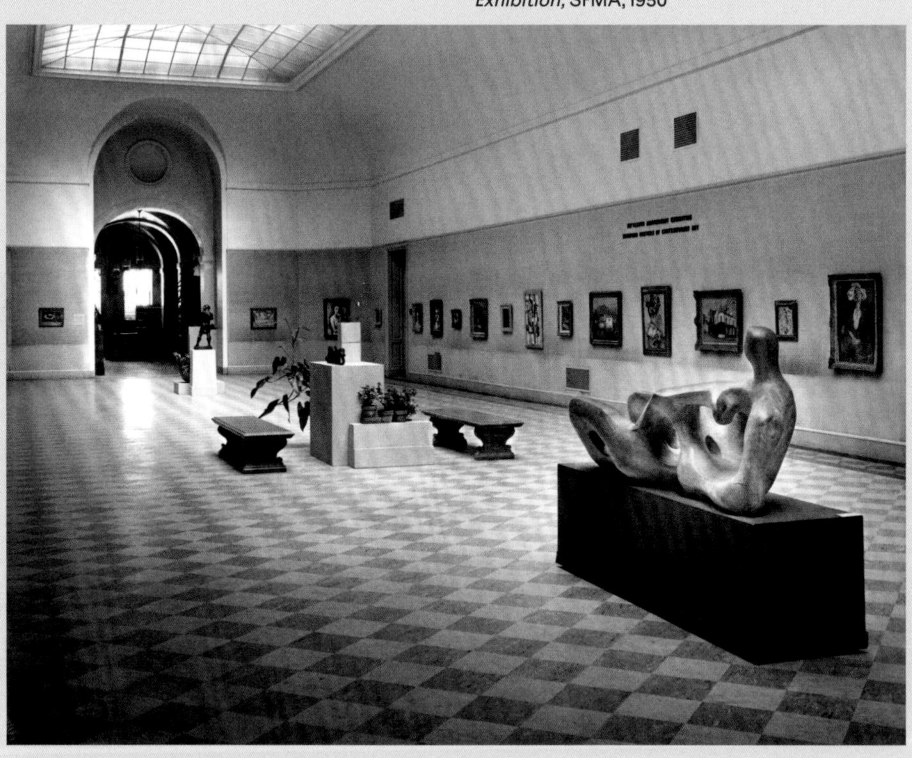

Installation view of *Modern Masterpieces of the Bay Region, 15th Anniversary Exhibition,* SFMA, 1950

JANUARY 11–FEBRUARY 24, 1936
⊷ Exhibited in *Henri-Matisse: Paintings, Drawings, Sculpture* at the San Francisco Museum of Art (SFMA, later the San Francisco Museum of Modern Art [SFMOMA]) (cat. no. 9), one year after the museum opens to the public. *Femme au chapeau* is reproduced on the cover of the exhibition brochure. Organized by the museum's founding director, Grace L. McCann Morley, the exhibition features 35 of Matisse's paintings, drawings, and bronzes. *Femme au chapeau* is one of 12 works loaned by Sarah and Michael Stein.

1938
⊷ Upon Michael Stein's death, Sarah Stein assumes sole ownership of *Femme au chapeau.*

OCTOBER 7–28, 1945
⊷ Exhibited in *French Modern Painting* at the Thomas Welton Stanford Art Gallery at Stanford University in Palo Alto, where it is seen by 3,158 visitors alongside the work of Fernand Léger, Pablo Picasso, Vincent van Gogh, and other influential painters who lived and worked in France.[8]

JANUARY 6, 1948
⊷ The San Francisco arts philanthropist Elise S. Haas purchases *Femme au chapeau* from her close friend Sarah Stein for $20,000, per a handwritten note in Haas's records.[9] Elise and her husband, Walter A. Haas, whose great-uncle founded Levi Strauss & Co., own the painting jointly until his death in 1979.

JANUARY 12–FEBRUARY 5, 1950
⊷ Exhibited in *Modern Masterpieces of the Bay Region, 15th Anniversary Exhibition* at the SFMA. The exhibition features 17 works by Matisse, alongside 84 works by American and European artists including Max Beckmann, Alexander Calder, and Pablo Picasso.

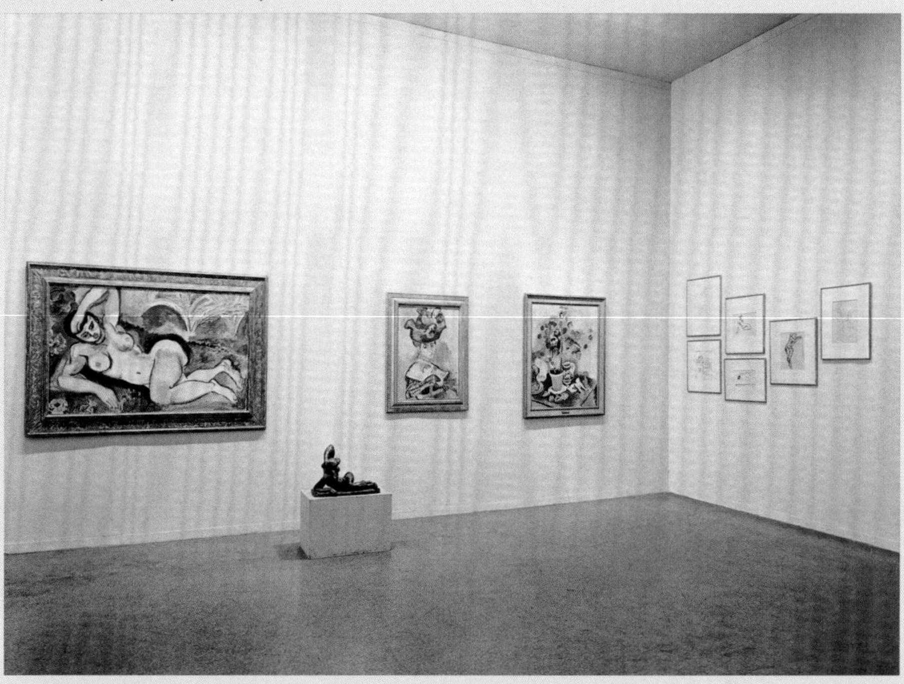

Installation view of *Henri Matisse*, MoMA, 1951, with *Femme au chapeau* exhibited to the right of Matisse's *Blue Nude (Memory of Biskra)*, 1907

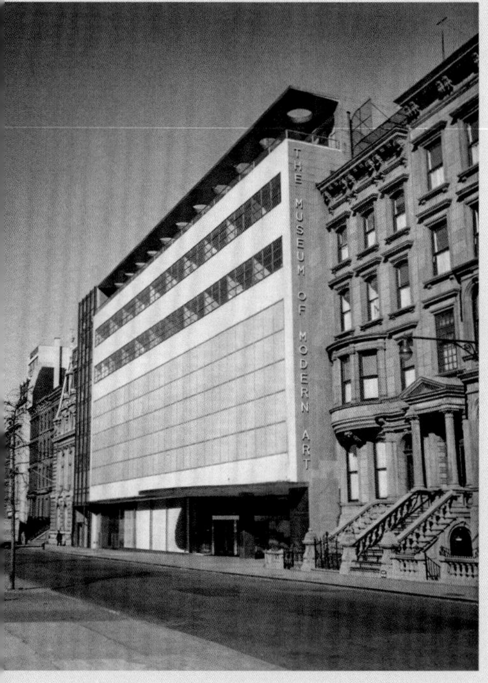

Exterior of The Museum of Modern Art, New York (MoMA), 1951

SEPTEMBER 6–30, 1951

Exhibited in *French Paintings of the 19th and 20th Century Lent by California Museums and Private Collections* at the Santa Barbara Museum of Art, an exhibition marking the museum's tenth anniversary.[10] In addition to paintings by Matisse, the show features works by Georges Braque, Paul Cézanne, Paul Gauguin, Georges Rouault, and Édouard Vuillard, among others.

NOVEMBER 13, 1951–JANUARY 13, 1952

Exhibited in *Henri Matisse* at The Museum of Modern Art, New York (MoMA). Organized by the museum's founding director, Alfred H. Barr Jr., the retrospective features 145 paintings, works on paper, sculptures, and illustrated books. The exhibition travels to the Cleveland Museum of Art (February 5–March 16, 1952), the Art Institute of Chicago (April 1–May 4, 1952), and the SFMA (May 22–July 6, 1952). *Femme au chapeau* is loaned only to MoMA and SFMA at Elise S. Haas's request.

DECEMBER 1951

Alfred H. Barr Jr.'s monograph *Henri Matisse: His Art and His Public* is published. The nearly 600-page book prominently features *Femme au chapeau* as the frontispiece.[11] Matisse makes paper cut-out designs for the book jackets of both this larger publication and a smaller exhibition catalogue. The latter is developed to accompany the exhibition after the opening is moved up from February 1952 to November 1951.[12]

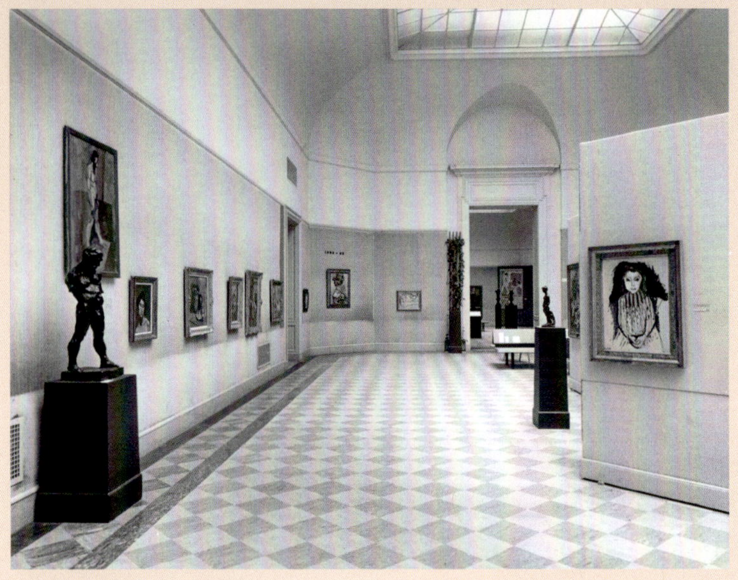

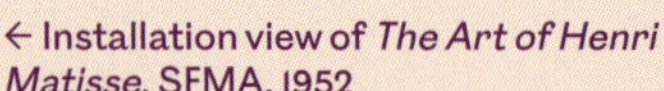

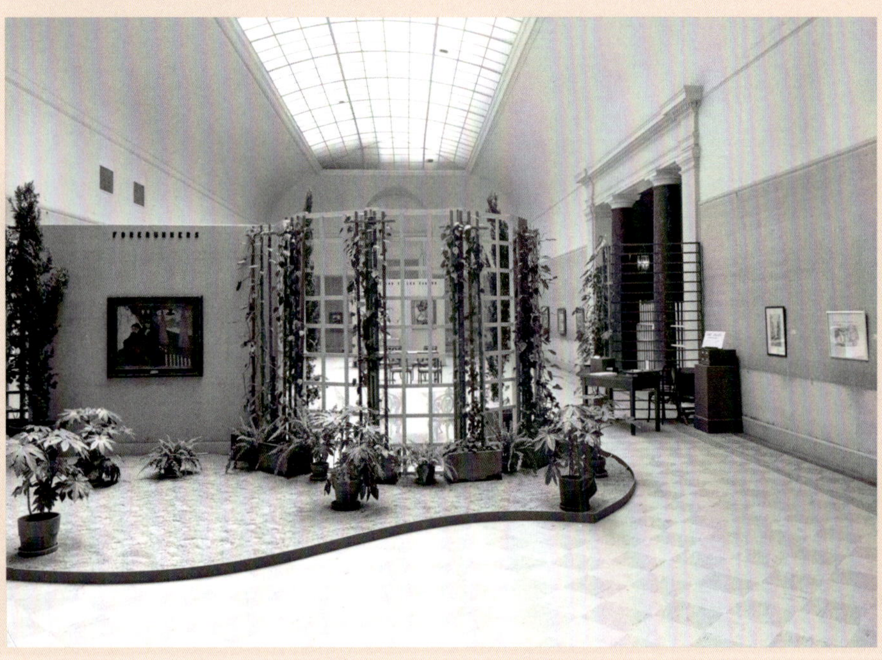

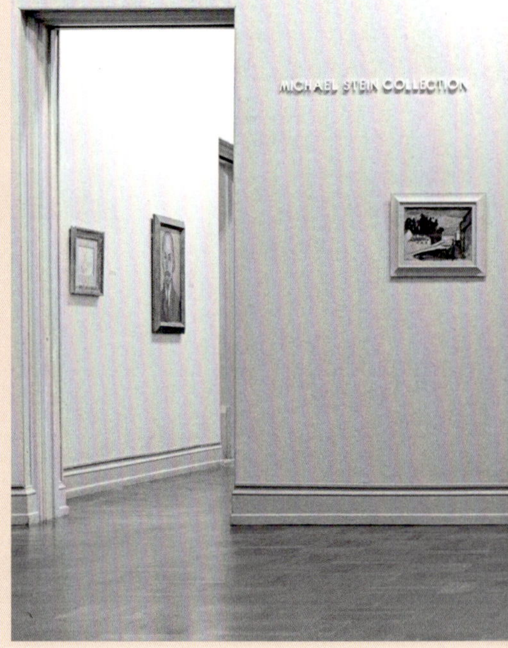

MAY 22–JULY 6, 1952

Exhibited in the SFMA's presentation of the touring retrospective, titled *The Art of Henri Matisse.*

MARCH 12–APRIL 12, 1953

Exhibited in *Les Fauves* at the SFMA. While the exhibition travels to MoMA (October 8, 1952–January 4, 1953), the Minneapolis Institute of Arts (January 21–February 22, 1953), and the Art Gallery of Toronto (May 1–May 31, 1953), *Femme au chapeau* is exhibited only at the SFMA.

JUNE 17–JULY 10, 1955

Exhibited in *Art in the 20th Century: Commemorating the Tenth Anniversary of the Signing of the UN Charter* at the SFMA. The exhibition is mounted on the occasion of the United Nations Commemorative Session held in San Francisco from June 20 to 26. *Femme au chapeau* is among the 270 paintings and sculptures exhibited.

1958

Exhibited in what Grace L. McCann Morley refers to as a "prelude" to a retrospective of Albert Marquet's work, which was on view at the SFMA from May 27–August 3, 1958.[15]

OCTOBER 28–DECEMBER 7, 1959

Exhibited in *Signposts of Twentieth Century Art* at the Dallas Museum for Contemporary Arts (now the Dallas Museum of Art). The exhibition is curated by Katharine Kuh and features *Femme au chapeau* alongside 24 other modern paintings and sculptures that mark new directions in the development of art.

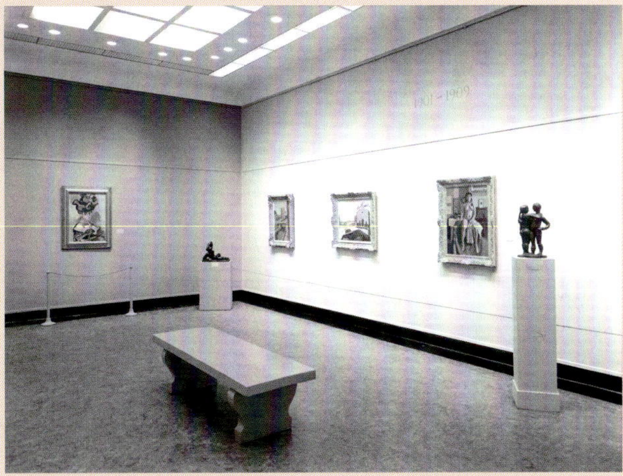

Installation view of *Henri Matisse Retrospective,* Museum of Fine Arts, Boston, 1966

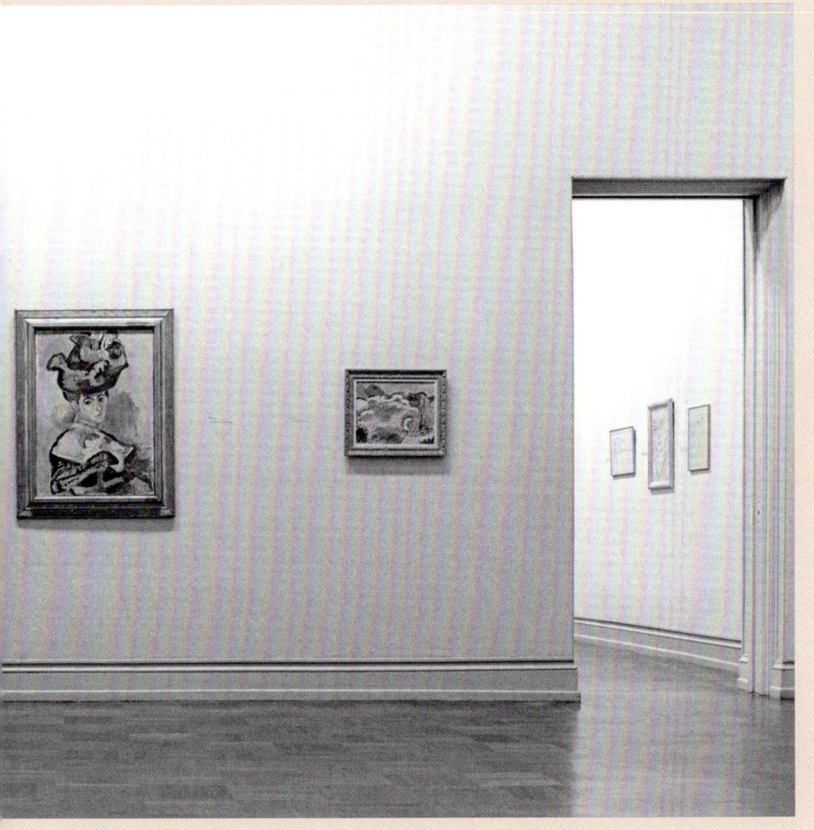

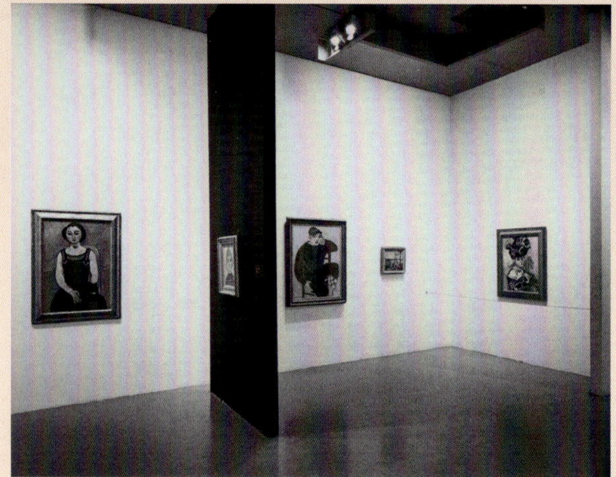

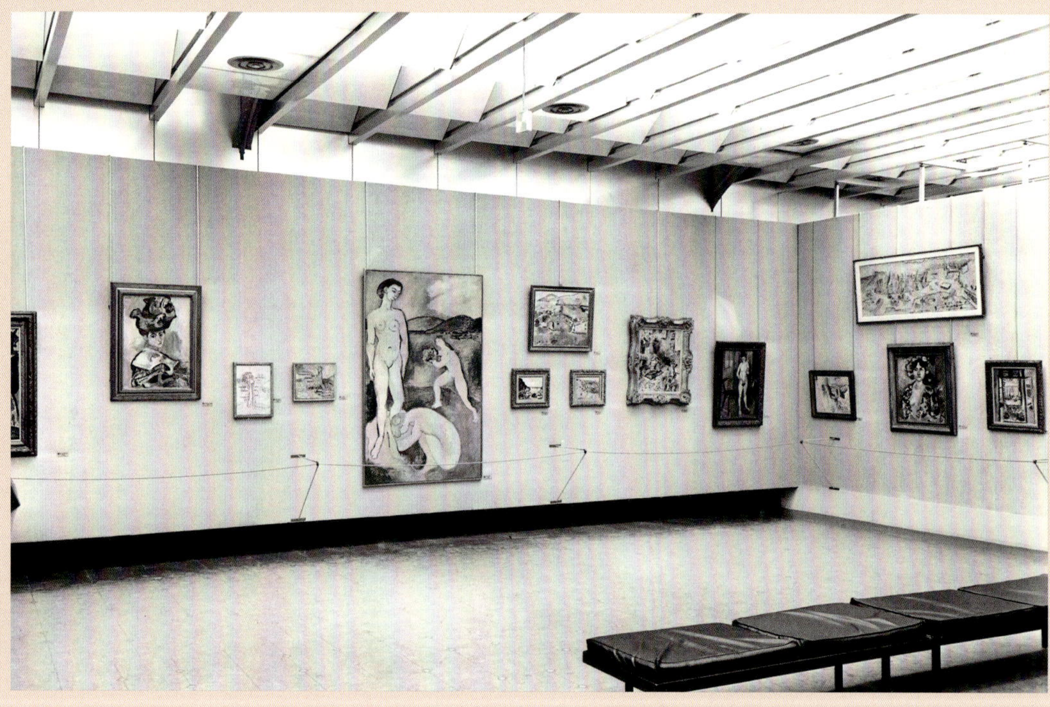

JULY 19–SEPTEMBER 25, 1966

Exhibited in *Henri Matisse: 64 Paintings* at MoMA. Unable to secure the tour of a smaller version of UCLA's exhibition, MoMA mounts its own exhibition of 62 paintings and 2 gouaches.[14] The exhibition is seen by 214,203 visitors.[15]

APRIL 22–SEPTEMBER 21, 1970

Exhibited in *Henri Matisse: Exposition du centenaire* at the Grand Palais in Paris—the first time *Femme au chapeau* returns to the place where it made its debut in 1905. The exhibition celebrates the 100th anniversary of Matisse's birth and features works from across his career, including 208 paintings, 28 sculptures, and 13 gouaches.

SEPTEMBER 9–OCTOBER 31, 1971

Exhibited in *Four Americans in Paris: The Collection of Gertrude Stein and Her Family* at the SFMA. The exhibition originates at MoMA and travels to both the SFMA and the Baltimore Museum of Art, but *Femme au chapeau* is shown only at the SFMA.

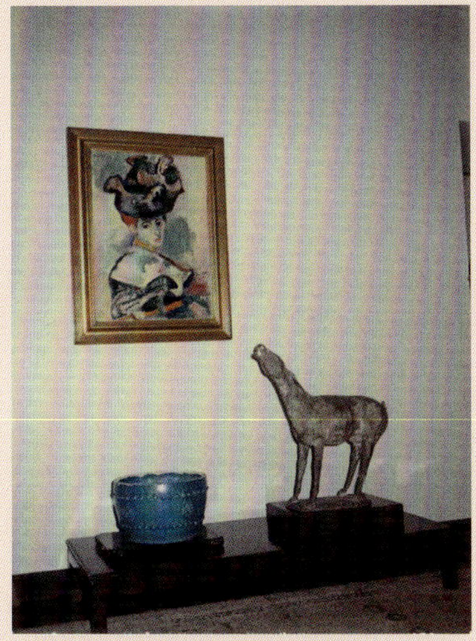

Femme au chapeau displayed alongside Marino Marini's *Cavallo* (Horse), 1947, in the Haas home at 2100 Pacific Avenue, San Francisco

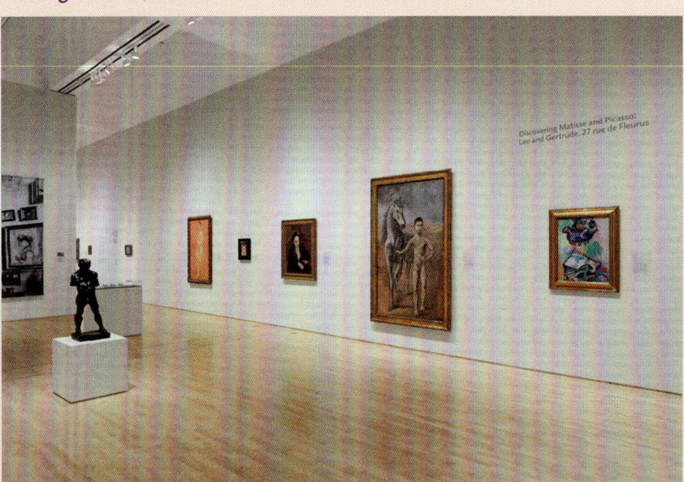

Installation view of *The Steins Collect: Matisse, Picasso, and the Parisian Avant-Garde,* SFMOMA, 2011, showing *Femme au chapeau* alongside Pablo Picasso's *Boy Leading a Horse,* 1905–6

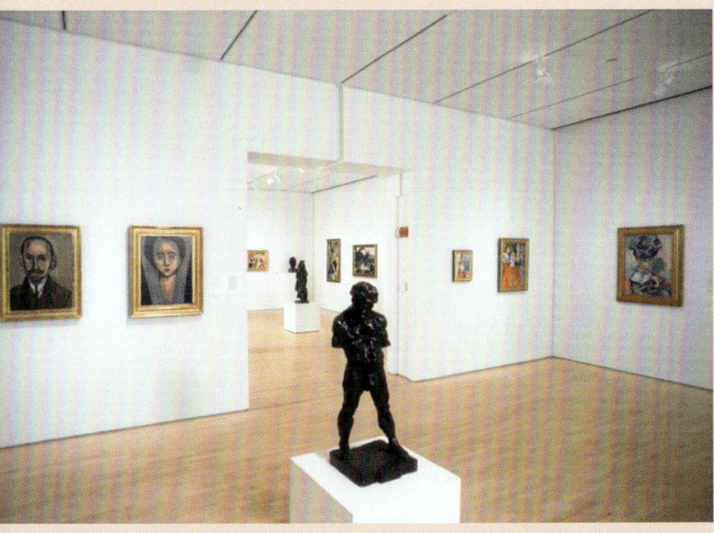

Installation view of *From Matisse to Diebenkorn: Selections from the Collection of Painting and Sculpture,* San Francisco Museum of Modern Art (SFMOMA), 1995

1979

Following Walter A. Haas's death, Elise S. Haas assumes sole ownership of *Femme au chapeau,* which she continues to display in their penthouse home at 2100 Pacific Avenue in San Francisco.

1991

Before her death in 1990, Elise S. Haas bequeaths the painting, along with a large part of her modern art collection, to SFMOMA. As a condition of the bequest, which enters the museum's collection in 1991, *Femme au chapeau* remains on permanent view at SFMOMA, appearing in temporary and permanent collection exhibitions including *Matisse and Beyond: A Century of Modernism, Open Ended: Painting and Sculpture Since 1900,* and *75 Years of Looking Forward: The Anniversary Show,* among many others.

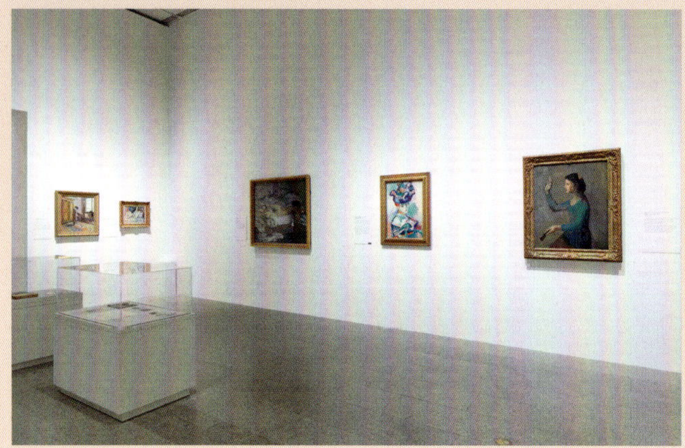

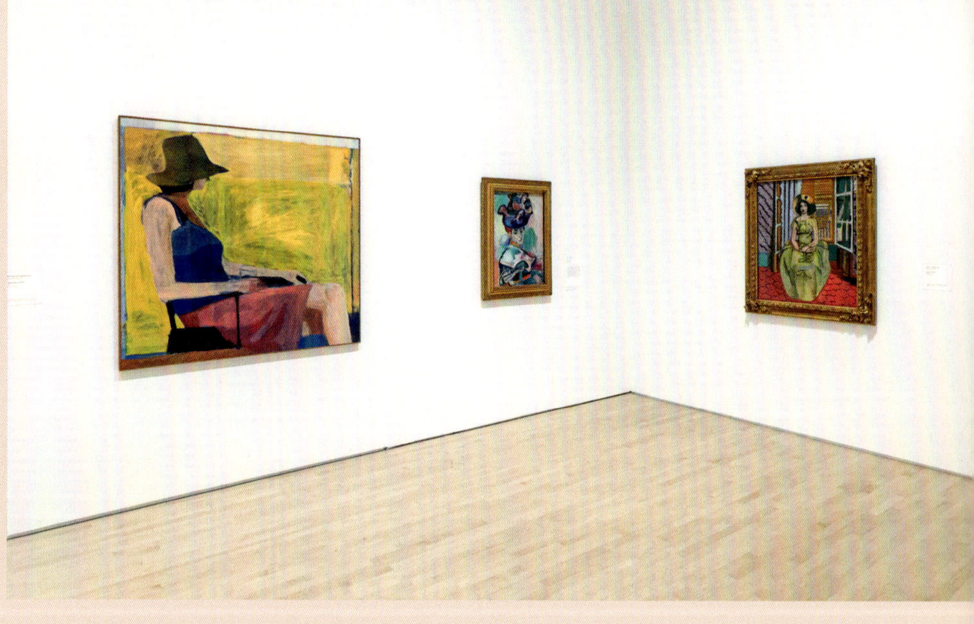

MAY 21–SEPTEMBER 6, 2011

🖼 Exhibited in *The Steins Collect: Matisse, Picasso, and the Parisian Avant-Garde* at SFMOMA, jointly organized by SFMOMA, the Réunion des Musées Nationaux–Grand Palais, and The Metropolitan Museum of Art, New York.

OCTOBER 3, 2011–JUNE 3, 2012

🖼 In a one-time exception to the terms of the bequest, permission is granted for *Femme au chapeau* to travel for *The Steins Collect.* The painting is exhibited in *Matisse, Cezanne, Picasso . . . L'aventure des Stein,* the French iteration of the show at the RMN–Grand Palais, Paris (October 3, 2011–January 16, 2012); and in *The Steins Collect: Matisse, Picasso, and the Parisian Avant-Garde* at The Metropolitan Museum of Art, New York (February 28–June 3, 2012).

MARCH 11–MAY 29, 2017

🖼 Exhibited in *Matisse/Diebenkorn* at SFMOMA. The show is co-organized with the Baltimore Museum of Art, where it debuts in 2016. *Femme au chapeau* is shown only at SFMOMA.

1   In a letter to "Messieurs Chaine et Simonson" dated November 18, 1905, Matisse turns down their offer of 300 francs, stating that the asking price for *Femme au chapeau* was 500 francs and that he could not let it go for less than 450 francs. Henri Matisse, signed letter, November 18, 1905. In Aguttes, *Les Collections Aristophil,* Hôtel Drouot, Paris, December 20, 2017, lot 8, https://www.gazette-drouot.com/en/lots/8262636-matisse-henri-. Leo Stein recalls that upon reviewing this correspondence, he "did not consider the price excessive either," thus likely purchasing the painting for either 450 or 500 francs. Leo Stein, *Appreciation: Painting, Poetry, and Prose* (New York: Random House, 1947), 126.

2   Details of the provenance of *Femme au chapeau* are drawn from Robert McD. Parker, "Catalogue of the Stein Collections," and Kate Mendillo, "Chronology," in *The Steins Collect: Matisse, Picasso, and the Parisian Avant-Garde,* ed. Janet Bishop, Cécile Debray, and Rebecca Rabinow, exh. cat. (San Francisco: San Francisco Museum of Modern Art; New Haven, CT: Yale University Press, 2011).

3   For additional details about the Stein residences, see "The Stein Residences in Photographs," in Bishop et al., *The Steins Collect,* 360–92.

4   Letter from Michael Stein to Gertrude Stein, February 12, 1915, in Donald Gallup, *The Flowers of Friendship: Letters Written to Gertrude Stein* (New York: Alfred A. Knopf, 1953), 106–7.

5   Mendillo, "Chronology," 324.

6   Mendillo, "Chronology," 323–24.

7   Carrie Pilto, "The Steins Build: Le Corbusier's Villa Stein–de Monzie, Les Terrasses," in Bishop et al., *The Steins Collect,* 167.

8   Annual Report of the President of Stanford University, Office of the President, 1945–46, Stanford University Archives.

9   SFMOMA Permanent Collection Object File, 91.161.

10 Exhibition Summaries, 1950s, Exh ID #A1951.09b, Santa Barbara Museum of Art Archives.

11 In a letter to Elise S. Haas dated November 20, 1950, Barr writes, "We hope more than we can say to include the *Woman in a Hat.* So far as I know it has never been exhibited here in the east and since it will be reproduced in color in my book, which is to be published at that time, we want to have it almost more than any other Matisse." The Museum of Modern Art Exhibition Records (hereafter MoMA Exhs.), 492.5, The Museum of Modern Art Archives, New York.

12 MoMA Exhs., 492.5. MoMA Archives, NY.

13 Letter from Grace L. McCann Morley to Adelyn D. Breeskin, May 24, 1958; Exhibition Records, *Retrospective – Albert Marquet,* May 27–August 3, 1958, San Francisco Museum of Modern Art Archives. An exhibition label on the painting's verso confirms *Femme au chapeau*'s inclusion in this presentation.

14 Letter from Mrs. Sidney F. Brody to Monroe Wheeler, January 18, 1965. MoMA Exhs., 803.14. MoMA Archives, NY.

15 Letter from Monroe Wheeler to Mrs. Walter A. Haas, October 6, 1966, MoMA Exhs., 803.6. MoMA Archives, NY.

COPYRIGHT CREDITS

IMAGE CREDITS

This book was produced by the San Francisco Museum of Modern Art on the occasion of the exhibition *Matisse's Femme au chapeau: A Modern Scandal,* organized by the San Francisco Museum of Modern Art (May 16 to September 27, 2026).

Lead support for *Matisse's Femme au chapeau: A Modern Scandal* is provided by Mimi and Peter Haas Fund.

Presenting support is provided by Bank of America and Dana and Bob Emery.

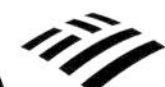

Major support is provided by Neal Benezra Exhibition Fund, Carolyn and Preston Butcher SFMOMA Exhibition Fund, and Davidow Family Fund for Exhibitions of Modern Art.

Significant support is provided by Mary Jane Elmore, Christine and Pierre Lamond, The Elaine McKeon Endowed Exhibition Fund, Deborah and Kenneth Novack, and Anonymous.

Meaningful support is provided by Alka and Ravin Agrawal, Dolly and George Chammas, Laurie and Jim Ghielmetti, Robert Lehman Foundation, Stuart G. Moldaw Public Program and Exhibition Fund, Nancy and Alan Schatzberg, Thomas W. Weisel and Janet Barnes, Bobbie and Mike Wilsey, Pat and Bill Wilson Exhibitions Fund, and Anonymous.

This book was produced by the publications department at the San Francisco Museum of Modern Art (Kari Dahlgren, director of publications; Amanda Glesmann, managing editor; and Katie Lindsey, publications and licensing coordinator).

Project editor: Kari Dahlgren
Designer: Barbara Glauber/Heavy Meta
Production manager: Amanda Glesmann
Editor: Jennifer Snodgrass
Translators: Fabienne Adler and Anne Levine
Proofreaders: Emily Bowles and Juliet Clark
Image permissions: Katie Lindsey
Printed in Italy by Verona Libri
Set in Mercure and Ostia Antica
Printed on GardaMatt Art 150gsm
Library of Congress Control Number on file
ISBN: 978-1-63681-189-5
10 9 8 7 6 5 4 3 2 1

Cover:
Henri Matisse, *Femme au chapeau* (Woman with a Hat), 1905. See page 46 and detail on pages 2–3.

Support for the catalogue is provided by Furthermore: a program of the J. M. Kaplan Fund.

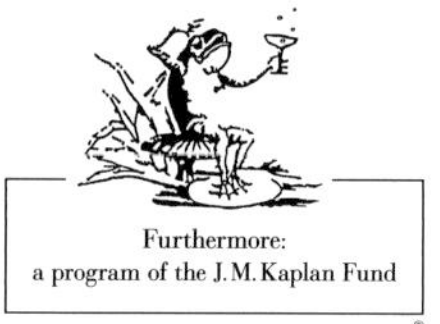